## *Quod scriptura, non iubet vetat*

**The Latin translates, "What is not commanded in scripture, is forbidden:'**

**On the Cover:** Baptists rejoice to hold in common with other evangelicals the main principles of the orthodox Christian faith. However, there are points of difference and these differences are significant. In fact, because these differences arise out of God's revealed will, they are of vital importance. Hence, the barriers of separation between Baptists and others can hardly be considered a trifling matter. To suppose that Baptists are kept apart solely by their views on Baptism or the Lord's Supper is a regrettable misunderstanding. Baptists hold views which distinguish them from Catholics, Congregationalists, Episcopalians, Lutherans, Methodists, Pentecostals, and Presbyterians, and the differences are so great as not only to justify, but to demand, the separate denominational existence of Baptists. Some people think Baptists ought not teach and emphasize their differences but as E.J. Forrester stated in 1893, "Any denomination that has views which justify its separate existence, is bound to promulgate those views. If those views are of sufficient importance to justify a separate existence, they are important enough to create a duty for their promulgation ... the very same reasons which justify the separate existence of any denomination make it the duty of that denomination to teach the distinctive doctrines upon which its separate existence rests." If Baptists have a right to a separate denominational life, it is their duty to propagate their distinctive principles, without which their separate life cannot be justified or maintained.

Many among today's professing Baptists have an agenda to revise the Baptist distinctives and redefine what it means to be a Baptist. Others don't understand why it even matters. The books being reproduced in the *Baptist Distinctives Series* are republished in order that Baptists from the past may state, explain and defend the primary Baptist distinctives as they understood them. It is hoped that this Series will provide a more thorough historical perspective on what it means to be distinctively Baptist.

The Lord Jesus Christ asked, *"And why call ye me, Lord, Lord, and do not the things which I say?"* (Luke 6:46). The immediate context surrounding this question explains what it means to be a true disciple of Christ. Addressing the same issue, Christ's question is meant to show that a confession of discipleship to the Lord Jesus Christ is inconsistent and untrue if it is not accompanied with a corresponding submission to His authoritative commands. Christ's question teaches us that a true recognition of His authority as Lord inevitably includes a submission to the authority of His Word. Hence, with this question Christ has made it forever impossible to separate His authority as King from the authority of His Word. These two principles—the authority of Christ as King and the authority of His Word—are the two most fundamental Baptist distinctives. The first gives rise to the second and out of these two all the other Baptist distinctives emanate. As F.M. Iams wrote in 1894, "Loyalty to Christ as King, manifesting itself in a constant and unswerving obedience to His will as revealed in His written Word, is the real source of all the Baptist distinctives:' In the search for the *primary* Baptist distinctive many have settled on the Lordship of Christ as the most basic distinctive. Strangely, in doing this, some have attempted to separate Christ's Lordship from the authority of Scripture, as if you could embrace Christ's authority without submitting to what He commanded. However, while Christ's Lordship and Kingly authority can be isolated and considered essentially for discussion's sake, we see from Christ's own words in Luke 6:46 that His Lordship is really inseparable from His Word and, with regard to real Christian discipleship, there can be no practical submission to the one without a practical submission to the other.

In the symbol above the Kingly Crown and the Open Bible represent the inseparable truths of Christ's Kingly and Biblical authority. The Crown and Bible graphics are supplemented by three Bible verses (Ecclesiastes 8:4, Matthew 28:18-20, and Luke 6:46) that reiterate and reinforce the inextricable connection between the authority of Christ as King and the authority of His Word. The truths symbolized by these components are further emphasized by the Latin quotation - *quod scriptura, non iubet vetat*— i.e., "What is not commanded in scripture, is forbidden:' This Latin quote has been considered historically as a summary statement of the regulative principle of Scripture. Together these various symbolic components converge to exhibit the two most foundational Baptist Distinctives out of which all the other Baptist Distinctives arise. Consequently, we have chosen this composite symbol as a logo to represent the primary truths set forth in the *Baptist Distinctives Series*.

# THE EVILS
## OF
# INFANT BAPTISM

# R. B. C. HOWELL
(ROBERT BOYTE CRAWFORD)
## 1801-1868

# THE EVILS
## OF
# INFANT BAPTISM

### BY R. B. C. HOWELL

AUTHOR OF

*THE TERMS OF COMMUNION AT THE LORD'S TABLE*

AND

**THE DEACONSHIP**

*With a Biographical Sketch of the Author by John Franklin Jones*

"*Finally, brethren, whatsoever things are true, whatsoever things are honest, whatsoever things are just, whatsoever things are pure, whatsoever things are lovely, whatsoever things are of good report, if there be any virtue, and if there be any praise, think of these things.*" (Philippians 4:8)

Charleston, South Carolina
The Southern Baptist Publication Society
1852

he Baptist Standard Bearer, Inc.
NUMBER ONE IRON OAKS DRIVE • PARIS, ARKANSAS 72855

Thou hast given a *standard* to them that fear thee;
that it may be displayed because of the truth.
-- *Psalm 60:4*

*Reprinted 2006*

*by*

# THE BAPTIST STANDARD BEARER, INC.
No. 1 Iron Oaks Drive
Paris, Arkansas 72855
(479) 963-3831

**THE WALDENSIAN EMBLEM**
*lux lucet in tenebris*
"The Light Shineth in the Darkness"

ISBN# 1579785034

TO THE

𝔖econd 𝔅aptist 𝔈hurch, and 𝔈ongregation,

IN THE

CITY OF RICHMOND, VIRGINIA,

THIS VOLUME

𝔍s 𝔎espectfully 𝔇edicated,

BY THEIR DEVOTED AND OBLIGED

PASTOR.

# PREFACE TO THE SECOND EDITION.

My gratitude is due to God, and to his people, for the kindness with which this little work has been received. A second edition is demanded at a much earlier period than I had anticipated. I have prepared it with as much attention as my circumstances would permit. Some portions of the book, as will be seen, have been recast, and a new Chapter has been added, on Infant Salvation. More perspicuity and conclusiveness have, as I think, been thus given to some of the arguments, and the whole work made much more complete. Again I send it forth, with the earnest prayer that it may prove a blessing to the cause of true religion.

Rob't Boyte C. Howell.

Richmond, Va., Dec. 17th, 1851.

# PREFACE.

The following pages were written with the specific design of considering, not the *"mode* of baptism," nor "the *subjects* of baptism," but "*the* EVILS *of* INFANT *baptism*." What baptism is, and who are authorized to receive it, have been questions of controversy during fifteen hundred years. The last two centuries have been especially prolific of essays and books on these subjects. Great learning and zeal have been called into requisition on both sides of the discussion. The conflict, as time passes, loses nothing of its interest, but grows each year, more and more warm. Nor will it ever cease until all christians fully understand the divine teachings in the premises, and submit themselves to the guidance of the word of God. The *evils* of infant baptism seem, however, to be a topic which has attracted heretofore, but very little attention. I have seen an occasional allusion to it in books, and periodicals, and sometimes a paragraph or two, affirming and sustaining the mischievous results of the rite. I myself wrote a small tract on the subject, more than twenty-five years ago, entitled "Plain Things for Plain Men," suggesting most of the propositions contained in this work. Beyond these almost nothing, so far as I know, has been published.* Consequently the advocates of infant baptism, driven from every other quarter, have here felt themselves safe. They affirm, and expect us to admit, that "If it does no good, it does no harm." It is innocent, and therefore may be practised. It was this very apology, offered in its behalf lately, by a friend in my presence, and which I had before so often heard, that called forth the book now before you. I thought it wrong to permit the public mind longer to remain involved in this error; and as I knew of no one who was likely soon to expose it, I determined to undertake the task myself. I have attempted, with what success

* Since the first edition of this work went to press, I have seen Dr. Gill's Tract, "Infant Baptism a Part and Pillar of Popery," edited by George B. Ide, D. D., and published in a handsome little volume, by the American Baptist Publication Society. This volume has a chapter by Dr. Ide on "The Influence of Infant Baptism on Protestant Churches, Historically considered." This is an able and conclusive chapter, of which, in this second edition, I have fully availed myself.

my readers will judge, to show that infant baptism is far from being harmless. On the contrary, that it is one of the most calamitous evils with which the church has ever been visited.

Permit, if you please, a word of explanation in the outset, regarding some terms, and phrases, of frequent occurrence. I have spoken of it as *baptism*, when only *sprinkling* was used, and *infants* were the subjects, not that I suppose any such thing *really baptism*, or that others than *believers* are capable of the ordinance, but simply as a matter of courtesy, and in compliance with common usage. In the same sense I have spoken of "the church," "the churches," and "the churches of Christ." In the use of these, and like expressions, I shall certainly, by all intelligent people, be perfectly understood.

One other prefatory remark will be pardoned. In this, as in every other book I have written, I have carefully sought the utmost simplicity and plainness. I write for "the million," and I have determined that "the million" shall understand me. I am unwilling to sacrifice force and directness to elegance of style. I do not enter in the presence of my readers, into labored criticisms, nor abstruse disquisitions, but give them the results simply, without fatiguing them with the process; and they have them in the plainest Saxon I can command. It has been my purpose to present the truth fully, fairly, and candidly, but at the same time, with all proper respect for the opinions of others. I have not introduced an argument which I do not believe to be logical and conclusive, a single passage of scripture which I am not persuaded is relevant, nor an authority from any writer, ancient or modern, which I am not assured is justly adduced, and applicable to the subject. My sole desire is the honor of truth, and the salvation of men.

With these observations premised, I send forth this little volume, earnestly praying that God our Heavenly Father, may make it a blessing to his cause and people.

Rob't Boyte C. Howell.

Richmond, Va., March 24th, 1851.

# CONTENTS.

### CHAPTER I.
Infant baptism is an evil because its practice is unsupported by the word of God .................................. 17

### CHAPTER II.
Infant baptism is an evil because its defence leads to most injurious perversions of scripture...................... 40

### CHAPTER III.
Infant baptism is an evil because it engrafts Judaism upon the gospel of Christ................................... 65

### CHAPTER IV.
Infant baptism is an evil because it falsifies the doctrine of universal depravity................................. 90

### CHAPTER V.
Infant baptism is an evil because the doctrines upon which it is predicated contradict the great fundamental principle of justification by faith.......................... 100

### CHAPTER VI.
Infant baptism is an evil because it is in direct conflict with the doctrine of the work of the Holy Spirit in regeneration ........................................... 117

## CHAPTER VII.

Infant baptism is an evil because it despoils the church of those peculiar qualities which are essential to the church of Christ.................................................. 130

## CHAPTER VIII.

Infant baptism is an evil because its practice perpetuates the superstitions that originally produced it............ 153

## CHAPTER IX.

Infant baptism is an evil because it subverts the scripture doctrine of infant salvation............................ 175

## CHAPTER X.

Infant baptism is an evil because it leads its advocates into rebellion against the authority of Christ................ 203

## CHAPTER XI.

Infant baptism is an evil because of the connection it assumes with the moral and religious training of children .................................................. 213

## CHAPTER XII.

Infant baptism is an evil because it is the grand foundation upon which rests the union of church and state ........ 225

## CHAPTER XIII.

Infant baptism is an evil because it leads to religious persecutions ............................................. 234

## CHAPTER XIV.

Infant baptism is an evil because it is contrary to the principles of civil and religious freedom ................... 253

## CHAPTER XV.

Infant baptism is an evil because it enfeebles the power of the church to combat error............................ 262

## CHAPTER XVI.

Infant baptism is an evil because it injures the credit of religion with reflecting men of the world................. 279

## CHAPTER XVII.

Infant baptism is an evil because it is the great barrier to christian union....................................... 284

## CHAPTER XVIII.

Infant baptism is an evil because it prevents the salutary impression which baptism was designed to make upon the minds both of those who receive it, and of those who witness its administration............................ 288

## CHAPTER XIX.

Infant baptism is an evil because it retards the designs of Christ in the conversion of the world .................. 293

## CHAPTER XX.

Recapitulation, with concluding addresses.................. 302

# THE EVILS OF INFANT BAPTISM.

## CHAPTER I.

INFANT BAPTISM IS AN EVIL BECAUSE ITS PRACTICE IS UNSUPPORTED BY THE WORD OF GOD.

Proposition stated; no authority in the Bible for infant baptism; confessions of its advocates; the great Protestant rule in religion; their arguments; it is no baptism; forms of the evil.

PERFECTION on earth, in its absolute form, unhappily no longer exists. "Man's first disobedience" brought sin into the world. Evil was its attendant. And since that fatal hour, evil has been connected with all that pertains to our race! It is like the air we breathe, an ever present influence. It corrupts all that is pure, and impairs all that is beautiful. Where are the natural beings whose perfections it has not disturbed? What rule of moral action is there, from compliance with which it has not turned men aside? But these are not its most lamentable developments. Evil is found prevailing even in the professed churches of Christ! Nor is its presence in the sanctuary seldom apparent. Scarcely is there a feature in our holy religion, which it has not somewhere, marred or distorted! *In no form, however, has it afflicted the cause of truth and salvation* more grievously, than in that of *infant baptism;* a rite generally prevalent, but without divine authority; repulsive in itself, and in its consequences always injurious. This declaration I hold myself bound, in the following pages, to sustain by adequate testimony. At present I solicit your attention to the proposition announced: *"Infant baptism is an evil because it is unsupported by the word of God."*

It is assumed that infant baptism is unsupported by the word of God. This is the *subject* of the proposition. If, upon examination, it be found true, the *predicate*, that it is an evil, follows as a matter of course. The forms and bearing of that evil may then be considered. Is *infant baptism supported by the word of God?* I aver that it is not. It is nowhere commanded. It is nowhere, in any form, divinely authorized. Examine the holy record, from first to last, and you will discover not a trace of infant baptism. If it *is* anywhere *commanded*, or *authorized*, the passages in which that fact appears, can be produced. Where are they? Let them be forthcoming. We have a right to see, and to examine them, for ourselves. We demand the texts. But this demand has before been often made, and always in vain. They have never been produced. They have not yet been found. They never can be found. They do not exist. The word of God, in all its length and breadth, contains not a syllable of authority for infant baptism, in the form of command, of precept, of permission, of example, or in any other form whatever. In that sacred book not one word in relation to it, is anywhere uttered. He who claims divine authority for infant baptism, must justify himself by adducing it. Until he does so, the least that can be said of it, is that "*it is unsupported by the word of God.*"

The authority demanded, has however often been essayed. Learned, ingenious, and protracted efforts have been attempted by every sect into which Pedobaptist christendom is divided. But as if God had determined to defend his own truth by the individual conflicts of its adversaries, it has turned out that no two of them have been able to harmonize either as to what may be regarded as testimony in the premises, or the class of infants divinely authorized to be baptized! Each is in collision with every other. Wall, Hammond, and others of that school, claim that Jewish proselyte baptism is its broad and ample foundation. Owen, Jennings, and many more, repudiate Jewish proselyte baptism, and predicate it upon circumcision as taught in the Abrahamic covenant. Beza, Doddridge, and their associates, teach that children are *holy*, and are therefore to be baptized. Wesley, and his disciples, teach that they are *unholy*, and must be baptized to cleanse them from their defilements. Burder, Dwight, and their class, permit no other infants to be baptized but those of christian parents, all of whom they contend, are born in the church, and are therefore entitled to its ordinances. Baxter, Henry, and those of similar faith, baptize infants to bring them into the covenant and church of the Redeemer. The evangelical divines of the Church of England, and of the Episcopal Church of America, tell us that "the doctrine of infant baptism is deduced by analogical reasoning, from statements of scripture applying more expressly, to the case of adult baptism." But those of the opposite character teach that baptism gives to the infant the regeneration of the Holy Ghost, and must therefore be administered. Many others receive and practise it, because, as they say, "It is in consonance with the general spirit of religion!" Each of these theories shows all the others to be wholly destitute of scriptural support. Among the several classes of religionists now indicated, are to be found very many men of the most extensive learning and research. Why are they all thus in hopeless conflict on the subject? The moment one brings forward his *scriptural proofs* of infant baptism, all the others clearly show them to be utterly false. Could this be the case were the ordinance anywhere enjoined or authorized? Every unprejudiced mind must see that, taken together, the arguments of all classes of Pedobaptists, destroy one another throughout. Like the builders at Babel, no two of them speak *the same* tongue, although every one protests that *he* utters the language of the Bible! It is true consequently, for any thing that yet appears to the contrary, that *infant baptism is unsupported by the word of God.*

But we have testimony in proof of our proposition still stronger if possible, than any which has yet been submitted. Very many of *the most learned and pious Pedobaptist Biblical critics, themselves candidly confess that infant baptism is not distinctly enjoined, nor directly taught, in the word of God.* Some of these I will now proceed to specify.

Martin Luther, the great father of the Reformation, says:—" It cannot be proved *by the scriptures,* that infant baptism was instituted *by Christ,* or begun by the first christians after the apostles."* John Calvin testifies thus:—"It is nowhere expressly mentioned *by the evangelists,* that any *child* was by the *apostles* baptized."† Bishop Burnet avers:—"There is no express *precept,* or rule given in *the New Testament,* for the baptism of infants."‡ Strarck says:—"The connection of infant baptism with circumcision deserves no consideration, since there were physical reasons for circumcising in infancy."§ Angusti says:—"The parallel between circumcision and baptism is altogether foreign to the New Testament."‖ Bishop Jeremy Taylor thus writes:—"For the argument from circumcision, it is invalid from infinite considerations. Figures and types prove nothing, unless a command go along with them, or some express to signify such to be their purpose."¶ Dr. Woods of Andover remarks:—"It is a plain case that there is no express precept respecting infant baptism in our sacred writings. The proof then, that it is a divine institution must be made out in some other way."** Prof. Stuart says:—"Commands, or plain and certain examples in the New Testament, relative to it [infant baptism] I do not find."†† And finally Dr. Neander declares:—"As baptism was closely united with a conscious entrance on christian communion, faith and baptism were always connected

---

\* Apud Van. Inf. Bapt., part 2, p. 8.
† Institutes of Religion, Liber 4, &c.
‡ Expos. 39 Arts., Art. 18. § Hist Bap., p. 11.
‖ Works, vol. 7, p. 329.
¶ Liberty of Prophesying, pp. 228–246.
\*\* Lect. on Inf. Bap., p. 11.
†† Biblical Repository, 1833, p. 385.

with one another; and thus it is in the highest degree probable, that baptism was performed only in instances where both could meet together, and that the practice of infant baptism was unknown" to the apostolic age.* In another work Neander says:—" Baptism was at first, administered only to adults, as men were accustomed to conceive baptism and faith as strictly connected. We have all reason for not deriving infant baptism from apostolic institution."† Multitudes of other similar declarations could, were they necessary, be readily produced, but these are amply sufficient. It is acknowledged that the word of God does not teach infant baptism. This acknowledgment is made candidly, by those who ought to know, since they were among the most learned men, and best Biblical critics the world has ever produced, made against themselves, voluntarily, freely, and of their own accord, and ought therefore to be considered decisive of the question. Infant baptism is not found in any form in the Bible. Every effort to deduce it from the sacred records, no matter how ingeniously conducted, has proved a wretched failure. It is confessed by its advocates that it is not found in the inspired pages. *Infant baptism is therefore, unsupported by the word of God.*

May I now, in view of all these facts, and considerations, solicit your attention to *the great Protestant principle in religion,* so familiarly known to all who are in the least conversant with sacred literature?—" *The word of God is a perfect rule of faith and practice.*" To this maxim every evangelical denomination professes

---

\* Planting and Training, p. 101.
† Church History, vol. 1, p. 311, Torrey's Translation.

to bow with entire submission. It avows the scriptures to be not the *supreme* authority only, but also the *sole* authority, in all that pertains to religion. It repudiates *all tradition*. It looks not to the *Fathers* of the church of whatever period, except in so far as they are sustained by the divine word. It relies exclusively upon *the scriptures*. If any doctrine or practice be there clearly taught, it must be received heartily, and fully. If otherwise, you dare not admit it. "The word of God is a perfect rule of faith and practice."

For myself, and for my brethren—although we are *not Protestants*—I declare for this christian law in religion the sincerest reverence. We receive it fully, and conform to it in every respect. We do this however, not simply because it is wise in principle, and safe in practice, but because it is really an embodiment in another form, of the law of God himself. It comes to us with the sanction not of men only, but of God. The language of Jehovah on the subject is this:—" What thing soever I command you, observe to do it. Thou shalt not add thereto, nor diminish from it."* And in another place he says:—" Ye shall not add unto the word which I command you, neither shall ye diminish ought from it, that ye may keep the commandments of the Lord your God which I command you."† Is not this a plain declaration, in other terms, that, "The word of God is a perfect rule of faith and practice?" Does any one suppose that since these precepts had a more direct reference to the law of Moses, that they are not equally applicable under the gospel? To such it may be replied, that the law was much less perfect

---

\* Deut. xii., 8.      † Deut. iv., 2.

than is the gospel. Did our Heavenly Father enforce the obligations of the former with the most jealous particularity, and is he less careful as to our compliance with the demands of the latter? Such an objection is *unreasonable*. It is also in direct conflict with apostolic teaching. To this very topic Paul refers, when he says:—" God, who at sundry times, and in divers manners, spake in times past to the *fathers*, by the *prophets*, hath in these last days spoken unto *us*, by his *Son*."* " *Therefore* we ought to give *the more earnest heed* to the things which *we* have heard, lest at any time we should let them slip. For if the word spoken by angels [messengers, in the law] was steadfast, and every transgression, and disobedience received a just recompense of reward, how shall we escape if we neglect so great salvation, which at the first began to be spoken by *the Lord*, and was confirmed unto us by *them that heard him*, God also bearing *them* witness, both with signs and wonders, and divers miracles, and gifts of the Holy Ghost?"† " See that ye refuse not him that speaketh. For if they escaped not who refused him that spake on *earth*, much more shall not we escape if we refuse him that *speaketh from heaven*."‡ Thus it is seen that if the inspired apostle knew whereof he affirmed, and reasoned not illogically, it is unquestionably true that the gospel requires to be obeyed, not with *less*, but with *more* carefulness, particularity, and fidelity than did the law. To no commandment of the *gospel* therefore, may you add any thing whatever; neither may you diminish aught from it. You are obliged to obey, and in the manner en-

\* Heb. i., 1. † Heb. ii., 1–4. ‡ Heb. xii., 25.

joined, all that Jehovah has there revealed for your guidance. It is "*the word of God*," and that "*is a perfect rule of faith and practice.*"

But we are constantly told that the gospel, unlike the law, is in many respects, indefinite in its instructions, giving only the outlines, and great principles of religion, and leaving the details to be filled up by the wisdom and pious discretion of the followers of Christ. He who has arrived at this conclusion has wholly mistaken the subject. If the word of God is a perfect rule of faith and practice, then the assumption cannot possibly be true. It is unreasonable in itself; it is in conflict with the inspired teachings just recited; and it proceeds on the false assumption that the gospel is less perfect than the law! On the contrary, in the gospel every duty required is distinctly enjoined. No one need mistake its authority, or its nature. That *rule* is certainly not *perfect*, to whatever department of life it may pertain, which only sketches general principles, and great outlines, and leaves the details to be supplied by each individual in such manner as may seem to him most proper. The word of God is no such rule. It is perfect. It is disfigured by neither redundancy nor defect. It must be obeyed in all things, without addition, diminution or change. You can never depart from it in any particular, without incurring imminent peril.

It is proper to remark in passing, that our pedobaptist brethren have yet *another* method of satisfying *themselves* that infant baptism is *scriptural*. When, as we have seen, Dr. Woods stated that since "It is a plain case that there is no express precept concerning infant baptism in our sacred writings," and that consequently, "The proof that it is a *divine institution* must be made out in some other way," you were perhaps, at a loss to conceive what that *"other way"* could be. By what process can any ordinance be proved "a divine institution," in regard to which not a word is said "in our sacred writings?" No such thing can be done. Since the Bible is our only authority in all cases, the proof proposed is clearly impossible. We will however hear Dr. Woods. He obtains his proof thus :—" It cannot with any good reason, be denied, or doubted, that those christian writers who have, in different ways, given testimony to the prevalence of infant baptism in the early ages of christianity, are credible witnesses. Nor can it be denied that they were under the best advantages to know whether the practice *commenced in the times* of the apostles. On this subject, as *they were not liable to mistake,* so their testimony is entitled to full credit!"* This is the method. It is by *tradition,* vouched by the Fathers, that *protestant* pedobaptists discover that the word of God teaches ordinances which are confessedly not in the word of God! These protestants will not allow the papists to prove, in the same way, the divine authority for the invocation of saints, prayers for the dead, the use of holy water, and such like "institutions," which they can do, readily and fully. *They* are popish. But *this* is protestant. If therefore the Fathers say, this was an apostolic tradition, it *was* an apostolic tradition! And more; *in this matter,* these same Fathers *"were not liable to mistake!"* Their au-

* Apud Hodges on Inf. Bap., p. 39.

thority therefore, though *entirely worthless* when in *favor* of the Catholics, is when infant baptism is to be proved *scriptural,* as *good* at least, as that of the *apostles,* since of *them* no more can be said than that *they were not liable to mistake!* Who would have supposed that theological professors could have been guilty of reasoning so absurdly? The argument, it would seem, needs not a word of refutation. I would not stop to consider it, if Dr. Woods alone, relied upon such testimonies. But it is a common pedobaptist resort. I will offer two or three examples.

Dr. Miller deposes thus regarding tradition:—" The history of the christian church from the apostolic age, furnishes an argument of *irresistible force,* in favor of the *divine authority* of infant baptism." He proceeds —" Can the most incredulous reader who is not fast bound in the fetters of invincible prejudice, hesitate to admit, first, that Augustine, and Pelagius, verily believed that infant baptism had been the universal practice of the church from the days of the apostles;' and secondly, that situated, and informed as they were, it was *impossible* that they should be mistaken?"* These men flourished *four hundred* years after Christ. The word of God says not a word about infant baptism. This however does not disconcert Dr. Miller. Augustine, and Pelagius, say it was an apostolic *tradition.* And *this* he says, is "an argument of *irresistible* force, in favor of the *divine authority* of infant baptism," and by which every one " not fast bound in the fetters of invincible prejudice," must be convinced. But these Fathers also declared that *infant communion* was an

* Inf. Bap., pp. 21, 26.

apostolic tradition. This Dr. *Miller* does not regard as of any importance. Their testimony makes infant *baptism* scriptural; but it has no such effect upon *infant communion!* Was Dr. Miller dreaming when he uttered this logic? Richard Watson says:—" The *antiquity* of infant baptism," taken together with the other arguments, " establish this practice of the church upon *the strongest basis of scripture authority!*" In another place he says:—"That a practice which can be traced up to the very first periods of the church, and has been till very modern times, its uncontradicted practice, should have a lower authority than *apostolic usage, may be pronounced impossible.*"\* To these I will add the declaration of Mr. Hodges. He says:—" Were there no other testimony but that of Irenæus alone, it seems to me, every *unbiased* and *conscientious* man must hold himself *bound* to continue infant baptism, were the scriptures even silent on the subject."† By these and such like arguments, our pedobaptist brethren essay to prove infant baptism scriptural, not by the *scriptures*, but by the Fathers. " It is a plain case," say they, " that there is no express precept respecting infant baptism in our sacred writings;" yet we are assured that the *traditions* of early times, vouched by the Fathers, " establish the divine authority of infant baptism with irresistible force." The Fathers say it was practised in the time of the apostles, and " it was impossible that they should be mistaken!" It is not in the scriptures, but it is undeniably scriptural! And these men who so contradict themselves, and abuse

\* Theol. Insts., vol. 3, pp. 382, 397, 399.
† Inf. Bapt., p. 125.

common sense, are *Protestants*, who proclaim that "The word of God is a perfect rule of faith and practice," and who clamorously join in the cry, "The Bible, the Bible alone, is the religion of Protestants." Yet totally *aside* from the Bible, and by *tradition* exclusively, they hold infant baptism. Thus they renounce, in this case at least, their professed protestant principles, and return to the old and exploded dogmatism of popery. Their position is utterly inconsistent, and cannot be maintained. They are in truth, compelled either to *reject* all the *traditions*, as they do all the *teachings* of the Fathers, which are not sustained by the word of God, and thus become Baptists; or, as in this instance, they must *receive* them all irrespective of their biblical character, and thus become avowed Roman Catholics. However this may be, by the confession that the Bible does not *in itself* teach it, they have surrendered the argument to us, and made the truth still more sure, that Infant baptism is unsupported by the word of God.

How unlike the reasoning of Woods, and Miller, Watson, and the rest, on patristic tradition, is that of their *brother pedobaptist*, the great Neander! He says:—"Not till so late a period as—at least certainly not earlier than—Irenæus appears a trace of infant baptism. That it first became recognized as *an apostolic tradition* in the course of *the third century*, is evidence rather *against*, than *for*, the admission of its *apostolic origin*, especially since, in the spirit of the age when christianity appeared, there were many elements which must have been favorable to the introduction of infant baptism." These were "the same elements from which [afterwards] proceeded the notion of the magical effects of outward baptism; the notion of its absolute necessity for salvation; the notion which gave rise to the mythus that the apostles baptized the Old Testament saints in Hades. How very much must infant baptism have corresponded with such a tendency, *if it had been favored by tradition!* It might indeed, be alleged on the other hand, that after infant baptism had long been recognized as an apostolical tradition, many other causes hindered its universal introduction, and the same causes might still earlier stand in the way of its spread, although a practice sanctioned by the apostles. But these causes could not have acted in this manner in the apostolic age. In later times we see the opposition between theory and practice, in this respect, actually coming forth. Besides, it is a different thing that a practice which could not altogether deny the marks of its later institution, although at last recognized as of apostolic founding, could not for a length of time, pervade the life of the church; and that a practice *really* proceeding from apostolic institution, and tradition, notwithstanding the authority that introduced it, and the circumstances in its favor arising from the spirit of the times, should not yet [in the third century] *have been generally adopted.* And if we wish to ascertain from whom such an institution was originated, we should say *certainly, not immediately from Christ himself.* Was it from the primitive church in Palestine, from an injunction given by the earlier apostles? But among the *Jewish* christians *circumcision* was held as a seal of the covenant, and hence they had so much less occasion to make use of another dedication for their children. Could it have been *Paul*, who first among *heathen* christians introduced this *alteration* in the use of baptism? But this would agree least of all with the peculiar christian characteristics of this apostle. He who says of himself that Christ sent him not to baptize, but to preach the gospel; he who always kept his eye fixed on one thing, justification by faith, and so carefully avoided every thing which could give a handle or support to the notion of a justification by outward things; how could he have set up infant baptism against the circumcision that continued to be practised by the Jewish christians? In this case the dispute carried on with the Judaizing party, on the necessity of circumcision, would easily have given an opportunity of introducing this substitute into the controversy, *if it had really existed*. The evidence arising from *silence* on this topic has therefore the greater weight."* Thus this distinguished scholar, and Ecclesiastical Historian, disposes of the question about which others are so confident, whether infant baptism was really an apostolical tradition. He fully proves the whole to be an utter fiction, not less gross than that which insisted that " the apostles baptized the Old Testament saints in Hades."

There is still one other argument however, which is supposed by many, to be sufficient to sustain infant baptism upon *a scriptural basis,* as " a divine institution." I am told *It is not forbidden in the word of God. It may therefore be practised.* Not forbidden, forsooth! Infant baptism not forbidden in the word of God! It may therefore, be practised! And is this

* Church History. On baptism.

the fashion of your argument? Upon this principle what may you *not* do? You are obliged to baptize all to whom God has commanded the ordinance to be administered; and you may also baptize *all others* whose baptism he has not expressly *forbidden!!* What shall I say of a proposition so monstrous? Its folly can be concealed from no one, who will think for a single moment on the subject. Need I enter into its formal refutation? This is surely unnecessary. Yet, since the argument is so easy and plain, it may be as well to prove that *infant baptism is in truth, actually prohibited by the word of God.*

It is prohibited, in the first place, by the fact that it is unrecognized in the sacred records, as a divine institution. The great christian axiom which teaches that "The word of God is a perfect rule of faith and practice," is, as we have seen, adopted by every protestant denomination upon the face of the earth. We have, besides this, seen that it is fully sustained by the teachings of divine revelation, and that no other principle in religion, can be true in theory, or safe in practice. Whatever God has revealed, we are bound to receive in the love of it, and to obey with reverence, and fidelity, without addition, diminution, or change. Infant baptism, we have clearly seen, is not taught in the Bible. Its friends and advocates confess that it does not there appear, and therefore they vainly seek to sustain it by tradition, and the authority of early Christian Fathers. Is all this true? Is the word of God not a perfect rule of faith and practice? Are you, as taught by Moses and Paul, permitted to add any thing to the commandments of God, or to diminish aught from them? Dare you receive any doctrine as an article of faith, or practise any rite as a christian ordinance, not taught, and instituted by Jehovah? To these inquiries who will venture an affirmative answer? No one, surely. Is infant baptism directly enjoined in the word of God? It confessedly is not. Then it is not by the word of God allowed. It is unlawful. And that which cannot be allowed, because it is not lawful, is clearly prohibited. Thus *God has, in his word, clearly prohibited infant baptism.*

Infant baptism is prohibited, secondly, by the apostolic commission. This is the "law of baptism" instituted by Jesus Christ himself, and "the only law," as Baxter justly observes, "he ever ordained on the subject." As recorded by Mark, it has the following reading:—"Go ye into all the world, and preach the gospel to every creature. He that believeth, and is baptized, shall be saved." This statute is perfectly simple and perspicuous. It ordains first, that the gospel shall *be preached;* secondly, that it shall be preached to *every creature;* thirdly, that all those who *believe the gospel* shall be *baptized;* and fourthly, it promises that those who so believe, and are baptized, *shall be saved.* These are all positive declarations. Every positive necessarily has its negative. And does not every one know that the *requirement* of the *positive* is, as a general rule, the *prohibition* of the *negative?* When God commands you to do a specified thing, the command embraces that particular thing only; and all that is not embraced is, by the very terms of the order, necessarily excluded. Especially is forbidden whatever is inconsistent with the faithful performance of the duty enjoined.

All these are self-evident truths. Let them be applied to the law of baptism as contained in the commission. Only those are permitted to preach who are called of God to the work; they are not allowed to preach, as coming from Christ, any thing but the gospel; and those, and those alone, *who believe the gospel*, they are required to baptize. The persons to be baptized are minutely described. They are believers. Believers therefore, and believers only, are to be baptized. A law to baptize believers is necessarily confined in its administration to believers. It embraces no others. To baptize any others is a violation of the law. It is unlawful. It is prohibited. Infants are **not** believers. The baptism of infants supersedes and prevents the baptism of believers, and is therefore inconsistent with a faithful compliance with the law. Every violation of the law is unlawful, and consequently prohibited. Infant baptism is a violation of the law; is therefore **unlawful**; and consequently by the law itself, clearly prohibited.

Infant baptism, thirdly, is prohibited by the very nature and design of baptism. This ordinance was instituted and enjoined as the form in which you publicly profess your **faith** in Christ, and devote yourself to his service. Paul so teaches when he says, "As many of you as have been baptized into Christ have put on Christ." Episcopalians and Methodists consent to this truth when they concur in the declaration that it "is **a** *sign of profession*, and a mark of difference, whereby christians are distinguished from others that are not baptized."* Presbyterians and Congregationalists, of

* Arts. of Rel., Art. 17.

all classes, regard it as "Not only for the solemn admission of the party baptized into the visible church, but also," of "his giving up unto God, through Jesus Christ, to walk in newness of life."* In this great fact, therefore, all parties are in theory agreed. I now submit the inquiry whether such a profession of faith, and devotion to Christ, as baptism expresses, must not necessarily be a voluntary and intelligent act, on the part of the baptized? To me no fact appears more certain. To those who are incapable of such voluntary and intelligent action, baptism can never be administered. Infants cannot profess their faith, even if they had any faith to profess. They cannot devote themselves to Christ. By the very nature of the ordinance therefore, since they are incapable of compliance with its demands, they cannot be baptized. Any baptism which is unreasonable and inconsistent, because it does not embrace the design, nor express the sense of the ordinance, is unlawful, and therefore prohibited. Infant baptism is unreasonable and inconsistent, because it does not embrace the design, nor express the sense of the ordinance. It is therefore unlawful. It is prohibited.

It must now, I think, be evident to every unprejudiced mind that infant baptism is by the word of God actually prohibited. It is prohibited by the fact that it is unrecognized in the sacred records, as a divine institution; it is prohibited by the terms of the apostolic commission; and it is prohibited by the very nature and design of baptism.

My proposition is thus fully established. We have

* West. Conf., chap. 28, sect. 1.

seen that "Infant baptism is not supported by the word of God," because it is not found to be instituted, or in any manner authorized in the inspired records; because the different sects who imagine that they find it there, prove the contrary by their mutual refutation of each other; because the most pious and learned among pedobaptists themselves, confess it is not directly taught in the sacred writings; because the great christian axiom which teaches that the divine word is our sole authority in religion, does not permit us to receive as scriptural what is not recognized in the scriptures; because the attempt to make it a divine institution by the testimony of the Fathers, through the medium of tradition, is a miserable failure; and because it is really and distinctly forbidden in the word of God. Infant baptism is, in truth, therefore, no baptism at all. God in his word, does not recognize it as baptism. It never can be recognized as baptism by the people of God. It is exclusively an institution of men foisted surreptitiously into the religion of Christ. It is therefore *a most appalling evil*. Some of the forms and bearings of this evil may now not improperly be considered.

It betrays *ministers* into most fearful presumption. When an infant is baptized the minister performs the rite professedly, in the name, and by the authority of Jesus Christ! But Jesus Christ never authorized any such thing! On the contrary, he has discountenanced and forbidden it! What then, shall be said of the act? What magistrate in civil society would venture, under pretence of law, to do a thing, and especially in his official capacity, for the sanction of which no law could be produced, and which by existing laws, according to any reasonable interpretation, is plainly prohibited? Such an officer would act most presumptuously. He would violate his trust. In what well-regulated community would his administration long be endured? And shall ministers of religion thus conduct themselves, and that too without compunction, and without rebuke? In this unauthorized and prohibited ceremony of infant baptism, shall they not only meet no discountenance, but on the contrary be sustained, and defended? How can a conscientious servant of Christ occupy a position so revolting, and abhorrent?

But *ministers* are not alone concerned in this evil. Infant baptism must create in the minds of the *people generally*, who are under its influence, a want of proper respect for the word of God. The habit of acting without law, and in opposition to law, leads to this result inevitably. This truth is so obvious that no argument is needed in its support. May men do, under pretence of law, the most important acts for which no law can be produced? May they indeed, do all these things, and be sustained in them, even in opposition to law? How long then, will it be to them a matter of any special concern what the law may require? They are not obliged to conform to its demands. They may do what they please with impunity, without regard to law! Do they any longer yield a due respect to the law? Do they feel for it any special deference? Assuredly they do not. In civil society this is true, and it is pre-eminently true in religion. Infant baptism necessarily destroys respect for the authority of the word of God.

The evil is still more striking in the fact, that it is a

bold attempt to perfect that which it is vainly conceived God has left imperfect. It is greatly more criminal to do in the name of Jesus Christ, what he has *not* commanded, than it is not to do what he *has* commanded, since when you fall short you thereby confess the difficulty of obedience, but when you go beyond, you impugn his wisdom. In the former case you acknowledge your own deplorable weakness. In the latter, and especially when you claim what he has not authorized or permitted as a part of his religion, you madly charge him with defectiveness, and attempt by additions of your own, to make his government more complete. Why did *he* not ordain infant baptism? Evidently because he did not design that his religion should embrace any such ordinance. *You* have discovered that it is necessary, and have therefore added it! *You* saw that it was demanded to make God's appointments complete! You know better than Jehovah, what is requisite to give perfection to his religion!

Who, in view of all these facts, can avoid the conclusion that infant baptism is a sin against God? What is sin? Is it not any thought, word, action, omission, or desire contrary to the law of God?* "Sin is the transgression of the law."† Infant baptism is not according to the law of God. It is a violation of the law of God. It is the *transgression* of the law of God. Therefore infant baptism is a sin against God.

These are some of the forms in which, as an ordinance not instituted, nor sanctioned by Jesus Christ,

---
\* Crudin on the Word. † 1 John, iii. 4.

the evil of infant baptism is developed. Its practice betrays ministers into fearful presumption; it creates a want of respect for the divine law; it charges imperfection upon the institutions of Messiah; and it is a sin against God. Infant baptism is unsupported by the word of God. It is therefore a great and fearful evil.

In conclusion permit me to entreat for these facts and arguments, your patient, unbiased, and prayerful consideration. You fervently desire to glorify God, and in all things to do his will. You have no wish to depart in any respect from the divine law. You would not encumber religion, much less pollute it, with any doctrines, or observances, not sanctioned from on high. You must therefore, remove infant baptism from its place in your theological system. While it remains there, it will continue to produce its natural fruits. Its extirpation only, can relieve you from its inherent evil. Humbly receive, and diligently practice the religion of Christ, guided in all things, exclusively by his most holy word, and infant baptism will be known no more. To the ascertained will of our Heavenly Father meekly submit yourself. Upon this principle alone is it possible for you to "keep the commandments of the Lord your God which he commanded you." "Behold to obey is better than sacrifice, and to hearken than the fat of rams." But "rebellion is as the sin of witchcraft, and stubbornness is as iniquity and idolatry."

# CHAPTER II.

INFANT BAPTISM IS AN EVIL BECAUSE ITS DEFENCE LEADS TO MOST INJURIOUS PERVERSIONS OF THE WORD OF GOD.

The general principle; instances in illustration, from the apostolic commission; from Peter's sermon; from Paul's instructions to the Corinthians; from Christ's blessing the children; forms of the evil

THE *defence of infant baptism, unsustained as it is by divine authority, necessarily leads to most injurious perversions of the word of God.* The same may be said also, of every other departure from truth, to support which a resort is had to the sacred record. The *evil resulting* will of course, be in proportion to the magnitude, and peculiar bearing, of the error sought to be established. Infant baptism is not a mere ceremony, which when performed, ceases to be of any further importance. Considered in itself, it may indeed seem of little consequence. It is not however thus isolated. Its relations, and influences extend themselves into every department of christianity. It is the process by which the churches which practise it, receive their entire membership, and must therefore enstamp upon them all, its own peculiar character. It leads to insidious and hurtful expositions of scripture; imposes upon the people false doctrines; subverts the true ecclesiastical polity; corrupts the spirit of religion; vitiates christian intercourse; weakens the power of the gospel; and hinders the conversion, and salvation of men. Like an error in the beginning of a mathematical calculation, it runs through the whole process, continually increasing in magnitude as it advances, until every part of it is involved in hopeless confusion. How then, can infant baptism be taught and defended without most injurious perversions of the word of God?

In proof of the proposition now before you, I will point you to appropriate examples. But these are so numerous that I know not where to begin. A proper exposition of them all would require a volume. In the space allowed to this chapter it is not practicable to do more than briefly to refer to a few instances. These, however, of themselves, will be sufficient to establish the truth of the proposition now before us.

The apostolic commission, which I had occasion in the preceding chapter to recite, has been confidently claimed as a law for the baptism of infants. "Go ye therefore, and teach all nations, baptizing them in the name of the Father, and of the Son, and of the Holy Ghost; teaching them to observe all things whatsoever I have commanded you; and lo I am with you alway, even unto the end of the world." This is the version of Matthew. That of Mark is as follows: "And he said unto them, Go ye into all the world, and preach the gospel to every creature. He that believeth, and is baptized shall be saved; but he that believeth not shall be damned." How plain! How perspicuous! How comprehensive! To mistake its sense would seem almost impossible. The solemn obligations thus imposed, are to be faithfully and always obeyed by both the teachers, and the taught. And let it not be forgotten that the several parts of the commission are to be observed in the order in which they are enjoined. The order is plainly as imperative as the commands themselves. A violation of the order is indeed a violation of the commands. This interpretation so evidently correct, is not peculiar to Baptists. Pedobaptists also give it their concurrence. Baxter, for example, says :—" This is not like some occasional historical mention of baptism, but is the very commission of Christ to his apostles, and purposely expresseth their several works in their several places and order." " To contemn this order, is to renounce all rules of order ; for where can we expect to find it if not here ?"* Each duty in the commission must therefore be observed in the order in which it is enjoined. Thus far all is simple and obvious. The commission is evidently, as before seen, a law to baptize believers, and believers only.

By what kind of process, we now inquire, can it be possibly made to appear, that this law to baptize believers is *a law to baptize infants?* Pedobaptists shall themselves answer, and in their own words. " In this commission to his apostles," says Dr. Worcester, " his direction was that *all nations* should be baptized, and children constitute a part of all nations ;" therefore children are to be baptized.† Dr. John Edwards remarks :—" This general commission includes all particulars. Go baptize all nations, is as much, and as full, as if Christ had said, Go baptize *all*, men, women,

---

\* Disp. of Rights to Sacr., pp. 91-149, 150.
† Letters on Bap., p. 115.

and children."* Matthew Henry observes:—"If it be the will and command of the Lord Jesus that all nations should be discipled by baptism, and children, a part of all nations, are not excepted, then children are to be discipled by baptism."† These are fair examples of their teaching, and of the manner in which they bring infant baptism into the commission of Christ to his apostles.

Consider these expositions attentively. How evident the perversions they contain! Were the apostles directed to *baptize all nations* without *respect to moral character*, or any other religious qualifications? Surely not. Is the commission a command in other words, to " baptize *all,* men, women, and children?" Preposterous claim! If infants are not in the commission "*excepted*" in express terms *from baptism*, are *they* therefore to be baptized? How surprising the pretension! Is *any one* ever " *discipled by baptism?*" To disciple is to *teach*. To teach is one thing. To baptize is another. They are not *the same* thing. To pretend then, that any one is "discipled by baptism" is nonsense. Here we have *four perversions* of this portion of the word of God, all palpable, and all made evidently for no other reason than to defend infant baptism. When great and good men, such as these, and the thousands of others who agree with them, thus interpret the commission, we cannot but lament the blindness of mind into which this pernicious error has betrayed them.

One striking instance is now before you of the perversion of the word of God, made for the sake of de-

* Theol. Ref., vol. i., p. 568.  † Treat. on Bapt., p. 114.

fending infant baptism. Take if you please, another. In a learned and very elaborate work recently published, by a distinguished clergyman of the Episcopal church, we have the following passage:—"The chief scripture ground upon which it [infant baptism] is placed, is the text, 'The promise is unto you, and your children.'—Acts ii., 39. And one of its best supports is St. Paul's statement that the children of a believing parent are in a certain sense *holy*.—1 Cor. vii., 14."* We have here therefore, as claimed by pedobaptists themselves, the two passages which are, the one their "*chief scripture ground*" for infant baptism, and the other "*its best support.*" We will therefore, briefly examine them both, and see to what extent they have been perverted for the defence of the rite in question.

"The promise is to you, and to your children."† This text we are told, is "*the chief scripture ground* upon which infant baptism is placed." That you may understand it perfectly, I will refresh your memory with the circumstances under which this inspired declaration occurred. It was uttered by Peter, in Jerusalem, during the ever memorable pentecost. Multitudes had on that day, been called together by "the signs, and wonders, and miracles" resulting from the fulfilment of the promise of God in the gift of the Holy Ghost. This intrepid apostle seized the occasion to preach Christ to the people. His sermon evinced great power, and was attended with singular success. Large numbers were convicted of sin, and in the anguish of their heart cried out:—"What shall we do?"

---

\* Goode on Bapt., p. 31.      † Acts ii., 39.

## PERVERSIONS OF THE WORD OF GOD. 45

In the strictest consonance with the apostolic commission, and almost in its very words, he answered:—
"Repent, and be baptized every one of you, in the name of Jesus Christ, for the remission of sins, and ye shall receive the gift of the Holy Ghost. *For the promise is to you, and to your children, and to all that are afar off, even as many as the Lord our God shall call.*"

What, I now inquire, was *the promise* of which the apostle here spoke? It was undoubtedly, *the gift of the Holy Ghost.* Peter himself so declares. "This is that which was spoken of by the prophet Joel:* And it shall come to pass in the last days, saith God, I will pour out of my spirit upon *all flesh;* and your *sons* and your *daughters* shall prophesy, and your young men shall see visions, and your old men shall dream dreams; and on my servants, and on my handmaidens I will pour out in those days of my spirit." " And it shall come to pass that *whosoever* shall call on the name of the Lord shall be saved."† It is decided therefore that the promise was the Holy Ghost, whose influences as predicted by Joel especially, were at that moment seen so conspicuously among the people. This truth is indubitable.

*To whom,* I next ask, was this promise made? Peter answers, "To you *Jews, and* to your *children,* and to *all that are afar off.*" The words of the promise in Joel, recited by Peter, are, To *you* Jews, and to "*your sons* and your *daughters.*" By "children" therefore, the apostle means "*sons and daughters,*" or in general terms, *posterity.*‡ The *gentile* nations are in

\* Joel ii., 28-32. † Acts ii., 16-21. ‡ τεκνα.

other places of the scriptures spoken of as "*them that are afar off.*" They are, therefore, the persons alluded to in that form of language. But was it the promise of God that *all* or *any* of these classes of persons, who in reality included "*all flesh,*" should receive the Holy Ghost in the times of Messiah—"the last days"—unconditionally? No one will surely maintain that it was, and especially since these very conditions were explicitly stated. They were according to *Joel*, that the persons in question should "call on the name of the Lord." *Peter* instructs us that by calling on the name of the Lord is implied, that they should "repent, and be baptized in the name of the Lord Jesus." The *promise* was to be fulfilled to all those who should comply with these *conditions*, and to none others. *If* you Jews repent of your sins, and by baptism profess your faith in our Lord Jesus Christ, you shall receive the gift of the Holy Ghost, *for the promise is to you. If* your "children," or as Joel calls them, "your sons and your daughters," repent of their sins, and by baptism profess their faith in the Lord Jesus Christ, they shall receive the gift of the Holy Ghost, *for the promise is to your children.* Nor are these privileges and blessings to be confined to your nation. They are to be extended to "them that are afar off," to "all flesh," to "every creature," to "all nations," to as many as the Lord our God shall call by his gospel, and who shall repent and be baptized, no matter to what people they belong. They also shall receive the gift of the Holy Ghost, *for the promise is to them.* To that anxious multitude how full of encouragement was this precious gospel message! It fell upon their hearts like gentle showers upon the parched earth. Hope sprang up in the bosoms of about three thousand, who " gladly *received* the word." They believed it; they acted upon it; they became the subjects of renewing grace, and received the Holy Ghost, according to the promise of God.

Thus, briefly, I have submitted the sense of the passage, and that it is the true sense it seems to me impossible to doubt. In what part of it is infant baptism taught? Not the remotest reference is found to any such thing. Yet say our friends, " It is *the chief* scripture ground for infant baptism!" How is it possible for them to make good this assertion? It cannot be done. But you shall hear their arguments. They shall speak for themselves. Mr. Henry gives the meaning of this passage as follows. Peter, he asserts, intends to say, in other words, to the people:— " Your children shall have, as they have had, an interest in the covenant, and a title to the external seal of it. Come over to Christ to receive those inestimable benefits; for the promise of *the remission of sins, and* the gift of the Holy Ghost, is to you, and to your children." " When God took Abraham into covenant he said, I will be a God to thee, and to thy seed;— Gen. xvii., 7—and accordingly every Israelite had his son circumcised at eight days old. Now it is proper for an Israelite, when he is *by baptism* to come into *a new dispensation of this* covenant, to ask, What shall I do with my children? Must they be thrown out, or taken in with me? Taken in, says Peter, by all means; for the promise, the great promise of God's being to you a God, is as much to you and your children now, as ever it was."*

Who that possesses any tolerable knowledge of the scriptures could readily imagine that learned and good men would *venture this* as the sense of the passage in question? It is crowded in nearly every line, with absurdities and perversions. Let them be separately, and more particularly designated.

In the first place, the representation that the word "*children*" in the passage means the *babes* of those then present is absurd for three reasons; first, because Joel says they were their sons and their daughters, who should then prophesy; and Peter did not intend to *contradict* Joel: secondly, because their babes could not fulfil the conditions upon which the promise was made: and thirdly, because of the nature of the promise itself, which was that they should receive the gift of the Holy Ghost, and prophesy. The word "*children*" is unquestionably used by Peter, in the sense of *posterity* simply. This fact is so obvious that it is frankly conceded by some of the best biblical critics among the pedobaptists themselves. Dr. Whitby says: —"These words will not prove a right of infants to receive baptism, the promise here being that of the Holy Ghost mentioned in verses 16, 17, 18, and so relating only to the times of the miraculous effusions of the Holy Ghost, and to those persons who by age were capable of these extraordinary gifts."† Limborch of Amsterdam, says:—" By children the apostle understands not infants, but posterity." "Whence it appears that the argument which is commonly taken

\* Comm. in loco. † Annot. in loco.

from this passage for the baptism of infants is of no force, and good for nothing."* With these distinguished interpreters agree Doddridge, Hammond, and many others. To represent Peter therefore, as referring to infant children, and inculcating their baptism, is a most injurious perversion of the word of God.

A second perversion is found in the implication that the *faith* and *baptism* of their *parents*, were the *conditions* upon which their *infant children* were to receive the *Holy Ghost*, and the remission of sins. This passage teaches no such thing. Our pedobaptist brethren however represent Peter as saying in other words, to the Jews there under conviction of sin, and whom they, singularly enough, suppose to be inquiring, " What must I do with my children ;" " Come over to Christ to receive these inestimable benefits ; for the promise of the remission of sins, and the gift of the Holy Ghost, is to you and to your children." Do you join the church of Christ, and your children, by virtue of their relation to you, shall be entitled to the same blessings you receive. They shall share with you every gospel blessing, and especially " the remission of sins, and the gift of the Holy Ghost." Do not hesitate therefore ; " come over to Christ." What a monstrous perversion !

A third perversion of this passage is committed. Our pedobaptist brethren insist that the promise in question, relates to the blessings pledged in the *covenant with Abraham*. The promise as stated by Peter, was the gift of the Holy Ghost to believers. But their version is wholly different. They interpret the

* Comm. in loco.

apostle as saying to the Jews :—" Your children [infants] shall [still] have, as they have had, an interest in the covenant [with Abraham] and a title to the external seal of it," all which the *gospel* gives to *you*, and consequently to them!

This short passage is subjected to a fourth perversion. They maintain that *the gospel* covenant is a continuance of the covenant of *circumcision!* Their language is, " When God took Abraham into covenant, he said, I will be a God to thee, and to thy seed ;— Gen. xvii., 7—and accordingly every Israelite had his son circumcised at eight days old. Now it is proper for an Israelite when *he is to enter into a new dispensation of this covenant,* to ask, What must be done with my children ?" And is the *gospel* a new dispensation of *this covenant* that God made with Abraham, according to which " every Israelite had his son circumcised at eight days old ?" The *gospel a new dispensation* of the covenant of *circumcision!* And does Peter so teach ? No such thing appears, either in this text, or elsewhere.

The fifth perversion of this passage, and the last I shall mention, is the claim that Peter means by " the promise," that infants are to be baptized, receive the Holy Ghost, and be taken into the church. " An Israelite" is represented as inquiring, If I " come over to Christ," and unite with this gospel church of yours, " What must be done with my children ? Must they be thrown out, or taken in with me ?" To this they represent the passage as answering :—" Taken in, says Peter, by all means ; for the promise, that great promise of God's being to you a God, is as much to you and your children now, as ever it was." How manifest a perversion is here! Strangely are good men blinded, *so* blinded by infant baptism, that they it seems, really believe that Peter teaches what they represent in the passage!

Having thus disposed of "the chief scripture ground upon which it is placed," and found that no allusion whatever is made in it to infant baptism, we now turn to the other passage, which is, "*one of its best supports.*" This "is St. Paul's statement that the children of a believing parent are in a certain sense holy." In *what sense* are they holy? To comprehend the whole matter perfectly, let us turn to the sacred record, and together with its context, read carefully the entire passage. "Now concerning the things whereof ye wrote unto me," says Paul, and proceeding, he gave various instructions to the Corinthians regarding marriage, and domestic duties. Among other things he says: "Let not the wife depart from her husband; but if she depart let her remain unmarried, or be reconciled to her husband; and let not the husband put away his wife." "If any brother hath a wife that believeth not, and she be pleased to dwell with him, let him not put her away. And the woman which hath a husband that believeth not, and if he be pleased to dwell with her, let her not leave him. For the unbelieving husband is sanctified by the wife, and the unbelieving wife is sanctified by the husband; *else were your children unclean, but now are they holy.* But if the unbelieving depart let him depart. A brother, or a sister, is not in bondage in such cases; but God hath called us to peace. For what knowest thou, O wife, whether thou shalt save thy husband? Or what knowest thou, O man, whether thou shalt save thy wife? But as God hath distributed to every man, as the Lord hath called every one, so let him walk. And so ordain I in all the churches."*

We will here pause if you please, until we have ascertained definitely, the true sense of this interesting portion of divine truth. Paul is without doubt, instructing the Corinthians regarding their conjugal, domestic, and social relations. This fact no one can rationally question. On these topics they needed to be enlightened, since they were evidently disposed to go astray. By some means, probably the instructions of Judaizing teachers among them, the church had, it seems, become agitated with the question whether the old Jewish law which required Israel to regard all gentiles as unclean, and their touch polluting, which in a word prohibited all familiar intercourse with them, ought not to govern christians in their relations with unbelievers. Should not the church regard all who are not members as unclean to them in the same sense that gentiles were formerly looked upon as unclean to Jews? To this opinion the brethren of Corinth appear to have strongly inclined. They soon saw, however, that such a rule of intercourse if adopted among them, must be attended with the gravest consequences. It would not only sever their social and domestic relations, but would actually break up and destroy their families, since some of them were married to unbelievers, from whom of course, they must instantly separate. That this was the true state of the case, and the actual question submitted by them to the apostle, is so plain, from his

* 1 Cor. vii., 1-17.

answer alone, that it is confessed by some of the pedobaptist commentators and divines themselves. Even Henry, for instance, could not avoid seeing it. He says:—" They thought that (the unconverted members of their families) would be common, or unclean, in the same sense as heathens in general were styled in the apostle's vision."* Dr. Miller, notwithstanding his prejudices, is still more full. He says:—" It appears that among the Corinthians to whom the apostle wrote, there were many cases of professing christians being united by the marriage tie with pagans; the former being perhaps converted after marriage, or being so unwise as after conversion deliberately to form this unequal and unhappy connection. What was to be deemed of such marriages seems to have been the grave question submitted to this inspired teacher."† Upon this point therefore, we are certainly right.

These were the perplexing circumstances under which they wrote to Paul for advice. He answered them in substance, that the old Jewish law regulating intercourse with gentiles, was not applicable to them, not only because the ceremonial dispensation to which it exclusively belonged had passed away, but also because in their case, (and the same was true of all other churches,) its observance was impracticable. Any attempts to enforce it, must have been attended with the most disastrous consequences. The christians, unlike the Jews, lived, and must live, in the *midst of unbelievers.* Many of them were connected with their families, and were a part of them. With such persons they could not *avoid* contact, and association. If such separation

* Comm. in loco. † Miller, Bapt., pp. 17–20.

was necessary to preserve their christian purity, then to retain it they "must needs go out of the world." But especially some of them were *married* to unbelievers, and if this abrogated Jewish law was to be enforced all such husbands and wives must part from each other. But this was not demanded by the gospel, and ought not to take place, unless the temper of the unbelieving party should render it necessary. "If any brother hath a wife that believeth not, and she be pleased to dwell with him, let him not put her away. And the woman which hath a husband that believeth not, if he be pleased to dwell with her, let her not leave him." "But if the unbelieving depart, let him depart. A brother or a sister is not under bondage in such cases; but God hath called us to peace." Believers and unbelievers who are husband and wife, may lawfully, and ought to continue to dwell together. No such rule of ceremonial *holiness*, and *uncleanness*, obtains under the gospel as that which characterized the Mosaic economy. The marriage tie makes the parties, though it unite a believer with an unbeliever, *holy* to each other. The unbelieving husband is not *unclean* so that the believing wife may not lawfully dwell with him. The unbelieving wife is not *unclean* so that the believing husband may not lawfully dwell with her. Why then separate? Let them remain together. And for their continued union there is yet another most important reason. God may perhaps, bless the efforts of the believing, to the conversion and salvation of the unbelieving party.

And yet more. Must the believing husband or wife separate from the unbelieving, for the reasons alleged?

Then it will follow that, for the very same reasons, the believing parent must also separate from his own children, since they also are not believers! Indeed, not a member of the church, if separation from all unbelievers is necessary to preserve his christian purity, must touch his own children, eat with them, or associate with them. The believing parent occupies, in this respect, precisely the same relation to his child that he does to his unbelieving wife. Must he separate from his wife? He must also separate from his child. But you do not, said Paul, consider your children unclean to you, but holy. You do not, you must not, humanity forbids that you should, consider their touch polluting. They are sanctified, holy, clean, to you. So also the unbelieving wife is sanctified, holy, clean to you. You must not separate from your child. Therefore you must not separate from your wife. "The unbelieving husband is sanctified $to$* the wife, and the unbelieving wife is sanctified $to$ the husband, else were your children unclean [to you], but now they are holy" to you. Therefore the unbelieving wife is holy to you. In the same way that the child is holy to the believing parent, the unbelieving husband is holy to the believing wife, and the unbelieving wife is holy to the believing husband. You may lawfully remain with your children. You may therefore lawfully remain with each other. Throw aside these absurd notions about the old Jewish law of ceremonial purity. Dwell together in the conjugal relation. "As God hath distributed to every man, as the Lord hath called every one, so let him walk. And so ordain I in all the churches."

* $εν$. Macknight in loco.

Is not this a true exposition of the sense of the apostle? It is self-evident. Some few of the more learned *pedobaptist* divines have seen and confessed it. Dressler, for example, says:—" According to Paul a holy pedigree is nothing in religion. Neither circumcision nor uncircumcision availeth any thing, but keeping the commandment of God. The passage 1 Cor. vii., 13, 14, [that now before us] does not support any such view. He says, if the christians would flee from every unbeliever, regarding him as unclean, they must flee from their own children, and hold them as unclean, for they were among the unbelievers. 'Otherwise your children would be unclean,' for they are not christians by birth merely. 'But now are they holy,' *i. e.*, you are not to consider yourselves polluted by them."\*

Such is the lesson, in response to their inquiry, taught by Paul to his brethren the Corinthians. How beautiful! How important! How simple! How easy to be understood! Not the remotest reference is made in it in any way, to infant baptism. Yet it is declared to be "*one of its best supports!*" Accordingly our brethren have chiefly predicated upon it this declaration in the Westminster Confession of Faith:—" Not only those that do actually profess faith in and obedience unto Christ, but also the infants of one or both believing parents are to be baptized."† Commenting upon the passage, "Else were your children unclean, but now are they holy," Mr. Henry says:—" That is, they would be heathen, out of the pale of the church, and covenant of God. They would not be of the holy

---

\* Doct. Sacra. Bapt., p. 137.   † West. Conf., pp. 21, 22.

seed." "The children born to christians, though married to unbelievers, are not part of the world, but of the church."* On the same passage Dr. Clarke remarks :—" If this kind of relative sanctification were not allowed, the children of these persons could not be received into the christian church, nor enjoy any rights or privileges as christians ; but the church of God never scrupled to admit such children as members." Dr. Miller, after admitting all that we have just seen, still says that Paul " pronounces under the direction of the Holy Spirit, that in all such cases, when the unbeliever is willing to live with the believer, they ought to continue to live together, that their connection is so sanctified by the character of the believing companion that their children are 'holy,' that is, in covenant with God ; members of that church with which the believing parent is in virtue of his profession united ; in one word, that the infidel party is so far, and in such a sense, consecrated by the believing party, that their children shall be reckoned to belong to the sacred family with which the latter is connected, and shall be regarded and treated as members of the church of God."†

These are specimens of the havoc made of the sense of the word of God for the sake of infant baptism. Look at the perversions here committed.

Paul teaches, as they contend, that the offspring of parents one of whom is a believer, are born members of the church with which the believing parent is connected ; that they are born in covenant with God ; that as such they are entitled to " enjoy the rights

* Comm. in loco. † Miller on Bap., pp. 17-20.

and privileges of christians;" and that were it not so their children "would be heathens!" Here are four palpable perversions. None of these propositions are true in themselves; they are not sustained at all in the word of God; and especially they are not found in the instructions of Paul to the Corinthians. But a still greater perversion of this passage, if possible, remains to be mentioned. Paul told the Corinthians that as they did not consider their children ceremonially unclean or unholy to them, but holy, and they therefore took care of them; so the unbelieving party in marriage, since she bore the same relation to the believing party with the child, was not to be considered by the other ceremonially unclean, or unholy, but holy, and they should therefore remain together. No, no, Paul! respond our pedobaptist brethren, this is not what you mean! You mean that the holiness of the *children* is *spiritual*, that it is "*ecclesiastical*," and more, you mean that this holiness is produced by hereditary transmission, so that the children are born in the covenant and church of God, and, since as such they are entitled to "enjoy the privileges and rights of christians," they are to be baptized! Thus boldly do they contradict the apostle himself, and greatly also to his injury; since if their interpretation is true they make Paul speak nonsense, and bring him into collision with himself, and other portions of divine truth. Are the terms unclean, sanctified, and holy to be understood in a spiritual, or an ecclesiastical sense? They so maintain. It is certain that these words are used in the same sense in their application to both parent and child. It follows thus, that if the child is to be baptized because that relationship makes it *holy*, as certainly is the unbelieving husband, or wife, to be baptized because by the same relationship he, or she, is *sanctified*. He who is sanctified is holy, and the sanctified have the same right to baptism with the holy.\* If then you baptize the child upon the faith of its mother, you must, to be consistent, baptize the unbelieving husband upon the faith of his wife, since if the child is *holy*, so also is the unbelieving father *sanctified*. But it is certain Paul teaches no such doctrine. Paul was wise. We have reason to lament that so much cannot be said of very many of his professed interpreters.

One other passage ought to be considered, and its false glosses briefly exposed, since much confidence has of late, been expressed that it contains evident authority for infant baptism. "Jesus said, Suffer little children, and forbid them not, to come unto me, for of such is the kingdom of heaven."† Let us, in the first place, carefully examine this text, and ascertain its exact sense.

The Saviour was in the midst of a discourse of surpassing interest. His disciples were absorbed in their attention to his instructions. Suddenly there "were brought unto him little children." The *object* of those who brought them—probably their parents—the evangelist fully states. It was, "That he should put his hands on them, and pray."‡ This was a very familiar observance among the Jews. Great importance was

\* In the original both words are the same, one the verb, the other the corresponding adjective.

† Matt. xix., 14. ‡ See context.

attached by them, and justly, to the benedictions of holy men. To obtain them therefore, when practicable, had been common from the earliest times.* These parents fully believed that Jesus was a prophet of God, and they desired for their children his prayers and blessing. This was what they sought, and all that they sought. They however, encountered in their approach, a *rebuke* from the disciples! This occurred, not certainly, from any want of respect on the part of the disciples for their motives, and wishes, but evidently because they were impatient of the interruption. Their feelings were deeply enlisted in the topic before them, and they were not willing that their Master should, on any account, be diverted from it. But he, observing what they did, "was much displeased,"† and immediately suspending his discourse, "Called the little children to him."‡ Thus he manifested his great love, patience, and condescension. What the Saviour did for these children is now distinctly and fully stated: —"He took them up in his arms, put his hands upon them, and blessed them." Meantime he compensated his disciples for the interruption, by imparting one of the richest lessons to be found in all his teachings. It is contained in the very passage now in question:—" Of such is the kingdom of heaven." And he adds:— " Verily I say unto you, Whosoever shall not receive the kingdom of God as a little child, shall in no wise enter therein."

By "the kingdom of heaven," and "the kingdom of God," here employed as convertible terms, our Sa-

---

\* Gen. xlviii., 14. Matt. ix., 18. Mark xvi., 18.
† Mark x., 14–16.                          ‡ Luke xviii., 16.

viour refers to the Gospel, the true principles of which in the heart, alone can qualify any one for the holy brotherhood of the church upon earth. This fact needs only to be stated. But what are we to understand by the phrase, " *Of such* is the kingdom of heaven ?" Is it not sufficiently explained by the other phrase, " Whosoever shall not receive the kingdom of God [the grace offered by Christ] *as a little child,* [in the spirit, and with the disposition of a little child] shall in no wise enter therein ?" This appears to me most evident. He does not say that the kingdom of heaven—the church—belongs to little children, or is composed of *these,* and other such little children. Certainly not. This is plain from our *present version,* but in *the original* it is still more obvious. The word rendered " *of such,*"* conveys the idea, as every *scholar* must see, of *comparison,* and does not therefore, signify *identity,* but *likeness.* The church therefore, is made up, not, as pedobaptists tell us, *of little children,* but of those who by divine grace are made *like* little children. Only "such" can have a place there, as are *spiritually,* what little children are *literally.* Little children love their parents supremely : To fit you for a place in his visible church, you must love God supremely. Little children receive as true, and implicitly believe, whatever is declared by their parents : You must receive as true, and implicitly believe whatever is declared in his word, by God. Little children submit themselves to such provisions as are made for them by their parents : You must submit yourselves to such arrangements as are made for you by God. Little children obey the com-

* τοιουτων, not αυτων.

mandments of their parents: You must obey the commandments of God. In these and other respects, to qualify you for a place in the kingdom, or church of God, you must be *like* little children. You "receive the kingdom of God as a little child" when you cherish the same love, faith, submission, and obedience towards God, that little children do towards their parents.

Such is undoubtedly, the true, and full sense of the passage. How evangelical! How rich! Never, as has been said, did the Redeemer himself, teach a more important lesson. Let it be observed, however, that neither in the passage, nor in the context, nor anywhere else in this connection, is there an allusion of any kind even remotely to baptism. With these facts and expositions before us, we turn to the interpretations of our pedobaptist brethren. What are they? Mr. Henry shall again serve as an example of them all.\* He speaks thus:—" Observe *the faith* of those who brought [these children to Christ. They were *believing* parents.] The *children of believing parents belong* to the kingdom of heaven, and *are members of the visible church*. Of such—not only of such in *disposition*, and *affection*, (that might have served for a reason why doves, or lambs should be brought to him,) but of such *in age*—is the kingdom of heaven; to *them* pertain the privileges of visible church-membership as among the Jews of old."
" Parents are trustees of their children's wills, are empowered by nature to transact for their benefit, and therefore Christ accepts *their* dedication of them as their [the children's] act and deed, and will own these dedicated things in the day when he makes up his

\* Comm. in loco.

jewels. Therefore *he takes it ill* of those who forbid *them*, and [who] exclude those [children] whom *he* has received;" " and who forbid water that they [infants] should be baptized, who if that promise be fulfilled (Isa. xliv., 3) [I will pour out my Spirit upon thy seed, and my blessing upon thine offspring] have received the Holy Ghost as well as we, for aught we know." Look at this gloss! Ponder it! How preposterous! Dr. Clarke's commentary is as follows :—" Let every parent that fears God, bring up his children in that fear; and *by baptism* let each be dedicated to the Holy Trinity. Whatever is solemnly consecrated to God, abides under his protection and blessing."\* These, and such like, are the pedobaptist interpretations of the passage in question! They are *published to the world*, and *received*, and *defended*, as expressing its *true sense!* Is it surprising therefore, that a vail is thus thrown over the gospel, and its great truths withheld from the faith of the simple?

And now mark if you please, the glaring *perversions* with which this whole pedobaptist "exposition" is crowded. I shall notice *six only*. It is here *denied* that Christ designs to *illustrate* the true christian character by *the disposition of children*, and it is asserted that this might have been done by the dispositions and affections of *doves*, or *lambs*, as well as by those of *children;* thus the *obvious truth is repudiated:* it is maintained that Christ here teaches the church-membership of literal infants, by natural birth; that parents have a natural right to "transact" in religion for their children—impose upon them the vows, and ordinance

\* Comm. in loco.

of baptism—and that God will accept it as binding upon the children; that in the last day, when God shall make up his jewels, persons will be "owned" by him, because they were in their infancy " dedicated to the Holy Trinity in baptism;" that Christ *takes it ill* of those who refuse to receive infants into the church, and to baptize them; and that "for aught we know, infants have received the Holy Ghost as well as we," and ought therefore to be baptized! *What perversions!* What falsifications of truth!

We have thus seen how the word of God is perverted in order to sustain this unauthorized rite, in the instances of the apostolic commission, the address of Peter on the day of pentecost, the instructions of Paul to the Corinthians, regarding social and domestic intercourse, and the blessing of children by our Lord Jesus Christ. Many, very many other examples equally striking, might be produced, but enough has been said to establish fully the proposition with which we set out. It is unquestionably true that the defence of infant baptism necessarily leads to *most injurious perversions of the word of God.* This is an evil, a most melancholy evil. It destroys all just principles of biblical interpretation; it covers the sacred oracles with impenetrable obscurity; it inculcates error, and withholds the truth from the cause and people of God; by it knowledge is abridged; faith is made weak; religion becomes less enlightened; and practical godliness is overwhelmed!

## CHAPTER III.

INFANT BAPTISM IS AN EVIL BECAUSE IT ENGRAFTS JUDAISM UPON THE GOSPEL OF CHRIST.

Form of church organization; pedobaptist theory; it proves too much ; is in conflict with christianity; violates true analogy; is at war with fundamental religion; is antiscriptural.

THERE are *two theories,* and two only consistent with themselves, *of church organization.* One of them models the church upon the spiritual plan developed in *the New Testament;* the other gives it the form of *the old Jewish Theocracy.* The former is Baptist. The latter is Roman Catholic. Between these two, and partaking more or less of both, stand *all the various protestant denominations.* Their evangelical spirituality is Baptist. Their other characteristics, and especially their *infant baptism,* is Roman Catholic ; or rather *Judaism,* of which popery is confessedly, a continuation. To obtain a basis for this ordinance, they have been obliged, with the papists, to assume *the unity of the Jewish church and the Christian church.* Thus they engraft Judaism upon the gospel of Christ. I shall state their argument in their own language, as elaborately set forth, in terms acknowledged by all, to be correct, and perspicuous. " Abraham and his seed, were divinely constituted a true visible church of God." "The Jewish society before Christ, and the Christian society after

Christ, are one and the same church in different dispensations." "Jewish circumcision before Christ, and Christian baptism after Christ, are one and the same seal, though in different forms." "The administration of this seal to infants was once enjoined by divine authority." "The administration of this seal to infants was never prohibited by divine authority." You will then perceive that we have "a divine command for baptizing infants."* To this statement may be added that of Rev. Dr. Peters. He says:—"When [circumcision] the ancient sign of the covenant which God made with his people for an everlasting covenant, was abolished, another [baptism] was instituted in the same church, under the same covenant, of precisely the same import, and for the same purpose." Such is the platform erected for the support of infant baptism. *It abandons the New Testament wholly, and assumes the old Jewish Theocracy as the true form of the gospel church!*

1. In the consideration of this argument, so specious to many minds, generally so successful, and therefore advanced with so much confidence, I shall, in the first place, show that *it proves immeasurably too much*.

Let us, for the sake of the discussion, admit for a moment that it is true, and what are the results? By all *Protestants* at least, as soon as its bearings and results are understood, it must be instantly renounced. It is really available for Papists, and for Papists only. But to the demonstration. "Abraham and his seed were divinely constituted a true visible church of God." "The Jewish society before Christ, and the Christian

---

* Dr. Maccalla in Debate with Rev. A. Campbell, pp. 55, 56.

society after Christ, are one and the same church in different dispensations." "Jewish circumcision before Christ, and Christian baptism after Christ, are one and the same seal, though in different forms." "They were instituted in the same church, and under the same covenant." "The administration of this seal to infants was once enjoined by divine authority." "The administration of this seal to infants was never prohibited by divine authority." "You will therefore perceive that we have a divine command for baptizing infants." Very well. Now you have infant baptism, and you have it by "divine command!" Presbyterians, Methodists, Congregationalists, and others are delighted. The argument is satisfactory. They embrace it with eagerness. It is true, every word true. The thought has not occurred that it is dangerous. But we shall see.

An Episcopalian perceives that it will serve *his design*. The other sects may protest against his use of it, but they cannot hinder it. All have an equal right to its benefits. He assumes as true, and admitted, all the propositions now before you, and then proceeds thus:—In the Jewish church there were three orders in the ministry, each a grade above the other in dignity and authority; the chief priests, the common priests, and the levites. There are therefore, three orders in the ministry in the Christian church. It is the same church, and under the same covenant. These orders in the ministry of the church were once enjoined by divine authority. They were never prohibited by divine authority. You will therefore perceive that we have a divine command for three orders in the ministry of the Christian church. They are bishops, priests, and deacons, and we have them by *divine right* and by *regular succession* from the apostles. Episcopalians are now fully gratified. Their episcopacy can be questioned no longer by any class of pedobaptists, since the argument for infant baptism and for episcopacy is the same, and you cannot overthrow one without at the same time destroying the other. Here, however, Episcopalians insist that the "analogy" shall cease. But no. The ball has been set in motion, and you must be content to see it roll on. The propositions are admitted, and they carry you resistlessly forward to other results.

A Roman Catholic reminds you that in the Jewish church there was one great high priest, who was the pastor or bishop of the whole visible church of God upon earth. In the Christian church therefore, there is one great high priest, who is pastor or bishop of the whole visible church of God upon earth. Although in different dispensations, it is the same church, and under the same covenant. The appointment of this universal pastor or bishop was once enjoined by divine authority. It was never prohibited by divine authority. You will therefore perceive that we have a divine command for one great high priest, who is the pastor or bishop of the whole visible church of God upon earth. This universal pastor or bishop we have, by "*regular succession from St. Peter.*" He is the Pope. His residence is Rome, the See of the Fisherman of Galilee, and the capital of the world, whence "*by divine right*" he rules the whole visible church of God upon earth. His name at present is PIO NONO.

You have obtained, from the argument before you, infant baptism; but the process by which this has been secured has also *forced* upon you, first *episcopacy*, and then *popery!* If you take the first you must also take the other two. And what else will you have? You must go still further. You must unite your *church* with the *state*, and have a national religion! This would be very convenient. It would give you dignity, and wealth, and power. The *Jewish* church was a *national* church, and the Christian church is *the same church.* Therefore the *Christian church* must be a *national church.* The union of church and state was once enjoined by divine authority. It was never prohibited by divine authority. You will therefore perceive that we have a divine command for the union of church and state! The *sacrifice of the mass* would probably be agreeable, if it only possessed divine authority. It is a very imposing rite. You have the wished-for sanction in the Jewish sacrifices. You want seventy cardinals? The seventy elders who composed the Jewish council will supply you. You are perchance fond of pageantry, and would willingly ornament the persons of your ministry with pontificals. The splendid robes and mitres of the Jewish priests, and especially the jewelled breast-plate of the high priest, will satisfy your vanity to the utmost. The Jewish church and the Christian church are the same church. All these were once enjoined by divine authority. None of them were ever prohibited by divine authority. You will therefore perceive that we have a divine command for the union of church and state, for the sacrifice of the mass, for the college of cardinals, and for priestly robes and ornaments.

The argument for the whole paraphernalia of popery is precisely the same with that for infant baptism. It has the same force and conclusiveness. Infant baptism, episcopacy, popery, the union of church and state, the mass, cardinals, robes, all, rest upon the same foundation and must stand or fall together. They are predicated not upon the gospel, but upon what our brethren *call* the analogy of the church, and really upon Judaism. Indeed such is, and has been the influence of Moses upon christianity, that pedobaptist churches of all classes, receive their members, and most of them are modelled, and governed, by his law rather than according to the gospel of Christ. Are you a Pedobaptist? To be consistent you must also be a Papist. The same law that requires infant baptism requires a pope, an established religion, and their adjuncts. Do you repudiate these? For the same reason you must also repudiate infant baptism. But renouncing them all, you are forced back upon Baptist ground. You adopt the New Testament as giving the true form of the church of Christ.

2. I, in the second place, remark that this Judaistic argument for infant baptism cannot be maintained, because it is directly *in conflict with christianity as taught by Christ and his apostles*.

Essays to commingle Judaism with the gospel commenced immediately after the ascension of our Redeemer. The Judaism then preached was precisely such as our pedobaptist brethren now claim as legitimate in religion. It did not indeed, include infant baptism, but advocated instead literal circumcision. The discovery that "Jewish circumcision before Christ, and Christian baptism after Christ, is one and the same seal, though in different forms," was not yet made, nor did it come to light until some centuries after. The principle however was the very same. Glance through the history of the first period of the church, as contained in the Acts of the Apostles, and you will find that, as soon as the gentiles began to embrace the religion of Christ, there were instantly among them christianized Jewish priests, urging upon the converts the absolute necessity of adding to the gospel the doctrines and rites of Moses. They said, in substance, to these disciples, The religion of Christ is true, and necessary, but it is not enough; "Except ye be circumcised after the manner of Moses, ye cannot be saved."* The agitations and proceedings consequent upon this teaching in the church at Antioch in Syria, and subsequently in the council at Jerusalem, with the numerous admonitions regarding them contained in all the epistles, will fully instruct you as to the rise of Judaism in the Christian church, its nature as then taught, and the manner in which it was met and resisted by the apostles. "Certain men that came down from Judea," says Luke, thus "taught the brethren." "When therefore Paul and Barnabas had no small dissension and disputation with them, they determined that Paul and Barnabas, and certain others of them, should go up to Jerusalem unto the apostles and elders about this question."† We saw in the last chapter an instance of the influence of Judaism among the Corinthians, and the painful perplexity it occasioned regarding domestic and social intercourse. Among the Galatians were those who desired to be under the law,‡ and they constrained their brethren to be circumcised.§ Indeed, the epistles evince conclusively, that the

---

\* Acts xv., 1.      ‡ Gal. iv., 21.
† Acts xv., 1, 2.      § Gal. vi., 12, 13.

churches of the Romans, the Corinthians, the Galatians, the Ephesians, the Colossians, and the others, were constantly excited, and agitated with Judaism. This fact cannot have escaped the attention of any intelligent christian. Perpetually repeated efforts were made by converted priests, and others, to engraft its forms, and ordinances, upon the gospel of Christ.

How was this subject regarded by the inspired apostles? Did they look upon the matter as of little importance? They taught the churches that it was *in conflict with christianity*, and could result only in confusion and disaster. Corresponding with these sentiments were the measures they adopted respecting it. Let us turn to their inspired instructions, and be enlightened. Protesting against the introduction of the doctrines and rites of Judaism, Paul, for example, thus admonishes his brethren. "O foolish Galatians, who hath bewitched you that ye should not obey the truth?" "Received ye the Spirit by the works of the law, or by the hearing of faith? Are ye so foolish? Having begun in the Spirit, are ye now made perfect by the flesh? Have ye suffered so many things in vain, if it be yet in vain? He that ministereth to you the Spirit, and worketh miracles among you, doeth he it by the works of the law, or by the hearing of faith?" You wish to conform to the law of Moses that you may be accounted the children of Abraham. Remember that "Abraham believed God, and it was accounted to him for righteousness. Know ye therefore that they which are of faith, the same are the children of Abraham." And further. "After that ye have known God, or rather are known of God, how turn ye again to the weak and beggarly elements whereunto ye desire to be again in bondage? Ye observe days, and months, and times, and years. I am afraid of you lest I have bestowed upon you labor in vain." And still further. " They [the Judaizing teachers] zealously affect you, but not well; yea they would exclude you that ye might affect them." " My little children, of whom I travail in birth again until Christ be formed in you, I desire to be present with you now, and to change my voice, for I stand in doubt of you. Tell me, ye that desire to be under the law, do ye not hear the law?" " It is written, Abraham had two sons, the one [Ishmael] by a bond maid, the other [Isaac] by a free woman. But he who was of the bond woman was born after the flesh; but he of the free woman was by promise. Which things are an allegory; [the two sons were typical] for these are [figures of] the two covenants; the one [that shadowed forth by Ishmael is the covenant] from Mount Sinai [the law] which gendereth to bondage, which is [the son of] Agar." The other, that prefigured by Isaac, is the covenant of grace in our Lord Jesus Christ. Isaac was by promise; Isaac was free; and " we, brethren, as Isaac was, are the children of promise," and like him we are free; " For the law of the spirit of life in Christ Jesus hath made us free from the law of sin and death."\* " What saith the scriptures? Cast out the bond woman and her son [this law of ceremonies and external observances from Sinai], for the son of the bond woman shall not be heir with the son of the free woman." " Brethren, we are not children of the bond woman, but of the free. Stand

---

\* Rom. viii., 2.

fast therefore in the liberty wherewith Christ hath made us free, and be not entangled again in the yoke of bondage ;" " the yoke which neither our fathers nor we were able to bear."* " Behold I Paul, say unto you that if ye be circumcised Christ shall profit you nothing." " Christ has become of no effect unto you, whosoever of you are justified by the law; ye are fallen from grace. For we through the Spirit do wait for the hope of righteousness by faith. For in Jesus Christ neither circumcision availeth any thing, nor uncircumcision, but faith which worketh by love. Ye did run well ; who did hinder you that ye should not obey the truth ?" " A little leaven leaveneth the whole lump." " He that troubleth you shall bear his judgment whosoever he be." " I would that they were even cut off which trouble you. For, brethren, ye have been called unto liberty."† Once more. In Christ " dwelleth all the fulness of the Godhead bodily. And ye are complete in him which is the head of all principality and power ; in whom also ye are circumcised with the circumcision made without hands, [purified in heart by the Spirit] in putting off the body of the sins of the flesh by the circumcision of Christ; buried with him in baptism, wherein also ye are risen with him through the faith of the operation of God, who hath raised him from the dead. And you being dead in your sins, and the uncircumcision of your flesh, hath he quickened together with him, having forgiven you all trespasses ; blotting out the hand writing of ordinances that was against us, which was contrary to us, nailing it to his cross ; and having spoiled principalities and powers, he

* Acts xv., 10. † Gal., chs. iii., iv., v.

made a show of them openly, triumphing over them in it. Let no man therefore judge you in meat, or in drink, or in respect of a holy day, or of the new moon, or of the sabbath days; which are a shadow of things to come; but the body is of Christ."* In this manner did the apostles meet, and resist Judaism in the church of Christ. If any conclusion can be drawn from their language which is beyond question correct, it certainly is that they regarded its introduction as in conflict with christianity, and portending destructive consequences. Judaism was thus suppressed for the time, but it was not cast out. As some of the Canaanites were left in Israel, so Judaism remained in the church, to try the faith of the people of God. Nor did it lie inactive, but as time passed, and piety waned, it gained strength; and at the present hour, though slightly changed in form from what it was originally, it has, as we have already seen, with all the sects, more influence in their ecclesiastical polity, and their administration of ordinances, than has even the gospel itself of the grace of God.

We have thus seen how Judaism is embodied in the argument before us, by which infant baptism is sustained and defended. We have seen how it arose in the church, how deleterious was its influence, and how it was met and resisted by the apostles. And are we after all, to be told that it is legitimate and scriptural? Are we now to hear it defended by grave and learned divines? That very corruption once so warmly deprecated by Paul, and James, and Peter, and John, and the others, as so insufferable that they spoke of *cutting*

* Col. ii., 9–17.

*off* those who troubled the churches with it, is it now to be assumed as granted, and made the foundation for infant baptism? No, we cannot. We will not. We repudiate it. We protest against it. We denounce it as condemned by the word of God, in conflict with christianity, and an offence to our adorable Redeemer.

3. This argument for infant baptism, in the third place, fails entirely, because it perverts, and renders wholly unintelligible, the true scriptural analogy of the church.

Pedobaptists call the argument for infant baptism, which we are now combating, *analogy;* but it is in truth *identity*, and not analogy, since they claim that the *Jewish* church and the *Christian* church are the *same church*, and that, although in different dispensations, they subsist under the *same covenant*. This is unquestionably *sameness*, as distinguished from *similitude* and *diversity*. This is *identity*. And what is *analogy?* If Webster be authority for words, it is " an *agreement* or *likeness* between things in *some circumstances* and *effects,* when the things are *otherwise* entirely different." A correspondence between the churches, of this character undoubtedly exists. But the *identity* claimed and advocated, and which is necessary to include and defend infant baptism, while, as we have fully seen, it also includes and defends popery in all its absurd extremes, is condemned and denounced by the apostles. There *is* a beautiful *analogy;* but the *identity* assumed is nothing more nor less than naked Judaism. Trace with me if you please, briefly, the *true analogy* between the Jewish church and the Christian church.

The relations between them are, I remark, precisely those subsisting between a figure and the thing signified, or a shadow and its substance. The *Jewish* church was a figure, a shadow, a type of the *Christian* church. No one with this proposition distinctly in mind, can read carefully the epistle to the Hebrews, and then seriously doubt its truth. To state this important fact, to establish it, and to illustrate its various bearings, much space, and carefulness, are employed in this admirable epistle. Indeed it seems to have been one of its main designs. The Hebrews were naturally more prone than others to Judaism, and to fall consequently into the error which supposes that " the Jewish society before Christ, and the Christian society after Christ, are one and the same church in different dispensations." Paul therefore instructs them that the people, the sacrifices, the priesthood, the temple, and all the ordinances and forms of the Jewish worship, were "figures for the time then present," and were ordained and instituted as "types of better things," "until the times of reformation," in other words, until the coming of Christ. "The holy places made with hands were the figures of the true" holy places.\* All the parts of the Jewish church and worship were figures of the Christian church and worship. What is true of all the parts, is true of the whole. The whole Jewish church therefore was a figure or type of the Christian church. This, as set forth in the word of God itself, is the true and exact analogy between the Jewish church and the Christian church.

The rules in Hermeneutics by which these corre-

\* Heb. ix., 9, 10, 11–23, 24.

spondences are governed, are obvious and definite. They are as follows. "No *external* institution or fact in the Old Testament is a type of an *external* institution or fact in the New Testament. *External* institutions and facts in the Old Testament are invariably types of *internal* and *spiritual* institutions and facts in the New Testament." These rules are, I am happy to say, recognized as legitimate by the learned among pedobaptists themselves. Turrettine, for example, the distinguished successor of Calvin, referring to doctrines of Cardinal Bellarmine, says:—"For what Bellarmine sets forth, that these [Jewish rites] were not so much sacraments as types of sacraments is absurd, inasmuch as a sacrament is an *external* thing, and whatever is a type of any *internal* or *spiritual* thing has no need of any other type by which it may be represented. Two types may indeed be given similar and corresponding to each other of one and the same truth, and so far the ancient sacraments were similar to ours;" "but one type cannot be shadowed forth by another type," since "both are brought forward to represent one truth. So circumcision shadowed forth not baptism, but the grace of regeneration; and the passover represented not the Lord's supper, but Christ set forth in the supper."*

With these fixed principles of exposition before us, we will pursue, in order that the subject may be rendered if possible still more plain and certain, "the analogy of the church" somewhat more in detail.

Abraham, the great type of Messiah, was the head of the Jewish covenant and church; Messiah himself is

* Opera., tom. iv., p. 342.

the head of the Christian covenant and church. The *natural* seed of Abraham were entitled by virtue of their carnal relationship to him as their father, to membership in the Jewish church, and to all the ordinances, rights, and immunities of that church; the *spiritual* seed of Abraham by virtue of their holy relationship to Jesus Christ as their father, are entitled to membership in the Christian church, and to all the ordinances, rights, and immunities of that church. The *natural* seed of Abraham in right of their father inherited the earthly Canaan; the *spiritual* seed in right of their father Jesus Christ, inherit the Canaan above. In the Jewish church sacrifices were *literal*. They were all types, and pointed to the great sacrifice in the person of Christ, to be in the fulness of time offered by him upon the cross. In the Christian church sacrifices are *spiritual*. "The sacrifices of God are a broken spirit; a broken and a contrite heart."* In the Jewish church offerings were presented to God in behalf of the people by priests only; in the Christian church all the *people* are *priests*, and through Jesus Christ, present to God their own offerings; for "*ye* are built up [not a literal house, as was the temple, but] a spiritual house, a holy *priesthood*, to offer up *spiritual* sacrifices, acceptable to God through Jesus Christ."† Every believer offers anew daily, the one infinitely glorious satisfaction of the Redeemer, by the power of which "he hath perfected forever them that are sanctified." In the Jewish church the high priest entered once a year into the most holy place, "made with hands," "not without blood, which he offered for himself, and for the errors

---

\* Psalm li., 17. † 1 Pet. ii., 5.

of the people;" "which was a figure for the time then present, in which were offered both gifts and sacrifices which could not make him that did the service perfect as pertaining to the conscience." In the Christian church "Christ being come a high priest of good things to come by [the ministry of] a greater and more perfect tabernacle, [than that upon earth] neither by the blood of goats and of calves, but by his own blood, he entered in once into the [true] most holy place, [heaven itself] having obtained eternal redemption for us. For if the blood of *bulls* and of *goats*, and the ashes of an *heifer*, sprinkling the unclean, sanctifieth [in the Jewish church] to the [ceremonial] purifying of the flesh, how much more shall the blood of *Christ* [the infinite sacrifice, and who is also the great and only high priest in the Christian church] who through the eternal Spirit offered himself without spot to God, purge your consciences [spiritually, and truly] from dead works to serve the living God?" "It was necessary that the *patterns* of things in the heavens should be purified with these [priestly services of the Jewish church] but the heavenly things *themselves* with better sacrifices than these. For Christ is not entered into the holy places made with hands, which are the *figures* of the true, but into heaven itself, there to appear in the presence of God for us," our adorable Intercessor, and Advocate. "And as it is appointed unto men once to die, but after this the judgment, so Christ was once offered to bear the sins of many, and unto them that look for him shall he appear the second time without sin unto salvation."

These are the teachings of the word of God. They

demonstrate that the *alleged analogy* does not exist, but on the contrary is the very essence of Judaism. The *figure* and the *thing* signified by it, cannot be one. The *type* and the *reality* are not identical. The *shadow* and the *substance* are never the *same thing*. The Jewish church and the Christian church are *not* therefore the same church. But the Jewish church, with its institutions and facts, were *external* and *literal*, and were types or figures of the Christian church, which with its institutions and facts, are *internal* and *spiritual*. That this is the doctrine of Paul it is impossible to doubt. So also are we instructed by the "rules of interpretation" before recited. No *external* institution or fact in the Old Testament is a type of an *external* institution or fact, but always of *internal* and *spiritual* institutions and facts, in the New Testament. The whole subject of *analogy* is thus perfectly plain. The Jewish church, the *type*, was *external*, and composed of all the *natural* seed of Abraham; the Christian church, the *reality*, must therefore be *internal*, and composed of all the *spiritual* seed. No one was permitted to enter the Jewish—the *external* typical—church, who was not, either by natural birth, or as a proselyte, already among the covenant people. The analogy therefore requires that no one be permitted to enter the Christian—the true *spiritual* church—who is not, by the new birth, and faith in our Lord Jesus Christ, already among the true covenant people of God. A correspondence exists in several respects between circumcision and baptism. By circumcision the *natural* seed were recognized as the children of Abraham, and received as members of the Jewish church; by baptism the *spiritual* seed are recognized as believers in Christ, and received as members of the Christian church. Circumcision was instituted expressly for *literal* infants,\* and it was commanded to be administered to them soon after they were born; baptism was instituted expressly for *spiritual* infants—believers in Christ—and it is commanded to be administered to them as soon as they are born again. Circumcision was an essential preliminary to the passover; baptism is an essential preliminary to the Lord's supper. All this is clear, but our pedobaptist brethren pervert the whole subject, and cover it with confusion, by supposing that because Abraham's *natural* seed was circumcised, that therefore the *natural* seed of christians should be baptized! How infinitely unworthy as you at once see, is this conclusion! It is unreasonable, evidently forced, and contradictory of the true "analogy of the church."

The pedobaptist doctrine is in fact, a misnomer; it is not analogy, but Judaism. It is confused, it is unintelligible. The true evangelical analogy is clear, reasonable, and scriptural. Nor does it even intimate infant baptism; but on the contrary teaches such great truths and principles, as are wholly inconsistent with the practice, and as indeed, must ever *forbid* the baptism of infants.

4. This pedobaptist argument, I remark in the last place, is *palpably antiscriptural*.

It maintains that the Jewish church and the Christian church are the same church, in different dispensations; or in the language of Dr. Peters:—"When

---

\* With the exception of servants purchased with money.

[circumcision] the ancient sign and seal of the covenant which God made with his people for an everlasting covenant was abolished, another ordinance [baptism] was instituted in the same church, under the same covenant, of precisely the same import, and for the same purpose." The Jewish church and the Christian church, the *same church!* If so, then the only *christian* church now existing, is as we have seen, the *Roman Catholic!* It is not the Episcopalian, the Presbyterian, the Congregational, the Methodist, nor any other *Protestant* church, since Judaized as all these are, they fall far short of the Jewish church. Only the Catholic is a tolerable copy of the original. But if they were the *same church*, why did Christ deny it, when he told the Jews that *his* was a church *unlike theirs*, and into which none could enter by virtue of carnal relationship to Abraham, or to any other good men, but only by repentance of sin, and faith in him? Why did Messiah deny it on another occasion, when he said: "The law and the prophets [the Jewish church] continued until John, since whom the kingdom of heaven [the Christian church] is preached, and all men press into it?" Why did Paul deny the identity of the Jewish and Christian churches by comparing the former to Hagar and her posterity, and the latter to Sarah and hers? Why did Nicodemus, and Paul, and the rest, trouble themselves about the Christian church? They were already members, and officers of the Jewish church, and that was the same church! Strange infatuation! How surprising that any man with the Bible before him should fall into an error so palpable! This however, has already been sufficiently elaborated.

But we are told that the Jewish church and the Christian church subsisted under the same covenant! Were this true, then there would be no distinction between the law and the gospel. They would be the same in every correct sense. Very different from this, however, are the teachings of the word of God. Abraham, as any one may see who will be at the trouble of examining the *Bible* on the subject, was concerned in *two covenants*, which were made at different times, and related to distinct things. The former had regard *to Christ;* the latter *to his natural posterity;* the one was called *the covenant of grace;* the other *the covenant of circumcision.* The original promise in respect to *the covenant of grace,* was made to Abraham when he was *seventy-five* years old, in these words :—" In thee shall all families of the earth be blessed."\* This *promise* was afterwards renewed, and ratified with an *oath* :— " By myself have I sworn, saith the Lord"—" In thy seed shall all the nations of the earth be blessed."† This Paul declares to have been the covenant of grace in Jesus Christ. He says :—" God willing more abundantly to show unto the heirs of promise, the immutability of his counsel, confirmed it with an oath, that by two immutable things [the *oath* and the *promise*] in which it was impossible for God to lie, we might have strong consolation, who have fled for refuge to the hope set before us."‡ The promises of this covenant, Paul teaches you, constituted the gospel, in relation to which he says :—" The scripture foreseeing that God would justify [not the Jews only, but also] the heathen through faith, preached before, the *gospel* unto Abra-

\* Gen. xii., 3.   † Gen. xxii., 16–18.   ‡ Heb. vi., 17–20.

ham, saying, In thy seed [Christ] shall all nations be blessed." It is proper to say in passing, that the gospel covenant now described was not really *made* with Abraham, but in the language of an apostle, was "*confirmed to* Abraham of God in Christ." It was therefore previously made. The same covenant was announced to *Adam* in Eden, immediately after the fall, in a promise the language of which strikingly resembles that to Abraham, and which was repeated to Isaac, to Jacob, and to David:—" The seed of the woman shall bruise the serpent's head." The nature of this covenant was indicated to our first parents, by the institution of *sacrifices*, pointing to the great atonement afterwards to be accomplished for man, in the blood of Messiah. Who, I now ask, were *the parties to this covenant* for the redemption and salvation of men? Were they God and *Abraham?* No more than they were God and Adam, or God and David. They were God *the Father*, and God *the Son*; the latter of whom "took on him" for the purpose of our redemption, "not the nature of angels, but the seed of Abraham;" and in relation to this event it was that the *promise* was given, to "the Father of the faithful," which *promise* pedobaptists have so generally, and unhappily *mistaken for the covenant itself!* So much for the covenant of grace.

The *covenant of circumcision*, received this name because of the peculiar ordinance attached to it. This covenant was *made*, in the true sense of that word, *with Abraham, twenty-four years* after the promise above referred to, and when he was *ninety-nine* years old, for *himself*, and for all his *natural seed*. In it nothing whatever is said regarding Messiah. It stipulated, in the first place, that his descendants should be numerous, prosperous, and happy; in the second place, that they should possess a specified territory; and in the third place, that so long as they observed the laws of God, he would surround them with security and happiness. This covenant, as is acknowledged, received its *organized* development at Sinai, and was consequently really and truly identical with that "covenant which God made with Israel, when he took them by the hand to lead them out of the land of Egypt." The Mosaic law was the formal exhibition, the possession of Canaan was the practical fulfilment, and the national religion of the Hebrews was the visible presentation, of the covenant of circumcision.

Thus it is seen that there were *two covenants*, distinct from each other, of different dates, designed for different purposes, and dissimilar in their characters. Accordingly the apostles speak familiarly of " *the covenants;*" of "the *old* covenant;" of "the *new* covenant;" and these "*covenants*" they everywhere represent, consider, and contrast, as separate and distinct from each other. Paul, employing the language of Jeremiah,* thus speaks in relation to this important topic :—" Behold the days come, saith the Lord, when I will make a *new covenant* with the house of Israel, and with the house of Judah; *not according to the covenant which I made with their fathers* when I took them by the hand to lead them out of the land of Egypt." And "in that he saith ' a *new* covenant,' he hath made the *first* old."† There are therefore two covenants; the one the covenant of the *law*, the organized development of the

* Jer. xxxi., 31-34. † Heb. viii., 8-12.

covenant of circumcision made with Abraham, which is "*the old covenant;*" the other the covenant of the *gospel*, the covenant between God the Father and the Son, the promise of which was announced to Abraham, which is "*the new covenant.*" The covenant of the law constituted the dispensation of Moses, and was the covenant of the Jewish church; the covenant of the gospel is the covenant of grace and redemption, the covenant of the Christian church. The covenant of the law had circumcision annexed; the covenant of grace, in Christ Jesus, which was not visibly administered until after the law, or old covenant, had passed away, has baptism annexed. And yet pedobaptists declare in the face of all these facts, that the Jewish and the Christian are the same church, and subsist under the same covenant! Never was there a conclusion more palpably *antiscriptural*.

Pedobaptists also declare that circumcision and baptism "were instituted in the same church, under the same covenant;" that they are "of the same import, and for the same purpose." But the declarations of our Lord Jesus Christ on the subject contradict them in every particular. He asserts distinctly, that circumcision belonged to the law of Moses, and was identified with the covenant of Sinai. It never was therefore of the gospel, since the gospel covenant is "not according to," or like "the covenant" of Sinai. To the Jews the Saviour said:—"Moses gave you circumcision." And again. "A man on the sabbath day received *circumcision* that *the law of Moses* be not broken."* Did *Moses* give them circumcision? Then circumcision was a part of his ceremonial law. Is it objected that the rite was in existence before Moses? Sacrifices were

* John vii., 22, 23.

also in existence before Moses. Circumcision may therefore be said to have belonged to his law, as properly as sacrifices may be said to have belonged to his law. Or if it is still insisted that circumcision belonged to the gospel, and was succeeded by baptism; with the same truth may it be asserted that the offering of slain beasts in sacrifice belonged to the gospel and is now succeeded by the sacrifice of the mass. Circumcision and baptism are both types; but they are not the same type in different forms, since circumcision according to Paul, was a type of regeneration by the Spirit, and baptism, as John avers, is a representation, or type, of the burial and resurrection of Christ.* And since circumcision and baptism are both types, the former is not a type of the latter, because one type cannot be a type of another type. Nor can one type ever be substituted for another type. Baptism, therefore, cannot take the place of circumcision. They are distinct things, and must ever so remain. The claim of pedobaptists that circumcision " was instituted in the same church, under the same covenant, and for the same purpose," with baptism, that is, in the gospel church, amounts to the declaration that the gospel church is in fact, built upon the law of Moses! We have now seen that the Jewish church and the Christian church are not the same church in different dispensations, that they are not under the same covenant, that baptism does not come in the place of circumcision, and that the pedobaptist argument that maintains the opposite of our conclusions, *is palpably antiscriptural.*

I have been necessarily somewhat prolix in this discussion, but I could not in a narrower compass present

* 1 John v., 8.

the subject clearly and intelligibly. I have shown conclusively how for the support of infant baptism Judaism is engrafted upon the gospel of Christ. It has been seen that the argument, by which this great evil is perpetrated, proves vastly too much, and leads directly into all the extremes of popery; that it is in conflict with christianity as taught by Christ and his apostles, who deprecated Judaism as destructive of true religion; that it perverts and renders unintelligible the true analogy between the Jewish church and the Christian church, and which I have explained at some length, showing that it does not intimate the legitimacy of infant baptism, but teaches such doctrines as necessarily forbid it; and that it is utterly antiscriptural, confounding the law and the gospel, and leading men into confusion and error. Judaism in the gospel church is what Hagar and Ishmael were in the family of Abraham, a shame, and an offence. "Therefore cast out the bond woman and her son." Sever the chains by which the bride of Messiah is manacled, and bound to the chariot of Sinai. Be it ours to contemplate the church of the Redeemer, not under the clouds of Judaism in which infant baptism has involved it, not obscured among the shadows of a former dispensation, but as developed in the gospel, distinct, spiritual, sanctified, the glory of our Lord Jesus Christ.

In conclusion, I will only observe that by how much the gospel is thus corrupted, rendered difficult of comprehension, its forms changed, and its benevolent designs rendered inoperative, by so much is infant baptism, to which all this may be justly ascribed, a lamentable, a most melancholy evil.

# CHAPTER IV.

## INFANT BAPTISM IS AN EVIL BECAUSE IT FALSIFIES THE DOCTRINE OF UNIVERSAL DEPRAVITY.

Statement of the subject; nature of alleged infant claims; their conflict with the doctrine of depravity; incompatibility of these sentiments.

THE children of those parents "who profess the true religion," are *born*, it is alleged, in *the covenant*, and *church* of our Lord Jesus Christ! On this ground mainly, Presbyterians, Congregationalists, and other Calvinists, maintain their right to baptism. A glimmering of the same doctrine runs through the teachings of all the other sects. It is true as Bushnell justly remarks:—That "no *settled* opinions of the *grounds*, or *import* of infant baptism has ever been attained to" by them all.* In this, however, they agree as nearly as they do in any other doctrine regarding that ordinance. It is my purpose in the present chapter, to show that this aspect of the subject develops prominently, *another of its evils*, since *it falsifies the doctrine of universal depravity*.

Pedobaptists claim that the infant offspring of believers enjoy hereditary rights to the covenant of grace, and their attendant privileges of baptism, and membership in the visible church. The truth of this statement

* Christian Nurture, p. 60.

I shall now certify in such a manner as to render it indisputable.

"It is an important inquiry," says a distinguished writer upon the Symbols and Rubric of the English church, "to *what* infants that title belongs. For not all even in the sight of man, can be considered as fit subjects for that holy rite," baptism. "Are the children of *infidels* fit subjects?" "Baptism administered to them is not warranted by our church."* Bishop Jewell says:—"No person which will profess Christ's name ought to be restrained or kept back therefrom, no not even the *babes* of *christians*, forasmuch as they" "do pertain unto the people of God."† Nowell, Beveridge, and the other British fathers, teach the same doctrine. "We see then," says Mr. Goode, "the necessity of inquiring whether the child [brought to be baptized] is the offspring of parents who are at least professed christians." "Here is a question not decided by the church." More unscrupulous ministers will baptize any child for whom sponsors can be procured. "But it is at least reasonable to think that our church, administering baptism on the grounds stated by Jewell and Nowell, administers it on the supposition" that the parents are believers. "The faith of the parent is to the infant, as an infant," "mercifully reckoned by God as imputable to the infant, and on the strength of this it is baptized; *faith* and *baptism together*, as in the case of adults, perfecting the work of *infantine regeneration*."‡ We have in these passages, the doctrine on the subject of the more *evangelical* of the English

\* Goode on Bap., p. 80. † Works, p. 216.
‡ Goode on Bap., pp. 31-33.

church, and her doctrine in the premises is the doctrine of the Methodist church, and of the Episcopal church in the United States. Dr. A. Clarke therefore confidently says :—" Though infants have not, and cannot have actual faith, yet they are sanctified by being born of religious parents. They are already in some sense, within the limits of the church and covenant of promise."\* The Westminster Confession, however, is definite. Its language is :—" The visible church, which is also catholic, consists of all those throughout the world that profess the true religion, *together with their children ;* and is the kingdom of our Lord Jesus Christ, the house and family of God."† The Directory is still more explicit. It is there affirmed that the children of believers are " *Born within* the church, have *by their birth* inheritance in the *covenant*, and right to [baptism] the seal of it ;" " that they are *christians*, and federally *holy* before baptism, and therefore are they baptized." On this subject Mr. Baxter remarks :—" God hath made, and offered to the world a covenant of grace, and in it the pardon of sin to all true penitent believers, and power to become the sons of God, and heirs of heaven. *This covenant is extended also to the seed of the faithful* to give them the benefits suitable to their age, the parents dedicating them to God, and entering them into the covenant, and so God in Christ will be their God, and number *them* with his people." Mr. Baxter further says —" As children are made sinners and miserable by their parents without any act of their own, so they are delivered out of it by the free grace of Christ, not through their own faith, but upon

\* Essays, p. 31.  † Chap. xxv.

conditions performed by their parents."* And still further. "Of those baptized in infancy, some do betimes receive the secret seeds of grace, which by the blessing of a holy education is stirring in them according to their capacity, . . . . . *so that they never were actual ungodly persons!*" The late Dr. Miller says:— "The children of professing christians are already *in the church*. They are *born* members. They are *baptized* because they were members. They receive the *seal* of the covenant because they are already *in the covenant* by virtue of their birth."†

From these expositions we learn that, according to our pedobaptist brethren, the children of believers are born in the covenant of grace, and have, by right of birth, the enjoyment of all its blessings; are born members of the church, and by hereditary descent are entitled to the privileges of membership in the house of God, and to the promises of salvation. These are prerogatives arising exclusively from their hereditary relations. Their parents are holy. Therefore their children are holy. Of all such Dr. Hopkins says:—" The church receive and look upon them as *holy*. So they are as visibly holy, or as really holy in their view, as their parents are."‡

With these doctrines distinctly before us we turn to consider the subject of *universal depravity*, that we may ascertain to what extent these two principles harmonize with each other.

*Depravity*, I remark, consists essentially in a state of mind the opposite of that which is required by the law

---

\* Works, vol. xv., p. 486, vol. xix., p. 261-264.
† Miller on Bap.          ‡ Theol., p. 319.

of God. The law commands, and the obligation is imperative upon every human being, "Thou shalt love the Lord thy God with all thy soul, with all thy mind, and with all thy strength, and thy neighbor as thyself."* The want of this love on the one hand, and the love of the world on the other, places the soul in that moral position known as depravity. By nature, men prefer the world and its sinful gratifications, to the love of God and of their neighbor. The creature usurps in their affections the place of the Creator. The moral powers are perverted, and turned aside from God. This is depravity. And I now remark that it is *universal*. It attaches to every human being. All are naturally affected by it in the same manner, and to the same extent. In this respect no material original difference exists between the children of the rich and the poor, the free and the bond, the holy and the unholy, the believer and the unbeliever. In subsequent life their characters are often very different. But this arises not from any difference in moral qualities, but in constitutional temperament, in instruction, in discipline, and in associations. These facts are apparent to every intelligent observer. We see in the children of all classes, the same inclination to evil, and the same estrangement from God, more or less strongly developed. But they are fully confirmed by the word of God. "The lusts of the flesh, the lusts of the eye, and the pride of life," all by nature pursue in preference to "the things of the Spirit" of God. The children of religious parents are involved in this depravity, to an extent fully as great as the children of others,

---

* Matt. xxii., 37.

who occupy with them the same social position. "*All have sinned and come short of the glory of God.*"* " By one man sin entered into the world, and death by sin, and so death passed upon all men, for that *all* have sinned."† "The scripture hath concluded *all* under sin, that the promise *by faith* of Jesus Christ might be given to them that believe."‡ Than this what language can be more conclusive? It is therefore undeniably true that all are corrupt; that all are alike depraved.

Our brethren themselves, notwithstanding their doctrine of the holiness of the children of believers, maintain, and emphatically teach *universal depravity*. The Episcopal church thus expresses herself:—" Original sin" " is the fault, or corruption of *every man* that naturally is engendered of the offspring of Adam, whereby *every man* is very far gone from original righteousness, and is of *his own nature* inclined to evil."§ The Methodist church says:—" Original sin" " is the corruption of the nature of *every man* that is naturally engendered of the offspring of Adam, whereby man is very far gone from original righteousness, and of his own *nature* inclined to *evil*, and that continually."‖ Calvinism in all its sects speaks thus:—Our first parents by sin " fell from their original righteousness and communion with God, and so became dead in sin, and wholly defiled in all the faculties and parts of soul and body. They being the root of all mankind, the guilt of their sin was imputed, and the same death in sin, and corrupted nature, were conveyed to *all their posterity*, descending from them

---

* Rom. iii., 23. † Rom. v., 12. ‡ Gall. iii., 10–22.
§ Thirty-Nine Art. ‖ Discip. Art. Rel., vii.

by ordinary generation. From this original corruption, whereby we are naturally indisposed, disabled, and made opposite to all good, and wholly inclined to all evil, do proceed all acts of transgression."* All other evangelical denominations hold the same principles. They all teach *universal depravity*. *Every man* therefore, *descended of Adam, all* the posterity of our first parents, are *naturally indisposed to good, wholly* inclined to *evil*, and that *continually*.

Let the doctrine of infant baptism, as based upon hereditary claims of the children of believers to the covenant of grace, be now compared with the doctrine of universal depravity. We take them both as set forth by pedobaptists themselves. On the one hand they earnestly teach that the children of believers " are sanctified by being born of religious parents," are "born within the church, and have by their birth inheritance in the covenant," " are federally holy," and for these and like reasons, are baptized. Persons cannot have, at birth, all these endowments, and be at the same time wholly corrupt. Therefore the infant offspring of believers are not naturally depraved. On the other hand, they all earnestly teach that "*every one*" is wholly depraved. "*Every man*" descended of Adam, is "defiled in all the faculties and parts of soul and body," *all* " are naturally indisposed, disabled, and made opposite to *all* good, and wholly inclined to all evil." With this corrupt nature "all that are naturally engendered of the offspring of Adam" are born. The children of believing parents are not excepted, but fully included, since they too " are naturally engen-

* Westmin. Confes., ch. vii.

dered of the offspring of Adam," and are a part of " *all men.*" Are such corrupt and depraved persons *holy?* Are *they* born members of the church? Are they naturally inheritors of all the benefits of the covenant of grace? It is impossible. They cannot at the same time be *holy* and *corrupt, sanctified* and *depraved,* in the gospel covenant and " naturally indisposed, disabled, and made opposite to all good, and wholly inclined to all evil." Both these propositions cannot be true. The one falsifies the other. But that all are born in sin, and are by nature, depraved, *is true.* The word of God emphatically declares it. The whole doctrine of hereditary claims to the covenant of grace, therefore, upon which our brethren so confidently predicate infant baptism, falsifies the doctrine of universal depravity ; it is baseless in itself, and upon their own principles ; and it is fraught with mischief, " full of deadly evil."

There are at least, I may now add, two other, and collateral disastrous consequences which arise from this aspect of infant baptism, and which must here be briefly noticed. The former is the *absurdity* that religion is hereditary ; and the latter that the children of believers have no need of the regenerating influences of the Spirit of God !

In the first place, if children are " holy," are " in the covenant of grace," are " members of the church" " *by being born of religious parents,*" then these children inherit " *by their birth,*" all the blessings of religion, and of course, *become religious by natural generation.* The infant children of believers are in the covenant and church of Christ, because their parents are in the covenant and church of Christ. The infant children of unbelievers are not in the covenant and church of Christ, because their parents are not in the covenant and church of Christ. Religion and irreligion therefore are results of natural generation. Paul the apostle declares this whole hypothesis untrue. "The children of the flesh," he affirms, " are not [therefore] the children of the covenant."* But pedobaptists allege, that the children of the flesh of believers, *are* the heirs of the covenant, and for the very reason that they are the children of the flesh. Which shall we believe? Paul, or our pedobaptist brethren? The Bible or the Confessions of Faith? We cannot believe both, since, in the plainest terms, they contradict each other.

In the second place, if the infant children of believing parents are "holy," are "in the covenant of grace," are "born in the church," then of course, *their* nature is pure. The work of the Spirit is not necessary to cleanse their hearts, and fit them for a higher life. They are the children of believing parents, and therefore "sanctified." They are born holy! All this they are carefully taught from childhood. Are they not likely to believe it? If they do, they cannot also believe that they have a depraved and corrupt heart. Consequently they can never feel very deeply, their miserable condition as sinners, nor appreciate highly the grace of God in the gift of a Saviour. They are thus, and by their teachers, made ignorant of their own hearts, and deceived in a most vital point. I will not say that they never will be converted. It is evident, however, that their salvation is thus placed in fearful jeopardy.

* Gal. iii., 12-20.

It is now demonstrated that, by arrogating hereditary claims to the covenant of grace, infant baptism falsifies the doctrine of universal depravity, teaches that religion is propagated by natural generation, and that the children of believing parents have no need of the renewing power of the Holy Spirit of God. Thus infant baptism inculcates a religion that is neither moral nor spiritual, but merely physical. It is therefore a most revolting evil.

# CHAPTER V.

INFANT BAPTISM IS AN EVIL BECAUSE THE DOCTRINES UPON WHICH IT RESTS CONTRADICT THE GREAT FUNDAMENTAL PRINCIPLE OF JUSTIFICATION BY FAITH.

Justification by faith; infant baptism; the two contrasted; reciprocal influence in the primitive churches; justification by faith restored at the Reformation; embodied with infant baptism in all the Confessions of Faith; effect upon protestantism; one or the other must be abandoned.

The doctrines upon which infant baptism rests, and the great fundamental principle of justification by faith, are in irreconcilable contradiction. They are throughout, the antagonists of each other. To them both no church, nor individual, can consistently adhere. One or the other must, sooner or later, be abandoned. Their opposite characters indicate this result, and the history of the church, primitive, popish, and protestant, evinces that it is inevitable. Let the doctrines in question be separately stated, and compared.

The great fundamental principle of justification by faith, is taught in the word of God, in terms perfectly full and explicit. We are, says an apostle, "Justified freely by his grace, through the redemption that is in Christ Jesus, whom God hath set forth to be a propitiation through faith in his blood, to declare his righteousness for the remission of sins," "that he might be just, and the justifier of him that believeth in Jesus."* And "being justified by faith, we have peace with God through our Lord Jesus Christ."† Justification is the act of God by which he declares a man just and righteous. The justified are accepted, and approved, as if they had never sinned. This is an act of God's own free and sovereign grace, and therefore necessarily irrespective of any works or worthiness on the part of the justified. It is *by faith*, not as a meritorious agency to procure justification, but as the medium through which it is bestowed. We are not justified *for faith*, as if it were of itself a sufficient righteousness, since faith no more than works can constitute such righteousness, but by faith through grace. "It is of faith, that it might be by grace;" faith being characterized by a peculiarity which harmonizes with grace, and which looks not to itself, but to Christ for righteousness and salvation. This, briefly, is justification by faith, as taught in the word of God.

How shall we ascertain the doctrines of infant baptism? They are not made known to us in the Bible. Revelation is silent on that whole subject. We must, of course, rely upon the statements of protestant Pedobaptists for our authority. With Papists I have at present nothing to do. Dr. Wall is more definite on this topic than any other writer now before me. He says:—"Most of the Pedobaptists go no further than St. Austin does. They hold that God by his Spirit, does, at the time of baptism, seal and apply to the infant that is there dedicated to him, the promises of the covenant of which he is capable, viz.: adoption, pardon of sins, [and] translation from the state of nature to that

---

* Rom. iii., 24–26. † Rom. v., 1.

of grace."\* The doctrines upon which infant baptism rests teach, therefore, that in that ordinance the child receives adoption, pardon, and translation into the state of grace, and of course that he receives justification! Davenant, the Bishop of Salisbury, thus speaks on this subject:—" The *justification*, regeneration, and adoption of little children baptized, confers upon them a state of salvation."† Archbishop Usher writes thus:—" The branches of this reconciliation [received by infants in their baptism] are *justification*, and adoption."‡ So teach all the other divines, and all the protestant Confessions of Faith and Catechisms. Infants are therefore, according to this doctrine, justified before God in baptism.

Let now the great principle of justification by faith and the doctrines of infant baptism be compared. If you are justified by faith in our Lord Jesus Christ, through grace, you are not justified by baptism, either in infancy, or at any other time; and if you are justified by baptism, then you are not justified by faith. This conclusion is perfectly plain. These doctrines are therefore as opposite as darkness and light. They emphatically contradict and falsify each other.

Justification by faith, I have said, is a fundamental doctrine of the gospel. It is vital. It is "the faith once delivered to the saints." No system from which it is excluded, can ever be justly regarded as embodying the religion of Christ. It was taught by the apostles, and early ministers, constantly, forcibly, emphatically. It was cherished by the primitive churches

---

\* Hist. Inf. Bap., vol. ii., p. 148.
† Letters to Dr. Ward, p. 25. ‡ Brief Method, &c.

as a priceless truth. How can we account for its abandonment by the professed followers of Jesus Christ? There is, I answer, an inherent tendency in human nature, renewed though it may be, to pass from the substance to the forms of religion. The transition is so easy that it can only be prevented by perpetual vigilance. The influence of this propensity the early churches did not very long escape. Among the first of the corruptions they admitted and embraced, was the undue importance which became attached to religious ceremonials. They gradually exalted the rites above the doctrines of christianity, while both were perverted and misapplied. Baptism, especially, was imagined to possess great and peculiar virtues. Thus justification through grace by faith, was ultimately displaced by justification through grace by baptism. Popery was the result, the doctrine of which, on this subject, is thus expressed by the Council of Trent :—
"Justification is by means of the sacraments, either originally infused into us, or subsequently increased, or when lost, again restored."* Thus the christian world was plunged into darkness, which remained unbroken for a thousand years.

But justification by faith was restored at the Reformation. Noble efforts to give back to men this truth had previously been made by Tindall, and Wicliff, and Huss, and others, but they all fell martyrs to their benevolent designs. Finally arose "the monk of Wittenberg," the iron-nerved Luther. He was previously a blind slave of popery, and in his own esteem "irre-

* Concil. Trid., Sess. vii., decret. Sacram., apud Moehler, p. 279.

proachably holy." His penances, mortifications, and obedience, were exemplary; but of true religion he knew nothing. In his monastery, apparently by accident, he found a copy of the Bible. It was the first he had ever seen. He read it with mingled surprise and delight. He began to be enlightened, but his soul rebelled against its teachings. Referring to his state of mind at this period, he himself says:—"I could not endure the expression, 'The righteous justice of God.' I did not love that just and holy being that punishes sinners." But the study of the Bible, with prayer, was continued daily. At length that striking passage attracted his attention, "The just shall live by faith." It originated a train of thought, and feeling, wholly new. "There is then," it occurred to him, "another life for the just than that possessed by other men, and this life is the fruit of faith!" Thus dawned upon his mind the great doctrine of justification by faith, which led first to his own reconciliation to God, and then to other consequences of infinite moment. In allusion to this event Luther remarks in another place:—"When by the Spirit of God I understood these words, 'The just shall live by faith;' when I learned how the justification of the sinner proceeds from God's mere mercy, by the way of faith; then I felt myself born again as a new man, and I entered by an opened door into the very paradise of God. From that hour I saw the precious and holy scriptures with new eyes. I went through the whole Bible. I collated a multitude of passages, which taught me what the work of God was, and as I had before heartily hated that expression, 'The righteous justice of God,' I began from this time to value and love it, as the sweetest and most consolatory truth. Truly this text, 'The just shall live by faith,' was to me the very gate of heaven."*

Was Luther now free from those delusions which had so long led men to rely for justification upon works of various kinds, ordinances, penances, and mortifications? It would be very natural to suppose that he was. But he had gained no such freedom. The profoundest ignorance rested in those days, upon the minds of men. Thick darkness, in many respects, still covered his own soul. He dared not quit his secluded cell, and very naturally hesitated to act in opposition to the whole religious world. His fetters were not broken until some years after, when on business of his monastery, he visited Rome. While there he determined, for the sake of the indulgence promised, to ascend in the prescribed manner "la Scala Santa," a sacred staircase preserved in that city, up which our Saviour is said to have passed when brought before Pilate. "He began, but had not dragged his prone body many steps before a voice arrested him in tones of thunder, 'The just shall live by faith.' Startled at these accents of terror, he hurried like a guilty thing, from the spot, and from that hour the doctrine, although mingled with other and contradictory doctrines, took full possession of his soul. He planted himself upon it as upon a rock, and looked serenely back on the wild sea through which he had been struggling. The last rivet in his chain was severed, and he stood up a freeman."† Justification by faith was thus recalled from the oblivion into which it had been so long driven, and through the instrumental-

* D'Aubigné's Reformation.   † Headley.

ity of the leading mind, became the central principle of the Reformation.

All the denominations that then sprang out of popery, did not agree as to the details of religion. Hence their separate organizations. But they all concurred in the doctrine of justification by faith, whether Lutheran, Calvinist, or Episcopalian. They each embodied it fully in their separate Confessions, and other standards. And strange as it may appear, they also embodied in the same symbols, that opposite and contradictory system, infant baptism. Why they did this will more fully appear hereafter. I now speak of facts only. I am not attempting to account for them. Thus they threw together conflicting elements, which, as they had before done, gradually destroyed the blessings which had been gained. To the sublimest truths they united the rankest corruption. To the gospel of Christ they chained the main supports of Popery, ignorance, and worldly conformity. These facts are most readily demonstrated by reference to the standards themselves.

In the first place, I shall show that the Confessions of all the protestant sects embody the doctrine of justification by faith. The Augsburg Confession is the symbol of Lutheranism. Its fourth article is in the following words:—" They teach also that men cannot be justified before God by their own efforts, merits, or works, but are justified freely through Christ by faith, and are received into favor, and enjoy the remission of sins, through Christ, who by his death presented a satisfaction for sin."*

In full agreement with this is the Westminster Con-

---

* Cox's Melancthon.

fession, which doctrinally is embraced by all classes of Calvinists, Presbyterians, Congregationalists, Independents, and others :—" Those whom God effectually calleth he also freely justifieth ; not by infusing righteousness into them, but by pardoning their sins, and by accounting, and accepting their persons as righteous; not for any thing wrought in them, or done by them, but for Christ's sake alone; not by imputing faith itself, the act of believing, or any other evangelical obedience to them as their righteousness, but by imputing the obedience and satisfaction of Christ unto them, they resting on him as their righteousness by faith ; which faith they have not of themselves, it is the gift of God. Faith thus received, and resting on Christ, and his righteousness, is the alone instrument of justification."\*

The doctrine of the Episcopal Church in all its sects, is contained in the eleventh of the Thirty-Nine Articles, in the following language :—" We are accounted righteous before God only for the merits of our Lord and Saviour Jesus Christ by faith, and not for our works or deservings. Therefore that we are justified by faith only, is a most wholesome doctrine, and very full of comfort."

Of the doctrine of the Methodist church in all its departments, the "Articles of Religion," in the Discipline, is the symbol. Their ninth article speaks thus :—" We are accounted righteous before God only for the merits of our Lord and Saviour Jesus Christ by faith, and not for any of our own works or deservings. Wherefore that we are justified by faith

\* West. Conf., ch. ii., sects. 1, 2.

only, is a most wholesome doctrine, and very full of comfort."

These are the principal Confessions of Faith of all the Protestant sects, and we have now seen their teaching on this subject. If they are to be believed, we are justified before God, not by our own efforts, merits, or worthiness, not by any thing done by us, or in us, not of course by baptism, or by any other act of obedience whatever, but alone through grace by faith in our Lord Jesus Christ. How great, how vital, how evangelical, how infinitely important this truth! Who could have supposed that they would have inserted in each one of these very formularies any principle directly and plainly contradicting that already so fully and elaborately stated? Yet they did so. Infant baptism finds a place there, sustained by all the doctrines with which Popery had surrounded it. For proof in the premises we retrace these several Confessions.

The Augsburg is as follows:—"They teach concerning baptism that it is necessary to salvation, because by baptism the grace of God is offered. Infants are to be baptized, who being brought to God by baptism, are received into his favor."*

The Westminster Confession says:—" Baptism is a sacrament of the New Testament, ordained by Jesus Christ, not only for the solemn admission of the party baptized into the church, but also to be unto him a sign and seal of the covenant of grace, of remission of sins, and of his giving up unto God through Jesus Christ, to walk in newness of life."† " By the right

* Aug. Conf., art. ix.     † Conf., ch. xxviii., sect. 1.

use of this ordinance the grace promised is not only offered, but really exhibited,* and conferred."†

The Thirty-Nine Articles teach thus:—"Baptism is not only a sign of profession, and a mark of difference wherein christian men are discerned from others that be not christened, but it is also a sign of regeneration or the new birth, whereby as by an instrument, they that receive baptism rightly, are engrafted into the church. The promise of the forgiveness of sins, of our adoption to be the sons of God by the Holy Ghost, are visibly signed and sealed." "The baptism of young children is in any wise to be retained in the church, as most agreeable to the institution of Christ."‡

"The Methodist Articles of Religion" speak as follows:—"Baptism is not only a sign of profession, and mark of difference whereby christians are distinguished from others that are not baptized, but is also a sign of regeneration, or the new birth. The baptism of young children is in any wise to be retained in the church."§

Thus we have the teachings of all these Confessions on baptism. The summary may be embraced in a few words. Lutherans declare that baptism is necessary to salvation, and that by it infants are received into the favor of God, and saved. Presbyterians, with all their kindred sects, maintain that baptism is to the child a sign and seal of the covenant of grace, of his engrafting into Christ, of regeneration, and of the remission of sins, and that all these are by baptism not only offered to the child, but really exhibited and conferred upon

---

* Used in the technical sense of the Latin *exhibere*, to apply or convey. † Conf., ch. xxviii., sect. 6.
‡ Thirty-Nine Art., 27. § Discip., Art. of Relig., xvii.

him. And Episcopalians and Methodists affirm that by baptism the new birth, the forgiveness of sins, and adoption, are all to the child, visibly signed and sealed. The child therefore in baptism, is pardoned of sin, is regenerated, is adopted, is received into the church, received into the favor of God, and saved. All this certainly involves justification, or the declaring the person innocent of crime. These Confessions teach, therefore, the justification of the sinner by baptism. Consequently on the doctrine of justification by faith, and the doctrines upon which they rest infant baptism, the Confessions, each and all of them, plainly, palpably, unmistakably contradict themselves. If you are justified, pardoned, and saved through grace by faith, and not by works, merit, or obedience of any kind, then you cannot be justified, pardoned, and saved by baptism. But it may be objected that infants are not capable of faith. Neither therefore, I answer, are they capable of baptism. They are saved by grace through Christ, and without baptism. Is baptism necessary to their salvation? God forbid. Why then baptize them, since the act is without authority, and without benefit? And especially why teach that baptism gives them pardon, regeneration, adoption, and salvation?

Do I deal unjustly with these several sects when I thus represent them as in collision with themselves? Their inconsistencies on this point have been noticed and condemned by others as well as Baptists. Moehler, a Catholic priest, and recently Professor of Divinity in Munich, one of the most eminent Roman Catholic scholars of the age, says:—" At the commencement of the Reformation, Luther and Melancthon evinced on this matter the most decided opposition to the Catholic church; and the internal ground of their opposition lay entirely in their one-sided conception of the justification of man before God. Hereby especially the communication of *really sanctifying* graces by means of the sacraments was thrown into the background, nay even totally called in question." "The highest point to which they could rise was the one-sided view of the sacraments considered as pledges of the truth of the divine promises for the forgiveness of sins. The sacraments accordingly were to have no other destination than to make the faithful receiver assured that his debt of sins was remitted, and to console and quiet him." "So mean a conception of the sacraments necessarily led to the view that they operate only through faith in the divine promise of the forgiveness of sins. It was only in course of the disputes with the fanatics, as Luther called them, or with the Sacramentarians, that the reformers of Wittenberg approximated again to the doctrine of the [Papal] church. Already the Confession of Augsburg expresses itself, though indefinitely enough, yet still in a manner to enable Catholics to declare themselves tolerably satisfied with it." "By degrees the Lutherans [and all other protestants] again adopted the entire notion of the *opus operatum*, although they continue even down to the present day to protest against it." "Thus in course of time no important difference [in the premises] inherent in the nature of things, could be pointed out" between Catholics and Protestants.* This testimony from an enemy is true. Still Protestants of all classes, as everywhere

* Symbolism, pp. 282–285.

else, so among us, in their sermons, and their conversations, from the pulpit, and the press, continue to protest that they do not attribute to baptism any justifying or saving power. And do they not? I have fairly recited the *very words of their Confessions of Faith!* Do they believe these Confessions? Let us turn to some of their standard writers, and see how they express themselves on this subject.

"The gospel," says Henry, the distinguished Presbyterian commentator, "contains not only a doctrine, but a covenant, and by baptism we are brought into that covenant. Baptism wrests the keys of the heart out of the hand of the strong man armed, that the possession may be surrendered to him whose right it is. The water of baptism is designed for our cleansing from the spots and defilements of the flesh. In baptism our names are engraven upon the breast-plate of the High Priest. This, then, is the efficacy of baptism; it is putting the child's name into the gospel grant. We are baptized into Christ's death; that is, God doth in that ordinance seal, confirm, and make over to us, all the benefits of the death of Christ,"[*] among which, of course, must be embraced *justification*. Professor Charles Hodge, one of the Theological Instructors at Princeton, says:—"We are baptized in order that we should die with him, [Christ] i. e., that we should be united to him in his death, and partakers of his benefits. This baptism unto repentance, Matt. iii., 11, is baptism in order to repentance; baptism unto the remission of sins, Mark i., 4, that remission of sins may be obtained."[†] Bishop Bedell says:—"This I

---

[*] Treat. on Bapt.     [†] Comm. on Rom. vi., 3.

yield to my Lord of Sarum most willingly, that the *justification*, and adoption which children have in baptism is not *univoce* the same with that which adulti have. And this I likewise do yield to you, that it is *vera solutio reatus, et veraciter, et in rei veritate* performed in all the like emphatical forms, etc."* Bishop Burnet says :—" Here, then, is the inward effect of baptism ; it is a death to sin, and a new life in Christ." "We are not only 'baptized into one body,' but also saved by baptism."† The Episcopal Catechism affirms that the child is by his "baptism, made a member of Christ, the child of God, and an inheritor of the kingdom of heaven."

These are the expositions of standard writers among pedobaptists themselves, of all classes, explanatory of the efficacy of baptism as taught in their Confessions. They effectually shield me from the charge of misrepresentation, and at the same time evince that their doctrine is such, in the language of Moehler, as "to enable *Catholics* to declare *themselves* tolerably satisfied with it." They inculcate, as do their Confessions, justification by *faith*, and also justification by *baptism*. Thus they contradict in one place what they teach in another. But Presbyterians, Congregationalists, and Methodists, do not *surely believe* these baptismal doctrines ! Many of them, I admit, earnestly deny it ! Gladly would we credit their disavowals. But we take up their standards, catechisms, and writers of authority, and there, word for word, are the passages I have recited, and much, very much more of the same character. They

* Letters to Dr. Ward, Letter 161.
† Expos. Thirty-Nine Arts., pp. 395, 396.

deny that they believe their doctrines, and yet they continue to *publish* them to the world as expressing truly *their faith*. From the pulpit and from the press they disclaim and repudiate them; but when called to the sacred altar, in their *vows of office*, they solemnly declare before God and men, that they *do* believe them "*ex animo!*" What now shall we say? They *deny;* they *affirm;* they again deny; and again affirm! The *same* contradictions which so strikingly mark their Confessions and Catechisms, we find pervading all their teachings, and practice! I lament these facts, but they are so natural to their position, that from them there seems to be, without changing their ecclesiastical relations, no way of escape.

We now turn to consider briefly, the results of the condition of things submitted. They are *evil*, and evil *only*. Look over the protestant christian world as it exists at the present moment, and you will find that infant baptism is again rapidly expelling, as it did in early times, the doctrine of justification by faith from the churches. Among the Lutherans of Germany, the Calvinists in continental Europe, the Episcopalians in England, and others—I speak of them as communities— the baptism of infants is observed with the utmost carefulness, but justification by faith has no practical influence whatever. It is still in their Confessions, but it has been banished from their pulpits, from their hearts, and from the faith of their people. Justification by faith they receive from the Bible. Infant baptism and its accompanying doctrines, they receive from Popery. The former is of God. The latter is of men. They cannot continue to exist together. All those churches, now regarded as evangelical, will, sooner or later, give up justification by faith, or they will give up infant baptism. What has been will be again. "Coming events cast their shadows before." Justification by faith from one direction, and the doctrines of infant baptism from the other, like opposing currents in the ocean, meet and form a whirlpool, in which no church exposed to its violence can long survive.

We have now seen the doctrine of justification by faith, and the principles of infant baptism, and contrasting them, have found that they are wholly contradictory and irreconcilable; we have seen that it was infant baptism mainly, which expelled the doctrine of justification by faith from the early churches, and brought on Popery, by which the world was shrouded in darkness for a thousand years; we have seen through what providential agency this great doctrine was restored, and how it became the central principle of the Reformation; we have seen that though justification by faith is embodied in all the Protestant Confessions, Catechisms, and other formularies, it is placed in them side by side with infant baptism, and its doctrines, and that, as elsewhere, they reciprocally contradict, refute, and nullify each other; we have seen, in the history of protestantism, the practical results of uniting these conflicting elements, and have found that they cannot exist together, but that the destruction of this fundamental doctrine is the inevitable result of maintaining infant baptism; and we have seen that the tendency of all the other protestant sects is in the same direction, and that they also, must ultimately abandon practically, if not professedly, either justification by faith, or infant baptism, with the principles upon which it is maintained, and defended. It is now demonstrated fully, that the doctrines, upon which infant baptism rests, contradict the great fundamental principle of justification by faith. It is therefore, in all its bearings and influences, an alarming and most disastrous evil.

## CHAPTER VI.

INFANT BAPTISM IS AN EVIL BECAUSE IT IS IN DIRECT CONFLICT WITH THE DOCTRINE OF REGENERATION BY THE HOLY SPIRIT.

Nature of regeneration; its early identity with baptism; popish doctrine on the subject; true principle restored at the Reformation; again confounded; Confessions of Faith, Catechisms, standard writers; contradictions; evils inflicted.

THE relations of infant baptism to the doctrines of justification by faith, and regeneration by the Holy Spirit, are in many respects the same. In the preceding chapter we considered the former. We now proceed to examine the latter. This also is a vital topic. It must not be summarily dispatched. It is necessary to both your happiness, and your safety, that you should understand it. You may easily be misled. God forbid that any obstruction should be thrown in the way of your obtaining a full knowledge of all that concerns your everlasting life.

Our brethren of all the protestant denominations* *teach that we are regenerated by the Spirit of God;* and they also *teach that we are regenerated by baptism!* Both these propositions cannot be true. This is self-

---

\* Baptists are not protestants. That you are aware of this is taken for granted. See the proof in my work on Communion. All protestants are pedobaptists.

evident, since they are in direct conflict with each other. By the word of God, we are instructed that, while, on the one hand, regeneration is a spiritual change wrought in the soul by the Holy Ghost, baptism, on the other, is merely an outward ordinance of our religion. The one is the work of God; the other is the work of man. Believers only, can be admitted to baptism; every believer is regenerate: consequently none but the regenerate can be lawfully baptized. Regeneration must then, as you perceive, come before baptism. And besides, the supposition that baptism is essential to regeneration, or ever produces it, is absurd. He who is regenerate is "born again," "born of God," "born of the Spirit," "quickened" into new life, has "Christ formed in him the hope of glory," and is "made a partaker of the divine nature." The moral image of God, lost by sin, in regeneration is restored to the soul. Is baptism, or any other ordinance, or all the ordinances together, competent to this great work? Why should it be effected in baptism rather than in any other christian duty? Is it obtained by these, or by any similar acts? Then it is certainly, in part at least, the work of man. But can regeneration be so accomplished? The supposition is at war equally with reason, and the word of God. He only who created us originally, has power to renew, and so to change our nature that we shall be conformed to the character of our Lord Jesus Christ, enabled to love him supremely, to delight in his service, and to overcome all our corrupt propensities, and dispositions. Regeneration is one thing, and baptism is another and wholly different thing; nor are they, in any sense, dependent the one upon the other. How profoundly to be deprecated the fact that they should be confounded, and that, by any class of men, the latter should be substituted for the former! This deplorable evil, to all who truly love our Lord Jesus Christ, and have any just conceptions of the gospel, is matter of the deepest regret. Regeneration is essential to salvation. "Except a man be born again he can in no case enter into the kingdom of heaven." "Ye must be born again." But he who has mistaken baptism for the new birth is never regenerated. How then can he be saved?

Dangerous, however, and fearfully fatal, as is this insidious error, it nevertheless arose in the church at a very early period. Its appearance was simultaneous with the perversion of the doctrine of justification by faith. It was a result, evidently, of a misconception of the design of baptism. According to the apostles, baptism is one of the witnesses of God, for our Lord Jesus Christ, (the other two being the Spirit, and the blood, that is, the sacred supper,) and it bears testimony to the amazing facts that he died for our sins, and was buried, and rose again for our justification. In receiving baptism we express our faith in the primary truth that "we have redemption by his blood, the forgiveness of sins, according to the riches of his grace." Had the church adhered unwaveringly to apostolic instruction on this topic, the defection we now deplore never could have occurred. But the fathers became, unhappily, wiser than the apostles, and they determined that it was necessary to have some sacramental emblem of the work not only of God the Son, but also of God the Holy Spirit. The Lord's supper being commemorative of the sufferings and death of Christ, they thought that sufficient for him, and so removed baptism from its legal place, as a concurring witness, and not only without authority, but expressly against authority, made it a witness, and significant of regeneration. They accordingly defined it, "the outward and visible sign of the inward and spiritual grace." Here the perversion commenced. It was soon established. The work of deterioration then rapidly progressed. Ere long all distinction was forgotten, and the church and her teachers confounded hopelessly, what they called "the sign," with "the thing signified." With them baptism was now regeneration, and regeneration was baptism! This delusion fixed itself permanently, and remains to the present hour the strong fortress of popery. Both by Papists of the West, and Greeks of the East, it is uncompromisingly maintained. The Council of Trent accordingly decreed thus:—"If any man shall say that baptism is not essential to salvation, *let him be accursed*. Sin, whether contracted by birth from our first parents, or committed ourselves, is by the admirable virtue of this sacrament, remitted and pardoned. In baptism not only our *sins* are remitted, but also all the *punishments* of sins and wickedness are graciously pardoned of God. By virtue of this sacrament we are not only delivered from these evils, but also we are *enriched* with the best and most excellent endowments. For our souls are filled with divine grace, whereby being made just, and the children of God, we are trained up to be heirs of salvation also. To this is added a most noble train of virtues, which, together with grace, is poured into the soul. By baptism we are joined and knit to Christ as members to the head. By baptism we are signed with a character which can never be blotted out of our soul. Besides the other things we obtain by baptism, it opens to every one of us the gate of heaven, which before through sin was shut."*

These facts sufficiently explain the manner in which regeneration and baptism were at first confounded, and the fatal extent of the consequent delusion. Baptism was a panacea which cured every malady. This was the condition of things everywhere prevailing, when the Reformation dawned upon the world. Spiritual religion—except among a few who were denounced as heretics, and hunted down with fire and sword—was lost, and grace, and salvation, were communicated, and obtained, only through sacraments. "Darkness covered the earth, and gross darkness the people. The Reformation poured a flood of light upon the world. It restored the doctrine of justification by faith, as we saw in the last chapter; and it restored also, though much less perfectly, the doctrine of regeneration by the Holy Spirit. It did both by giving back to the people the Bible, of which for many centuries, priestly jealousy, and priestly domination, had deprived them. The minds of men were recalled to first principles. True penitents turned to God, and obtained as in primitive times, by faith in Christ, assurance of the divine favor, the Spirit bearing witness with their spirit that they were born of God. Luther, and Melancthon, and Calvin, and Zuingle, and Ridley, and

* Concil. Trid., Sess. 7, Can. 5.

Latimer, and their compeers, were themselves doubtless regenerated.

In Germany, and England, and France, and even in Spain, men awoke as from a sleep of ages. They shuddered when they beheld the gulf from which they were barely delivered. They commenced the work of reform. They exposed the abuses of popery in terms of indignant eloquence. They stated some of the doctrines of Christ with great clearness, but *this*, it must be confessed, is exhibited with painful obscurity. In none of the German Confessions is it presented with satisfactory distinctness. Nor is it set forth with more plainness in the Thirty-Nine Articles, or in the Articles of Religion of Mr. Wesley. The Calvinists had evidently a better comprehension of the doctrine than the other protestants. The Westminster Confession thus speaks :—God is pleased " effectually to call [men] by his word and Spirit, out of that state of sin and death in which they are by nature, to grace and salvation by Jesus Christ; enlightening their minds spiritually and savingly to understand the things of God, taking away their heart of stone, and giving unto them a heart of flesh; renewing their wills, and by his almighty power, determining them to that which is good."*

I am gratified to say, however, that all these denominations, but especially those portions of them who have preserved their evangelical character, have gradually acquired, as they became better instructed in the word of God, more distinct and full conceptions of the work of the Spirit in regeneration, and especially

* Art. x., sect. 1.

is this true of the various classes of Methodists, Congregationalists, and Presbyterians in our country and in Europe. Apart from infant baptism, they recognize amply the great truth as stated by us, that regeneration is a change of heart, effected exclusively by the Holy Ghost. More than this; they give in their life and character, most gratifying evidence that they are themselves the subjects of this heavenly renovation. Thus happy, in its influence upon the character and destiny of the church and people of God, has been the Reformation.

But has any portion of the protestant pedobaptist world fully renounced the old popish dogma which teaches that infants are regenerated in baptism? Do they believe in the doctrine of regeneration as exclusively the work of the Holy Spirit, *and also* in the antagonistic and conflicting doctrine of regeneration by baptism? Such inconsistency, it would seem, is almost incredible. Yet when infant baptism is to be administered, or defended, all their evangelical principles are apparently forgotten. This relic of popery can only be sustained by the dogmas of popery. Baptism and regeneration are not now esteemed by them as separate and distinct things, but are declared essentially identical. This statement is not hazarded carelessly. It is made after mature thought, and full investigation. I am aware that it is not a light imputation. I shall therefore sustain it by the amplest evidence.

What kind of testimony may be regarded as satisfactory in proof of so grave a proposition? The declarations of Confessions of Faith, Catechisms, and accredited writers, must, of course, be conclusive. To these, therefore, I direct your attention. The Augsburg Confession says:—" Our church likewise teaches that since the fall of Adam, all men who are naturally engendered, are born with a depraved nature, that is, without the fear of God, or confidence towards him, but with sinful propensities; and that this disease, or natural depravity, is really sin, and still condemned, and causes eternal death to those who are not *born again by baptism* and the Holy Spirit."\* The earlier Helvetic, another Lutheran Confession, is still more explicit. Its language is:—"*Baptism* is, by the institution of the Lord, the *law of regeneration*. With which holy law, we, *on that account*, baptize our infants." The Thirty-Nine Articles embrace in substance the declarations of the Augsburg Confession, and add, "There is no *condemnation* to them that believe, and are *baptized*."† For this reason *they* also baptize *their* infants! The Articles of Religion of the Methodist church assert that, baptism is "a sign of *regeneration*, or the new birth," and is to be administered *to infants*.‡ The Westminster Confession says: —"*Regeneration*," with various other blessings, is "*offered*" in baptism, and that "by the right use of this ordinance the *grace* promised is not only *offered*, but really exhibited and *conferred* by the Holy Ghost, to such, whether of age, or *infants*, as that grace belongeth unto according to the counsel of God's own will, in his appointed time."§ Other Confessions not yet noticed concur with these. The Belgic Confession

\* Conf., Art. 11.     † Art. 9.
‡ Art. 17.     § Art. 28, sects. 1, 6.

says:—"The sacraments are signs, and visible symbols of things internal, and invisible, by which, as by means, God himself works in us by the power of the Holy Ghost." The Heidelberg Catechism, or Confession, written by Zachary Ursinus, says:—"Christ commanded the external laws of baptism with this promise annexed, that [in it] I am not less certainly washed by his blood and Spirit, from the pollutions of the soul, that is, from all my sins." The Gallican Confession says:—"God really, that is, truly and efficaciously, does whatever he there [in our baptism in infancy] sacramentally shadows forth, and therefore we annex to the signs the true possession of that thing [regeneration] which is thus offered us."* The same doctrine is maintained in the Bohemian, the Saxon, and all the others.

These are the teachings of the Confessions. Their lessons cannot readily be mistaken. The Catechisms maintain the same doctrine. The Bishops of the English church, in their "Answers to the Ministers of the Savoy Conference," remark:—"We may say in faith, of *every child that is baptized*, that it is regenerate by God's Holy Spirit; and the denial of it tends to Anabaptism, and the contempt of this holy sacrament, as nothing worthy, nor material whether it be administered to children or no."† The present Bishop of Exeter thus states the doctrine of his church:—"The grace of God so certainly attends this ceremony of baptism, that *regeneration* and *baptism* are contemporaneous, and *the terms are convertible*, and may be used inter-

---

\* Sylloge Conf., p. 74, et seq.
† Caldwell's Conf., pp. 325, 356.

changeably."* And did not Mr. Wesley express himself in similar terms? He says:—"By baptism we who are by nature the children of wrath, are made the children of God. And this *regeneration* which our church in so many places ascribes to baptism, is more than barely being admitted into the church, though commonly connected therewith." "By water then as a means, the water of baptism, *we are regenerated and born again*, whence it is called by the apostle, 'the washing of regeneration.' In all ages the *outward baptism* is a means of the *inward*. Herein we receive a title to and an earnest of the kingdom, that cannot be moved. In the ordinary way, there is no other way of entering into the church, or into heaven." " If infants are guilty of original sin, then they are proper subjects of baptism, seeing in the ordinary way, they cannot be saved unless this be washed away in baptism."† Mr. Henry, Prof. Hodge, and others of their class, teach, as we saw in the last chapter, doctrines essentially the same. Mr. Ainsworth says:— " Thus to whom God giveth the sign and the seal of righteousness by faith, and of regeneration, *they* [the infants] *have faith* and *regeneration;* for God giveth no lying sign; he sealeth no vain or false covenants." " If we cannot justly object against God's work in *nature*, but do believe that our infants are reasonable creatures, and are born not brute beasts, but men, though actually they can manifest no reason, or understanding more than beasts, then neither can we object to God's work *in grace*, but are to believe that

---

\* Gorham Trial.
† Works, N. Y. edit., vol. i., pp. 15, 16.

## IN CONFLICT WITH REGENERATION. 127

our infants are sanctified creatures, and are *born believers,* not infidels, though actually they can manifest no faith, or sanctification."* But Calvin himself ought to be heard in behalf of his followers. He says:— "We agree that sacraments are not empty figures, but do truly supply whatever they represent; that *the efficacy of the Spirit is present in baptism to cleanse and regenerate us.*"† With the divines of Zurich, he had however, in this matter, one sad difficulty, which is more than intimated in the Westminster Confession. In "The Argument," drawn up in 1549, Calvin says: —" We diligently teach that God does not put forth his power without distinction to all who receive the sacraments, but only to the elect." If then the child is not one of the elect, it is not regenerated in baptism. If it is elect, it is certainly regenerated in baptism.

A volume might be filled with similar passages, but further proof is deemed useless. The Catechisms, and standard writers, even more conclusively than the Confessions of Faith, demonstrate, as you must plainly see, all that I have alleged. The fact is now placed beyond question that, whatever they may avow, or maintain at other times, whenever this ordinance is in question they all connect infant baptism and regeneration. With the Lutherans infants are born again by baptism; with Episcopalians baptism and regeneration are contemporaneous, and the terms are convertible; with the Methodists baptism is the means by which their infants are regenerated and born again; and with Presbyterians, since God gives no lying signs, nor seals, *infants of be-*

---

\* Hanbury's Histor. Memor., vol. i., pp. 413, 414.
† Epist. ad Melanc. Op., vol. ix., Epist. 82.

lievers *are believers*, and *if they are elect infants*, they are *regenerated*, sanctified, adopted, have conferred upon them, in a word, "*all* the benefits of the death of Christ." "The denial of this tends," in the language of the bishops, "to *Anabaptism*, and the contempt of this holy sacrament as nothing worthy, or material whether it be administered to children or no." They all teach, therefore, that we are regenerated exclusively by the Holy Spirit of God; *and* they also teach that we are regenerated by baptism! These propositions are the *opposites* of each other. They *cannot both* be true. But the doctrine of regeneration by the Holy Spirit is true. Therefore the doctrine of infant baptism is not true.

I am here again met, however, with the declaration, that the best and most pious of all these classes utterly deny that *they* believe at all, as charged, in baptismal regeneration. To this disclaimer I have already replied in such terms as I think appropriate. I have said that their positions are irreconcilably at variance. I have myself often heard them assure these same baptized children when grown up, who had been regenerated in their infancy, that they must yet be regenerated or they could not be saved! The attitude in which they are thus placed is most perplexing, and pitiable. They solemnly declare to the world that they *do not* believe the very dogmas that in their books they solemnly declare that they *do* believe! They repudiate them, and adhere to them! In this dilemma they have involved themselves. I lament it sincerely, and trust that they may yet see their inconsistencies, and embrace the whole "truth as it is in Jesus."

In these facts and considerations we have revealed another of the evils of infant baptism. It withdraws the mind from truth, and places it upon a fiction. It seduces men from the reality to the mere forms of religion. It attributes to an ordinance, which since it is despoiled of its form, and applied to unlawful subjects, is no ordinance of Jesus, a work which the Holy Ghost only can do. It is utterly subversive of the fundamental doctrine of the work of regeneration by the Spirit of God. It is a most deplorable evil.

# CHAPTER VII

INFANT BAPTISM IS AN EVIL BECAUSE IT DESPOILS THE CHURCH OF THOSE PECULIAR QUALITIES WHICH ARE ESSENTIAL TO THE CHURCH OF CHRIST.

Qualities essential to the church; how destroyed by infant baptism; examples drawn from protestantism in its various forms; recovery of the church hopeless.

THE true visible church of our Lord Jesus Christ upon earth, is necessarily *spiritual*, and *pure*. If deprived of these qualities, it is evidently no longer *his* church. Its form, and organization, may still be retained; it may be great, and powerful, and honored; but it is a mere *worldly corporation*. It is not the church of Christ.

Do you inquire what I mean by spirituality, and purity? By *spirituality* I mean, that disposition of mind implanted by the Holy Ghost, by which men are inclined to love, delight in, and attend to the things of the Spirit of God. Those who are spiritual seek spiritual blessings, engage in spiritual exercises, pursue spiritual objects, are influenced by spiritual motives, and experience spiritual joys. Paul describes their character in terms, as clear as they are comprehensive. "They that are after the flesh, do mind the things of the flesh; but they that are after the Spirit, the things of the Spirit. For to be carnally-minded is death, but to be spiritually-minded is life, and peace. Because the carnal mind is enmity against God ; for it is not subject to the law of God, neither indeed can be. So then, they that are in the flesh cannot please God."* Such is spirituality. And *purity* is a fixed habit of abhorrence of whatever holiness forbids, whether in the heart or in the life. It is the disposition that discovers itself by a cautious fear of all that leads to sin, and by perseverance in prayer, devotion, and the service of God. Where these two qualities exist, all the others that distinguish true christians, will ever be present. A congregation of such will be "living stones, built up a spiritual house, a holy priesthood, to offer up spiritual sacrifices, acceptable to God by Jesus Christ."† All those from whom they are absent, are carnal and unholy. And can men of this class legitimately compose Christ's church upon earth ? The supposition is preposterous. Spirituality, and purity, must distinguish those who are entitled to a place in the sanctuary of God.

Of this character were all those who formed the church in its original organization. The King in Zion intended and required that the holiness of his church should be preserved, and perpetuated. But how can this be done ? Its accomplishment demands evidently, *the strictest regard to appropriate laws of membership.* That the required character cannot otherwise be attained must, to every thinking man, be perfectly obvious. Who does not know that the *character of any association*, among men, is determined, and ever must be determined, by its laws of membership ? These

---

\* Rom. viii., 5–8. † 1 Pet. ii., 5.

laws decide the qualifications of the *individuals* of whom the association is composed. The *aggregate* is made up of the individuals. The character of the individuals will inevitably be the character of the *association*. This truth is self-evident. That would not be a *Temperance* society, however vehemently it might demand the name, which should receive, and retain, large numbers of men who continue in the daily use of ardent spirits as a beverage. A *Literary* society would not remain such, in any proper sense, when filled up with *uneducated* men, who neither study, nor intend to study literature. Nor would a *Medical* society deserve the name, if composed mostly of planters, merchants, and lawyers, who designed to give no special attention to medicine. If the specific character of the association is preserved and perpetuated, those only must be admitted to membership, and retained in the body, who are qualified by the necessary acquirements, and disposed to prosecute the objects had in view in its formation. These great truths are especially applicable to the church of Christ. Her *spirituality* and *purity* as a *body,* can be preserved and perpetuated no otherwise than by admitting to membership, and retaining in communion, *those individuals only* who are *spiritual* and *pure.*

In accordance with these facts, and corroborating their truth, the laws of membership enacted by our Lord Jesus Christ, are fixed with the greatest possible plainness and particularity. Baptism is the outward form in which this membership is given and assumed. This ordinance is essential to admission into the visible church, and of that church all who receive it are members. Paul so teaches us when he says :— "As many of you as have been baptized into Christ, have put on Christ."* All the denominations around us receive, and act upon this truth. At the baptism of a child in the Episcopal church, the minister says :—"We receive this child into the congregation of Christ's flock."† The Methodist minister says when a child is baptized, it is done that:—"He [this child] being delivered from thy [God's] wrath, may be received into the ark of Christ's church."‡ And the Presbyterian says :—" Baptism is a sacrament of the New Testament," "whereby the parties baptized are solemnly admitted into the visible church, and enter into an open and professed engagement to be wholly and only the Lord's."§ The laws of baptism, therefore, are confessedly included in the laws of membership. Let these laws, as enacted by Messiah, now be indicated. "*Teach*," said he, and "*baptize*" *the instructed.* "*Preach* the gospel," and "him that *believeth*" the gospel, "*baptize.*" In all your administrations let the fact be remembered, that "My kingdom is not of this world."∥ "The kingdom, and the dominion, and the greatness of the kingdom under the whole heaven, shall be given to the people of the saints of the Most High."¶ The language of the New Covenant describes truly, without doubt, the character of those who are in that covenant, and such only are legitimately, church members. "I will," says God, "put my laws into their mind, and write them in their heart; and I will be to them a God, and they shall be

---

* Gal. iii., 27.     † The Liturgy.
‡ Discipline, ch. 3, sect. 2.     § Larger Catechism, Quest. 165.
∥ John xviii., 26.     ¶ Dan. vii., 27.

to me a people; and they shall not teach every man his neighbor, and every man his brother, saying, Know the Lord; for all shall know me, from the least to the greatest."* By the laws of Christ, therefore, only those are to be admitted into the church who have been taught, who believe, who are not of this world, who are saints, in whose mind and heart the law of God is incorporated, and who know the Lord as their God. This character is required of them also by their relations to Jehovah. The church of God offer him acceptable worship, but this can be done by no others than those described; "for God is a Spirit, and they that worship him, must worship him in spirit and in truth."† It is also demanded by their relations to mankind. "Ye are the salt of the earth. But if the salt have lost his savor, wherewith shall it be salted? It is thenceforth good for nothing, but to be cast out, and to be trodden under foot of men. Ye are the light of the world. A city that is set on a hill cannot be hid. Neither do men light a candle, and put it under a bushel, but on a candlestick, and it giveth light unto all that are in the house. Let your light so shine before men, that they may see your good works, and glorify your Father which is in heaven."‡

These are some of the laws of membership in his church as fixed by Christ himself. How definite! How precise in all things! They describe, with the utmost clearness, the spiritual, and the pure. None others can enter his church, since it is his purpose to perpetuate in the body these holy qualities. The *execution* of these laws is confided to his ministers and people. If they

\* Heb. viii., 6.   † Rom. viii., 2-6.   ‡ Matt. v., 13-17.

swerve from their duty, the result is lost. The strictest obedience on their part, is consequently commanded, and enforced by the most solemn sanctions. He who fails in his fidelity, no matter who he is, or what may be his official position, sins against God, by disregarding his solemn injunctions; sins against the church, by corrupting and degrading it; sins against the world, because he removes and extinguishes the light by which it is to be guided to salvation; and sins against his own soul, covering himself with crime, and condemnation.

We are now prepared to inquire into *the effect produced upon the character of the church by infant baptism.* It sets aside all the laws of membership enacted by Christ for her preservation and glory; it proceeds upon others of its own creation, and substitution; it brings into the body, not the spiritual and pure only, but also all classes of men; and it thus impresses upon it such a character as effectually destroys its claims to be regarded as the true visible church of Christ. It is thenceforth necessarily carnal and unholy. *It is not the church of Christ.*

Infant baptism, I have said, necessarily leads to this melancholy result. Let this proposition be further considered. Does it not, to the extent that it prevails, throw the whole population of the country into the church? This fact no man will deny. Is it not also true, that great multitudes of these baptized children grow up to maturity in the church, worldly, sensual, wicked men? They are all members, and some of them ministers, and other officers, in the church! If, as we have seen, the character of an association as a body, is necessarily that of the individuals of which it is composed, then it follows with certainty, that infant baptism must soon despoil the church of its spirituality and purity, and render it carnal and unholy, since it is by this rite, filled with members, officers, and ministers, who are not themselves spiritual and pure, but carnal, unholy, and worldly. The church is what the members are of which it is composed.

But the evil influence in the connection in which I now speak of it, is not *negative* merely, it is *positive*, and overwhelming. It not only *excludes* spirituality and purity from the church, but it introduces *corruptions* of the most destructive character.

How it corrupts the church in her *membership* is sufficiently apparent. Its corrupting influence upon her *doctrines* has been seen in previous chapters. I will here recapitulate. It perverts the word of God to bring it apparently into its support; it engrafts Judaism upon the gospel of Christ; its principles contradict the doctrine of justification by faith; they are in conflict with the work of the Spirit in regeneration; and they falsify the doctrine of universal depravity. What fearful destruction it has thus wrought in all that is revered and holy! What now must be her general *temper*, and *disposition?* Will she be as designed by Jesus Christ, and represented by his apostles, "A glorious church, not having spot, or wrinkle, or any such thing, but holy, and without blemish?"* Will she "crucify the flesh, with its affections and lusts?" Will she "live in the Spirit, and walk in the Spirit," bringing forth the fruits of "love, joy, peace, long-suf-

* Eph. v., 27.

fering, gentleness, goodness, faith, temperance?" Will she not rather be guided by ambition, pride, and vainglory, relying for her advancement upon measures of mere worldly policy? Will she not prefer a learned, or an eloquent, to a converted ministry? Will she not be ready to embrace any false doctrines, or unscriptural practices, which may be found congenial with her unsanctified nature, and suited to her purposes of dominion, and power? With such a spirit infant baptism has always been found inspiring the church. Nor is this less true of *Protestantism* than it is of *Popery*. Whence originated the Neology of Lutheranism, the Puseyism of Episcopacy, and the Unitarianism and Universalism of Calvinism? Had these churches adhered to the laws of membership established by Christ Jesus, and admitted, or retained in their communion, none but the truly converted, could these miserable dogmas ever have covered them with shame and misery? They are all, therefore, the legitimate offspring of infant baptism. Its advocates have "sown the wind," and as a natural consequence, "they have reaped the whirlwind."

Nor does the evil of infant baptism terminate even here. *It blots out every vestige of the church itself, by wholly destroying its visibility!* This proposition may seem startling. Let us give it a candid investigation.

The doctrine taught by pedobaptists would bring every child upon earth into the church as soon as it is born! We will suppose, for the sake of the illustration, that from this hour, the gospel is known in every land, and these principles universally prevail. What would be the practical effect? Evidently that *in one generation the whole world would be in the church!* The Presbyterians would baptize all the children of believing parents; the Episcopalians would baptize "upon the faith of the church," all those for whom sponsors could be secured; and the Methodists, and others, would baptize the remainder! Not a living being would be out of the church! What now is the condition of things? The church is the world; and the world is the church! They are identical! Either there is no church; or there is no world! If the world is not the church—and we know that it is not—then *there is no visible church of God upon earth!* Its visibility is *destroyed;* and is destroyed *by infant baptism.* What do we now see? The *spirituality* of the church is gone! The *purity* of the church is gone! The *visibility* of the church is gone! The *church itself* is gone! It is despoiled of those peculiar qualities which are essential to the church of Christ. If there is no other than a Pedobaptist church, then there is no true visible church of Christ upon earth!

But is not this an overstatement of the case? Would not a laudable christian charity draw a much brighter picture than the one I have now sketched? I am reminded that the Methodist church, the Presbyterian church, the Congregational church, and several other churches in this country, and in England, are, in their numerous divisions, highly evangelical. All these, with infant baptism, still hold and teach the great fundamental truths of the gospel. I am happy to concede that this is true. It is, however, the result of a peculiar condition of things, and cannot, therefore, discredit any argument which has been submitted on the subject. *Four* causes, continually acting upon them all, have hitherto preserved them, in a great measure, from falling into the same destruction which has overwhelmed others.

The *first* is *the great Baptist principle*, with which they are unceasingly in contact. In North America the Baptist churches contain a million of communicants. Four millions more, at least, are of their opinion, and under their influence. Nearly one-fourth, therefore, of all our population are strongly Baptistical. All these regard infant baptism, and infant church membership, as wholly unauthorized, and treat them as nonentities in religion. These Baptists are diffused in all the families of the land, high and low, rich and poor, bond and free, learned and unlearned. They are associated with their Pedobaptist brethren upon equal, and most intimate terms. As a consequence of this state of things, the influence of infant baptism is, to a very great extent, neutralized, and destroyed.

The *second* of these causes is *the universal diffusion of the Bible*. The word of God is now carefully studied, in Sabbath-schools, in Bible-classes, in families, and in the closet, not by scholars only, but also by all classes of our people, and it is probably better understood by them all, than it has ever been at any period since the days of the apostles. The masses are enlightened; they exercise their own judgment; and their religious opinions are approaching, consequently, much nearer the scriptural standard. In all the teachings of that holy book they find not one word to justify infant baptism. Thousands, consequently, who have received the rite, refuse utterly, to act in accordance with it. They do not regard themselves as church members, or in any way privileged spiritually, because of their infant baptism. That, say they, was only a form. And indeed, so far has this conviction proceeded, that many, very *many members,* even of Pedobaptist churches, do not hesitate to avow their entire disbelief in the whole theory. Hence its wide-spread neglect throughout our whole land. In proportion as the Bible is understood, loved, and obeyed, does infant baptism, in all its relations and bearings, dwindle, and recede from public view.

The *third* cause is found in *the character of our Pedobaptist ministry.* The great body of them, and especially of those connected with the denominations I have named, are converted men. Their religion and good sense lead them involuntarily to discard, except in its forms, the puerilities of their distinguishing rite. They preach to all alike, and boldly declare to sinners of every class, that if they are saved at all, it must be alone by the grace of God in Jesus Christ our Lord, whom they can approach only as penitent believers, and whose Spirit must renew and sanctify their hearts. Thus preaching the fundamental truths of the gospel, they falsify infant baptism, keep it out of sight, and avert in part its deleterious influence.

The *fourth* and last cause is *the revivals of religion which have so long, and so extensively prevailed in our country.* Of these, in common with our churches, theirs have largely, and happily partaken. These revivals call the thoughts of men directly to the corruptions of their own nature, to the light of the word of

God, to the cross of the Redeemer, to regeneration by the Holy Ghost, and to pardon, justification, and salvation, through faith in Christ. True religion is thus everywhere spread abroad, and many, notwithstanding the errors of their standards, and other authorities, whose forms they still observe, are converted, and saved.

These, mainly, are the causes which in America, and the British dominions, have thus far averted from them, its natural and inherent evils, and preserved their churches from total overthrow. Take these away, and nothing can save them from utter disaster.

We have now established our proposition by scripture, reason, and facts. We proceed still further to illustrate and confirm it, by the history and *present state of the Pedobaptist world*.

Infant baptism swept the primitive churches into popery, with all its darkness, and horrors. The earthly "Head and Ruler," thus brought whole nations into the church, and made them subject to his authority. National governments were within, and subordinate to his, and all the people of which they were composed owed to the "Holy See" their personal and primary allegiance. Thus the pope ruled the nations with " a rod of iron." That all this is due to infant baptism is demonstrated by these two facts: in the first place, that he exercised this authority solely upon the ground that the people, and princes, were all members of his church; and in the second place, we all know that they never could have been of his church, but for infant baptism. May I not add, that it is *by the same means* that he still retains his influence over nations, and communities, keeps them in awe of his spiritual prerogatives, and holds them in servile subjection to his will? For what other purpose than to force them under his authority, does he so sedulously inculcate the pernicious dogma, that by their baptism received in infancy, they are brought into the fold of the *church*, *within* which they will be saved, and *out of which* they will be damned; and that therefore, if they renounce their baptism, or apostatize from popery, their everlasting destruction is certain? Do any of these nations, or communities, dare at any time, to oppose his authority, or disobey his orders? He immediately lays them under an interdict, suspending the sacraments, all public prayers, burials, and baptisms, the obsequious priests implicitly obeying his mandates. A superstitious dread of these prohibitions, and particularly of that which withholds baptism from their children, soon reduces the people to an humble compliance, since to parents it seems most horrible that their children thus deprived must, if they die, be inevitably lost. Whole kingdoms therefore yield to his exactions, however arbitrary or oppressive, because thereby, as they suppose, they save their own souls, and the souls of their children, which would be lost if they did not submit to the "Vicar of Christ!" What a tremendous influence does infant baptism give to popery! How cunningly is it adapted to uphold its power!*

Protestant Hierarchies in the old world were not, in adopting infant baptism, indifferent to the power which they would be able through its means, to exert over the people. But we are now considering its effect

* Consult Dr. Gill's Inf. Bap. a Part and Pillar of Popery, ch. 2.

upon the *spirituality*, the *purity*, and other *holy qualities*, which are essential to the *true* church of Christ. In these respects what, when uninfluenced by antagonistic causes, such as those I have recited, has been its effects upon *the churches of the Reformation?* Survey the present aspect of the *Episcopal* Church, and especially in England. Her creed was in the main, evangelical. Many of her early ministers were men of great learning, energy, and piety. She took a firm hold upon a large proportion of the people. She abolished the mass, and with it purged out most of the grosser abominations of popery, but *she retained infant baptism*, with its sacramental doctrines. It has had time to produce its mature fruits. And what are they? "The land which around the martyr-fires of Smithfield, swore eternal hatred to popery, is now full of popish dignitaries, popish priests, and popish proselytes!" Almost every week announces the conversion to Romanism of some of her ministers, and people! Infant baptism has destroyed her gospel faith, and transformed her worship into a beggarly imitation of Italian pageantry. Of the Methodist church, a late and vigorous offshoot of Episcopacy, it is proper to say, that it *has not yet existed long enough* to feel deeply, the evils in question. But since it is following in the same steps, it must, at length, reach the same results. How many already, of her ministers, and members, are found going over to the Episcopal church, and some of them go on to Puseyism, and to Rome! Thus Methodism evinces that the blood of the mother courses in the veins of the daughter.

Turn now to Lutheranism. The fabric reared by

the reformers of Germany, was originally, massive, lofty, and glorious. But infant baptism was left, apparently a little rill beneath its foundation. It has continued to flow on, slowly but certainly undermining the structure, and now it is overturned, and lies prostrate, in stately ruins! "For two centuries the doctrines taught by Luther, were rigidly maintained. But they were by many, held merely as a dead letter." They constituted " a theological creed for which men would buckle on the armor of controversy, but which had no place in their hearts, and no influence over their lives." "There came at last a change over the public mind." There was "a breaking away from old paths of thought, and a reckless pushing into new ones." What power existed to check this current of things? The whole of the people were in the church. Infant baptism had placed them there. Very few were converted. "Even her pastors, and theological professors, were in most instances, destitute entirely of any experimental acquaintance with the power of christianity. Such could have no inward witness of the truth of the gospel, and no illumination of the Spirit to guide them in their inquiries. Led exclusively, by unsanctified reason, and a skeptical philosophy, they plunged into speculations" the most wild and extravagant. The Bible was either perverted to sustain their infidel theories, or regarded by them as a mere mythical representation. Its inspiration they discarded as a fond conceit of former days. "This condition of things has continued until the church of Luther, the eldest daughter of the Reformation, has, to a great extent, become crowded in all her departments with men who, while partaking of her ordinances, and filling her offices, laugh at her doctrines," and trample upon the word of God! Tholuck, a distinguished minister of her own, says of the present state of the Lutheran church, that, it is "a huge mass, stiff, cold, and livid. What in many of its parts appears like life, is but the life of the corruption itself by which these parts are dissolving. Only here and there among its dying members is there a living one, that with difficulty averts death from itself."* This is the deplorable condition of protestant christianity in all the German states. By what means has it been produced? By infant baptism. The barriers with which Jesus Christ surrounded his church, were by this rite, thrown down, and the unregenerate, profane, and worldly filled her sanctuary.

The church of Calvin offers to our consideration, and from the same cause, a similar history. Like Luther, he did not return to the gospel laws of membership, but continued the initiatory ordinance as practised by popery. The light of his doctrines, with the piety of his people, gradually waned. The very city where he dwelt, is now covered by "*the black night of Socinianism!* Her radiance is quenched. Her voice of truth is hushed. The very pulpit in which he preached, is polluted by lips that deny the divinity of the Son of God, and the renewing agency of his Holy Spirit."

Such are the results to which infant baptism has already brought Episcopacy, Lutheranism, and Calvinism, in Europe. But a still more striking instance, if possible, of its pernicious effects is furnished in the history of Puritanism in our own country. "The founders of

* Predigten, Band 1, § 25.

the New England churches had cast off the fetters of a tyrannical Hierarchy in the old world, and they brought with them to the new, views respecting the spiritual nature of christian communities, and the simplicity of christian worship, much more correct than those generally entertained in that age. They were men profoundly read in the scriptures, of great faith and zeal, and of exemplary holiness." "Their situation removed them far from the corrupting influence of other less evangelical societies. They were alone in the wilderness, with themselves, their offspring, and their God." Here, then, if it ever can be anywhere, infant baptism would surely have been harmless. The process by which it inevitably leads to deterioration is thus described by Dr. Wisner, who being himself a Puritan Pedobaptist, cannot be suspected of having colored his picture too highly. " As to the promises [made at their baptism, by parents and friends] of educating children in the fear of the Lord," "they soon came to be alike disregarded by both those who exacted, and those who made them." " The most solemn and impressive acts of religion, came to be regarded as unmeaning ceremonies, the *form* only to be thought important, while the *substance* was overlooked, and rapidly passing away." " And now *another* and still more fatal step, was taken in this downward course. Why should such a *difference* be made [in the persons receiving them] between the *two* christian sacraments, which *reason* infers from the nature of the case, and the *scriptures* clearly determine, require precisely the same qualifications? If persons were qualified to make in order to come to one ordinance, [baptism] the very same profession, both in meaning and terms, required to come to the other, [the communion] why should they be excluded from that other? The practical result, every one sees, would be, that if the innovation already made [known among them as the Half-Way Covenant, according to which all the baptized, if not openly immoral, were regarded as church members*] were not abandoned, another would be speedily introduced. And such was the fact. Correct moral deportment, with profession of correct devotional opinions, and a desire for regeneration, soon came to be regarded as *the only qualification* for admission to the *communion*." The churches soon came to consist very considerably, in many places, of *unregenerate* persons; of those who regarded *themselves*, and were regarded by *others*, as unregenerate. Of all these things the consequence was, that within thirty years after the commencement of the eighteenth century, a large portion of the clergy throughout the country, were either only speculatively correct, or to some extent actually erroneous in their religious opinions; maintaining regularly the forms of religion, but in some instances having well-nigh *lost*, and in others having, it is to be feared, *never felt* its power."†

"To such a state," remarks Dr. Ide,‡ "had the Puritan churches of New England been brought by infant baptism within a single century! Silently, but surely, it had done its work!" Successively it had de-

\* Vide Mather's Magnalia, Book 5.
† History of the Old South Church.
‡ In his excellent chapter in Gill's Part and Pillar, ch. 4, from which I have here drawn my statements regarding Episcopacy, Lutheranism, Calvinism, and Puritanism.

stroyed the spirituality, and the purity of the church. Truth was abandoned. Religion expired. " Everywhere men avowedly *unconverted*, belonged to her communion, presided over her interests, and served at her altars. With such a *membership*, and such a *ministry*, both alike carnal, it was not to be supposed that the church would long retain even a theoretical belief in the grand teachings of revelation. These, however, were not at once repudiated. The forms of faith which have become fixed in a community, do not suddenly pass away. Truth leaves the heart, and the lips, long before it leaves the creed. For a considerable period, therefore, a dead, leaden orthodoxy hung over New England, hiding like a shroud the rottenness beneath. But this could not continue. An incipient change began to be perceived. The distinguishing doctrines of the gospel were not, indeed, denounced and opposed. They were *passed over*. While keeping their place in the Confessions, and Articles, they were quietly dismissed from the pulpit, to make room for moral essays, and panegyrics on the beauty of natural virtue. The downward progress having gone thus far, must go further. Men are never satisfied with what is merely negative. They demand a positive. When once they have discarded *positive truth*, their next step is to embrace *positive error*. Hence we find that as early as the middle of the last century, opinions involving a denial of the proper divinity of Christ, the depravity of human nature, the need of atonement, and the work of the Holy Spirit in regeneration, were extensively adopted in Massachusetts."
" They spread for fifty years through the country, per-

vading the graceless clergy, and more graceless laity." "At last the great *Unitarian apostasy stood revealed in all its hideous deformity!*"

All these facts are authenticated by the stern voice of impartial history. They afford a demonstration most perfect, that infant baptism, wherever it is not counteracted by mitigating influences, will destroy, and must destroy, the *spirituality*, the *purity*, the very *visibility* of the church. It inevitably despoils her of all those qualities which are essential to the true church of our Lord Jesus Christ.

Infant baptism, as must be seen, in the light of all the facts and considerations now before you, is not merely a question of *an ordinance*, it is also a question of *membership* in the church of Christ. In the former sense it is unlawful. In the latter it is fearfully destructive. It must always give character to the church in which it is practised. It inevitably fills it with the unregenerate, and unholy, with skeptics, and unbelievers. And still more. *Against this deterioration and moral death, there is for Pędobaptist churches, as such, no possible remedy.* They possess within themselves no power to throw them off. They *must* wither and expire under their influence. Not so with us. Do corruptions, no matter of what character, invade *Baptist churches? They* contain inherently all the elements of restoration. They have only to recur to first principles, to *their inspired laws of membership, and discipline*. By the former, no persons are admitted to a place among them, but those who are decided, in a judgment of charity, to be true penitent believers in Christ, born of the Holy Ghost;

and by the latter laws, all those who depart from piety in life, or truth in principle, are promptly separated from their communion. By this simple, but effective process, how often have they purged themselves from evils of all kinds! Striking instances are perhaps, within your own memory. Antinomianism attempted to fasten itself upon our churches. It was promptly thrown off. Campbellism came, with its Pedobaptist doctrine of sacramental efficacy. They arose and cast out this source of impurity. Thus they have acted in all ages. They have only to enforce the fundamental laws of their constitution, which require that God's spiritual house shall be composed of spiritual materials. While they do this, they will ever rejoice in a pure doctrine, a pure membership, a pure and able ministry, and a vigorous life. With *Pedobaptist churches* the case is wholly different. From a resort to first principles *they* can derive no help. These *very first principles*, embracing, as they do, infant baptism, and infant church membership, *have done all the mischief.* While they preserve and cherish the *source* whence they arise, they can never escape the *corruptions* that necessarily result. They may manifest occasional amendment. There may be in their history, intervals of revival. There have been such, in this country, among Presbyterians, and Congregationalists, and in the Methodist branch of the Episcopal church. Comparative spirituality and purity, will in such cases, for a while prevail. But these periods must be evanescent. The same prolific fountain is perpetually sending forth its streams, and they must soon again be deluged. *They have no remedy.* They must *renounce their first principles*, and adopt the laws of church membership contained in the word of God. The annals of history contain not an instance of a Pedobaptist church, that has continued a Pedobaptist church, which has radically and permanently reformed itself. The Church of England has not done it. The Church of Germany has not done it. The Church of Calvin has not done it. No Pedobaptist church ever has done it. None ever will, except those who cease to receive into their bosom the worldly and the profane. In a word, if they would be what the church was designed to be by Christ, *they must cease to be Pedobaptists.*

With Baptists, I remark in conclusion, are lodged, as you must plainly see, *the only conservative influences* now existing in the universe. It is ours, with the blessing of God, to save from being quenched that truth which is "the world's only hope." It is ours also, to save Pedobaptists themselves, of all classes, from the consequences of their own errors. If we do not save them, they must sink. It is ours to spread the gospel throughout the round earth. How exalted, therefore, how responsible, how far-reaching, is *our mission!* It is fearfully sublime. It has, however, been assigned us by our God. Sustained by his grace, let us discharge it with fidelity. He is even now, clothing us with strength for the work. How unexampled is our multiplication! How rapid our diffusion over the whole earth! Jehovah is evidently about to vindicate his gospel; to sweep away the clouds of ignorance, superstition, and error; to restore to man a pure and glorious christianity. Of this great conflict who will consent to remain an idle spectator? Who can refrain from participating in the Battle? Who does not involuntarily exclaim with the princely prophet, "For Zion's sake I will not hold my peace, and for Jerusalem's sake I will not be silent, until the righteousness thereof go forth as brightness, and the salvation thereof as a lamp that burneth?"

## CHAPTER VIII.

INFANT BAPTISM IS AN EVIL BECAUSE ITS PRACTICE PERPETUATES THE SUPERSTITIONS BY WHICH IT WAS ORIGINALLY PRODUCED.

Causes which produced infant baptism; hypothesis by which it was justified; protestants adopted it with all its ancient absurdities; its original superstitions still prevail.

INFANT baptism is the offspring of *superstition*. Nor has any of the progeny of that most prolific mother been more productive of evil to the cause of truth and salvation. In these respects it has amply justified its origin. It is not the eldest born, but it is the most popular and insidious of them all.

During the apostolic age, and until two hundred years of the church had been told, infant baptism was wholly unknown. The history of that period, whether sacred or profane, makes not the remotest allusion to such a practice. This of itself, is sufficient proof that it did not exist. But it is not the only testimony. The fathers in the church who then lived and wrote, often speak of baptism, and always in such terms as to convince us that it was not administered to children. One of them—Justin—contrasts the state of christians at their birth with their state at their baptism. "*Then* [at their *birth*, says he] they were involuntary and unconscious of what they experienced; but at their *baptism* they had choice, and knowledge, and illumination."* And Tertullian observes:—"The laver of baptism is the seal of *faith*, which faith begins from *penitence*. We are not washed [baptized] in order that we may cease from sinning, but because we have ceased, since we are already cleansed in heart."† Infant baptism, therefore, could not have as yet been introduced. Origen, who lived in the middle of the third century, was the first who defended it. It was, as he tells us, a subject of "frequent inquiry among brethren."‡ Consequently it must have been a new topic. "Brethren" did not understand it. Up to this time evidently, none received baptism, but such as with " choice and knowledge," made a credible profession of their " faith." In this ordinance they publicly " put on Christ." But now, whether infants, or persons too young to understand the rudiments of religion, should be baptized, excited "frequent inquiry among brethren." Thence onward the practice rapidly gained ground, and soon acquired universal prevalence.

Why, I may ask, should such a thing as the baptism of infants ever have suggested itself to the minds of men? It is not intimated in the word of God. Reason does not approve it. To religion it is plainly repugnant. From whence did it arise? It owes its existence, I answer, exclusively to blind superstition, which *first* persuaded men that there is a mysterious,

---

\* Christian Rev., No. 22.

† De Penitentia, sect. 5, p. 123.

‡ There is great uncertainty whether Origen wrote what is attributed to him. His works have been wholly vitiated by interpolations.

secret, inexplicable efficacy in baptism, which conveys the grace of God to the soul of the recipient; *then*, that without baptism no one, whether adult or infant, could be saved; and *lastly*, that infants really do, by some incomprehensible power of God, repent of their sins, believe in our Lord Jesus Christ, and therefore, according to the gospel, are entitled to receive baptism! We will examine each of these propositions separately.

1. The opinion began to prevail as early as the middle of the second century, that there is in baptism some mysterious, secret, inexplicable efficacy which conveys the grace of God to the soul of the recipient!
Of this fact testimony so ample has already been submitted that you need not here be detained with its repetition. This superstitious absurdity seems to have been first taught by the Gnostics, borrowed doubtless from the "Eugenia"* of the pagan Greeks. Gnosticism was a popular and inveterate heresy.† As a sect, it was nominally put down, and destroyed; but its dogmas lived. Many of them were embraced by the teachers reputed orthodox, and perpetuated in the faith of all subsequent ages. Among them, this is not the least striking or conspicuous. The spiritual benefits they attributed to baptism were supposed not to be in the ordinance itself, but through that as a medium conveyed to the soul by the administrator, in virtue of the prayers, and the faith of the church, and as readily to one individual as to another. No one, whether adult or infant, was considered safe who should die

* ευγενια. Vide Stovel on Discipleship.
† Vide Neander's Eccl. Hist.

without having obtained the benefits of these cleansing influences. Gregory Nazianzen, for example, supposing, in one of his discourses, that he might be requested to express his opinion in the premises, proceeds to advise that in case of any apparent danger of death, children should be baptized, "Inasmuch," says he, "as it were better they should be sanctified without knowing it, than that they should die without being sealed and initiated." In all other cases he prefers that baptism should be delayed until those who receive it are of sufficient age to allow the impression intended to be made by the recital of the mystic words.* On these accounts the ordinance continued to grow in importance until it assumed all the consequence with which it has been invested in subsequent ages.

2. A kindred doctrine grew up with this, and soon took possession of the general mind, that no one, of whatever age, without baptism could be saved.

And if indeed baptism conveys grace and salvation, which without it cannot be received, how can any one be saved to whom it has not been given? On this subject, Cyprian, the Bishop of Carthage, says:†— "As far as in us lies, no soul is to be lost. It is not for us to hinder any person from baptism, and the grace of God. Which rule, as it holds to all, so we think it more especially to be observed in reference to infants, to whom our help, and the divine mercy, are rather to be granted." Ambrose also, the Bishop of Milan,‡ remarks:—"No person comes to the kingdom

---

* Turney on Bapt., p. 138.     † Anno Dom. 250.
‡ A. D. 390.

of heaven but by baptism. Infants that are baptized, are reformed back again from wickedness to the primitive state of their nature." And Chrysostom, the Patriarch of Constantinople,* observes :—" The grace of baptism gives us cure without pain, and fills us with the grace of the Spirit." " If sudden death seize us before we are baptized, there is nothing to be expected but hell." Thus do these great men express the doctrine, which in their age prevailed among all who were considered orthodox. They believed that salvation without baptism was impossible. The effect upon the minds of parents and others, may readily be imagined. All, as we may suppose, were baptized without delay.

Concurrent with these movements arose an institution in the church, the workings of which had a powerful influence in hastening infant baptism. I allude to Catechumenical Schools, of which a full account may be seen in any extended ecclesiastical history. Concerning them I shall state but two or three facts. They originated in the second century, and were attached, as Sabbath-schools now are, to the several christian congregations. They proposed to instruct children, and proselytes in the principles of religion, preparatory to their admission to baptism and membership in the church. For several centuries they enjoyed boundless popularity. Into these schools were received children of all classes, and persons of all ages and circumstances. None of them, however, were baptized, except in cases of " danger of death," until they had passed through their regular novitiate, and could

* A. D. 400.

answer intelligibly the questions proposed in the rubric of the times. But as we have seen, the impression of the importance and necessity of baptism was constantly increasing in intensity, and the result was, proportionally to shorten the catechumenical period. The qualifications for baptism were also of course diminished in their number and extent, and finally, if the children could not themselves answer the questions, their friends were permitted to answer for them.

The liturgy then, as now, required that all who were baptized should, preparatory to receiving the ordinance, renounce the world, the flesh and the devil, profess their faith in Christ, and promise to walk in obedience to the gospel all the days of their life. This of course infants could not do. But the deficiency was supplied by *sponsors*, who did all this in their names, pledging themselves to the church and her ministry, that these little ones should subsequently receive the necessary instruction, admonition, and guidance, and at a suitable time, be brought before the bishop to be examined, and confirmed in their christian profession. In these facts we have the true history of the origin of sponsors, or sureties for infants, in baptism. Such sureties had previously been employed only for older, or adult catechumens, having been first used for Pagans, and afterwards for others on their baptism. Ask you for testimony in proof of this statement? It is abundant, and at hand. We satisfy ourselves with one only. The Edinburgh Encyclopædia says:—" In the second century christians began to be divided into *believers*, or such as were baptized, and *catechumens*, or such as were receiving instruction to qualify them for baptism.

To answer for these [last] persons, sponsors or God fathers were first introduced."* By this device the consciences of all were quieted. Infant baptism thus gradually extended itself. And since preparatory instructions were no longer necessary, the catechumenical schools were not wanted, and they at last ceased to exist. Murmurings were doubtless uttered occasionally, by those who knew any thing of religion as taught in the word of God. But for these there was a ready remedy. They were all silenced, and the policy of the Catholic church fixed, by decrees such as the following established at the Council of Trent:—" Whoever shall affirm that the sacraments of the new law [the gospel] are not necessary to salvation," " and that they do not contain the grace they signify," " let him be accursed."†

3. Infant baptism was now established, and justified, by the grace conferred in the ordinance, its necessity to salvation, and the expedient of sponsors to answer for the child. Yet the difficulty was not entirely overcome. In those early days, repentance for sin, and faith in our Lord Jesus Christ, were acknowledged as indispensable preliminaries to baptism. These conditions are so plainly set forth in all parts of the New Testament, that no Pedobaptist then pretended to call them in question. They felt, on the contrary, that they were obliged to comply with them. They knew also that the repentance and faith of the sponsor, were only those of the proxy or substitute, and not of the child. But it was the child who was to receive the ordinance, not the sponsor, and the Bible requires these

* Art. Sponsors. † Conc. Trid., Art. Bapt.

conditions of the very person to be baptized himself. Here, it would seem, was an insuperable impediment. What was to be done? A most convenient discovery was now made and announced to the world. It was an effectual remedy. It was found that infants do, by some unexplained and incomprehensible power of God imparted to them, really possess, truly exercise, and acceptably profess repentance of sin and faith in Christ, and are therefore, according to the conditions prescribed in the gospel, the proper subjects, and legally entitled to receive baptism!

This assumption is so monstrous that many may doubt whether it was ever made. Since then it may, perchance, be called in question, I shall here pause until the amplest proof has been submitted. When first announced, it is not surprising that the proposition did not, at once, command universal assent. It seemed, even to some high ecclesiastics, to be an absurdity. Bishop Boniface, for example, wrote on the subject, to St. Augustine, as follows:—" If I should set before thee a young infant, and should ask of thee whether that infant, when he cometh to riper years, will be honest and just," "thou wouldest, I know, answer, that to tell in these things what shall come to pass, is not in the power of mortal man. If I should ask what good or evil such an infant thinketh, thine answer would be with the like uncertainty. If thou neither canst promise for the time to come, nor for the present pronounce any thing in this case, how is it that when such are brought to baptism, their parents there undertake what the child shall afterwards do? Yea, they are not doubtful to say it doth [*believe*], which is impossible to be done by infants; at least there is no man precisely able to affirm it done. Vouchsafe me hereunto some short answer, such as not only to press me with the bare authority of custom, but also instruct me with the cause thereof." To this very modest and sensible address Augustine thus replies:—" In the infant there is *not* a present actual *habit* of faith. There is delivered unto them that sacrament a part of the due celebration whereof consisteth in answering to the Articles of Faith, because the habit of faith that doth afterwards come with years, is but further building up the same edifice, the foundation whereof was laid by the sacrament of baptism. For that which we professed without any understanding, when we afterwards come to acknowledge, do we any thing else but only bring into ripeness the very seed which was sown before? We are *then* [in infancy] *believers,* because we then begin to be that which process of time doth make perfect. And until we come to *actual* belief, the very *sacrament of faith* [baptism] is a shield as strong as after this, the *faith of the sacrament,* against all contrary infernal powers, which whoever doth think '*impossible*' is undoubtedly farther off from christian belief, though he be baptized, than are those innocents who at their baptism, albeit they have no concert or cogitation of faith, are notwithstanding pure and free from all opposite cogitations, whereas the other is not free. If, therefore, without any fear or scruple, we may account them, and term them believers, only for their outward professions' sake, who inwardly are farther off from faith than infants, why not infants much more at the time of their solemn initiation by baptism the sacrament of faith, whereunto they not only conceive nothing opposite, but have also that grace given them which is the best and most effectual cause out of which our belief doth grow. In sum, the whole church [infants and all] is a multitude of believers, *all* honored with that title, even *hypocrites* for their professions' sake, as well as *saints* because of their inward sincere profession, and *infants* as being in their first degree of ghostly motion towards the actual *habit of faith*. The first sort are faithful in the eyes of the world; the second faithful in the sight of God; the last in the ready, direct way to become both."\* Again :—" *Infants do profess repentance* by the words of those who bring them, when *they* do by them renounce the devil and this world."† Mr. Bingham of the Episcopal denomination, in his learned work on the Antiquities of the Christian Church, writing of this early period, says :—" Another sort of names given to *baptism* were taken from the conditions required of all those who received it, which were *the profession of a true faith,* and a *sincere repentance.* Upon this account baptism is sometimes called the *sacrament* of faith, and the *sacrament* of repentance. St. Austin uses this name to explain how children may be said to have faith, though they are not capable of making any profession of themselves." " And upon this account, when the answer [in the church] is made that an *infant believes* who has not yet the habit of faith, the meaning is that he *has* faith because of the *sacrament* of faith; and that *he turns to God* because of the *sacrament* of conversion." Fulgentius uses the same terms

---

\* Hooker's Works, vol. i., pp. 630–637.
† Wall. Hist. Inf., vol. ii., pp. 435, 438.

in urging the necessity of baptism :—" Firmly believe and doubt not, that excepting such as are baptized in their own blood for the name of Christ, no man shall have eternal life who is not here first turned from his sins by repentance and faith, and set at liberty by the sacrament of faith and repentance, that is, by baptism."*

Such are the teachings of the fathers on this subject. But we have still more indubitable authority. The whole doctrine, in all its absurdity, is embodied unmistakably, in the liturgy of the ancient church. The priest there asks the *child*, and the *sponsor* answers, as follows :

" *Question*.—Dost *thou* [the child] renounce the devil and all his works, all his angels, and all his service, and his pomps ?"

" *Answer*.—I [the sponsor in his name] do renounce."

" *Quest*.—Dost *thou* [the child] believe in Christ ?"

" *Ans*.—[By sponsor] I do believe." *And he repeats the creed.* The infant, after some other ceremonies, is baptized, and of course baptized as a penitent believer in Christ ! Thus the proof is complete that neither the ancient church nor the papacy ever abandoned the great truth that repentance and faith are unchangeable gospel preliminaries to baptism, and that from the fourth century up to the Reformation, infants were believed to possess the required repentance and faith, upon a profession of which they were baptized.

These were mainly, the superstitions that originally

* Antiq. Chris. Church, vol. iii., p. 120.

produced infant baptism; the belief of a mysterious cleansing power in baptism itself; the necessity in all cases of baptism in order to salvation; and the plea that infants who are baptized have the necessary preliminaries demanded in the gospel. From this accumulation of theological impurities, like Python from the mud of the deluge, sprang infant baptism.

I now proceed to the other branch of the proposition, and shall show conclusively, that the practice of infant baptism perpetuates the superstitions by which it was originally produced.

That all the sects of protestant pedobaptists are under the influence at this moment, to a greater or less extent, of the *first*, and the *second*, of these forms of superstition, is a fact that no man can successfully deny. Their standards and other authorities teach unquestionably, that baptism carries with it some mysterious cleansing power, and that it is connected somehow, with grace and salvation! The ancients believed, moreover, that little children brought to baptism are endowed with the graces of repentance and faith, and have therefore the gospel preliminaries required for baptism! Do modern enlightened protestant pedobaptists credit this absurdity? The inquiry is worthy of our attention.

We turn, first, to the great, and, in some respects, incomparable Martin Luther. He practises no concealments, but expresses himself boldly, and without equivocation. He remarks:—" We here say and conclude that *the children believe in baptism itself*, and have *their own faith* which God works in them, through the intercession and hearty offering of the sponsors, in the faith of the christian church, and that is what we call

## PERPETUATES SUPERSTITIONS. 165

the power of another's faith; not that any one can be saved by that, but he thereby (that is, through another's intercession and aid) may obtain faith of his own from God by which he [the infant] is saved." This faith is, he declares, *the infants'* "*own faith* in which *they* believe, and are baptized for themselves."* In his larger Catechism, published 1529, he further says:—"The great efficacy and usefulness of baptism being thus understood, let us further observe what sort of persons it is that receive such things as are offered by baptism. This, again, is most beautifully and clearly expressed in these words: 'He that believeth, and is baptized, shall be saved.' That is, faith alone makes a person worthy to receive with any profit, this salutary and divine water. Without faith baptism profits nothing, although in itself it cannot be denied to be a heavenly and inestimable treasure." "We bring *a child* to a minister of the church to be baptized in *this hope* and persuasion, that *it certainly believes*, and we pray that God may give it faith." And again. In the "Conference at Wittenberg," in 1536, when called upon to explain how infants who do not think at all, can believe, Luther answered:—"As we even when asleep, are numbered among the faithful, and are in truth such although we are actually thinking nothing of God, so a certain beginning of faith (which nevertheless is the work of God) exists in infants according to their measure and proportion, of which *we* are ignorant."† Thus we have the doctrine of Lutheranism on this subject. It cannot be mistaken. That church

* Hinton's Hist. Bapt., p. 339.
† Bucer's Notes of the Conf. in Goode on Bapt.

holds that it is lawful to baptize those only who exercise repentance of sin, and faith in Christ; that infants do exercise repentance of sin, and faith in Christ; therefore it is lawful, and indeed obligatory, to baptize infants!

Calvin next demands our attention. What did he teach, and what do his followers now hold, on this subject?

Two incompatible and contradictory theories struggled in his mind. The infants of believing parents, and these only, he taught, are to be baptized. He says:— "This principle must always be maintained," "that baptism is not conferred upon infants in order that they may *become* the children and heirs of God, but because they are already [their parents being such] in that rank and position. Otherwise Anabaptists would be right in excluding them from baptism."* The grace conferred upon children, and the faith upon which they are baptized, are therefore *hereditary!* This is the former theory. The latter refers to his doctrine of election. He taught that some infants are *elect,* and some *non-elect,* and that only the elect children receive any benefit by baptism! He remarks:— "We diligently teach that God does not put forth his power without distinction to all who receive the sacrament, but only to the elect."† "How, it is inquired, are infants regenerated, who have no knowledge either of good or evil? We reply, that *the work of God is not yet without existence, because it is not observed or understood by us.*"‡ Calvin says:— "Though these graces [repentance and

---

\* Agreement at Zurich, 1549. † Ut Supra.
‡ Calvin's Inst., xvi., 18.

faith] have not yet been formed in them, *the seeds of both* are nevertheless implanted in their hearts by the secret operations of the Spirit."* The grace and benefit are therefore *elective!* But if they be hereditary how can they be elective? And if elective how can they be hereditary? These two theories are radically the opposites of each other, and never can be harmonized, unless, indeed, God has elected to salvation only the infants of believing parents, whose faith and election are the faith and election of their offspring; in which case faith and election are propagated by *natural generation*, and no man can be saved whose parents before him were not believers in Christ. Thus does infant baptism overwhelm and destroy the scripture doctrine of Predestination!

Apart, however, from these considerations, the Calvinistic doctrine on the subject before us, may be stated in a few words, thus:—" Faith is necessary to baptism. No child can be baptized without it. The parents of the child have faith. What belongs to the parents belongs to the child. Therefore the child has faith, and upon that faith is baptized!" So taught Calvin, and so teach his disciples at this time. Of this fact I could introduce instantly a hundred witnesses. One, however, is sufficient. Dr. Miller, the late distinguished Professor at Princeton, to whom I have before several times referred, remarks:—" After all, the whole weight of the objection [to infant baptism] in this case, is founded on entire forgetfulness of the main principle of the pedobaptist system. It is forgotten that in *every case* of

* Institutes, xvi., 20. Examine Bushnell, p. 28; also p. 60

*infant* baptism *faith* is required, and if the *parents* be sincere is *actually exercised*. But it is required of the *parent*, not of the *child*. So that if the parent truly present his child in faith, the *spirit* of the ordinance is really met and answered." The Calvinistic doctrine is therefore substantially the same as that of the Papists and the Lutherans. Presbyterians, Congregationalists, and the others, arrive, although by a different route, at the conclusion that the gospel does require faith on the part of all those who are baptized as an indispensable condition of their receiving the ordinance; that the children to be baptized have faith, since their parents' faith is their faith; and that infants are therefore baptized upon a profession of their faith.

The only other great parent class of protestant pedobaptists whose principles remain to be examined, is the Episcopal, embracing Methodists of all sects. Turn, if you please, to the liturgy of that church, whether of England or America, and you will find the doctrine distinctly and unequivocally taught, that *infants are baptized upon a profession of their own faith!* "The office" of baptism prescribes that the minister shall ask, and the sponsor answer as follows :—

"*Minister.*—Dost thou in the name of this child, renounce the devil and all his works, the vain pomp and glory of the world, with all covetous desires of the same, and the sinful desires of the flesh, so that thou wilt not follow nor be led by them?"

"*Answer.*—I renounce them all, and by God's help will endeavor not to follow, nor be led by them."

"*Minister.*—Dost thou believe all the Articles of

the Christian Faith as contained in the Apostles' Creed?"

"*Answer.*—I do."

"*Minister.*—Wilt thou be baptized in this faith?"

"*Answer.*—That is my desire."

"*Minister.*—Wilt thou then obediently keep God's holy will and commandments, and walk in the same all the days of thy life?"

"*Answer.*—I will by God's help."

Will it be pretended that in these answers the sponsors speak only for themselves? This is a common plea, and very often made, but it is plainly preposterous, since it is the *child* and not the *sponsor* that is to be baptized, and it is the child who is asked, "Dost *thou* believe;" "wilt *thou* be baptized;" "wilt *thou* obediently keep God's holy will." It is the *infant*, therefore, that renounces the world, the flesh, and the devil; it is the *infant* that *believes* "all the Articles of the Christian Faith;" it is the *infant* that *desires* to be baptized; it is the *infant* that binds itself to perpetual obedience! These facts are so obvious, that no intelligent man will, I persuade myself, upon mature reflection, venture to call them in question. These are the professions of their *infants*, upon which they are baptized.

The fathers of all the protestant episcopal churches maintain infant repentance and faith at great length. Bucer, and Peter Martyr, taught the doctrine in the Universities of Cambridge and Oxford, and Archbishops, Bishops, and inferior clergy, in all the pulpits of the land. But it is necessary to particularize.

Cartwright, a distinguished divine of the Calvinistic

school, thought proper to "*admonish*" the British Parliament on this subject, and in a learned address, expressed his doubts whether all the infants baptized were *elect*, and in case any were not, he insisted that *they* could not with propriety be said to believe. " It can," he avowed, " no more be precisely said that it [the infant] hath *faith*, than it may be said precisely that it is elected."* This paper called forth a spirited reply from the famous Hooker, in which he severely rebukes the presumptuous Presbyterian. "Were St. Augustine now living," says Hooker, "there are [those] who would tell him for his better instruction, that to say of a child that it is *elect*, and to say it doth *believe*, is all one, for which cause sith no man is able precisely to affirm the one of any infant in particular, it followeth that precisely and absolutely, he ought not to say the other. Which precise and absolute terms are not necessary in this case. We speak of infants as the rule of piety alloweth both to speak and to think." " Baptism implieth a covenant or league between God and man, wherein as God doth bestow presently remission of sins, and the Holy Ghost, binding himself also to add (in process of time) what grace soever shall be further necessary for the attainment of everlasting life, so every baptized soul receiving the same grace at the hands of God, tieth itself likewise forever to the observation of his law, no less than the Jews by circumcision bound themselves to the law of Moses. The law of Christ requiring, therefore, faith and newness of life in all men by virtue of the covenant of baptism, is it toyish that the church in baptism exacteth at *every man's*

* Admonition to Parliament.

## PERPETUATES SUPERSTITIONS. 171

*hands* [infants included] an express profession of faith, and an irrevocable promise of obedience by way of stipulation?"* Bishop Beveridge asks, "Why are infants baptized?" and answers thus:—" The reason is, not only because they have the seeds of *repentance*, and *faith* in them, which may afterwards grow to perfection, but chiefly because they then promise to perform them, which is as much as we know adult persons, or those of riper years do."†

We may, however, appeal to still higher authority than that of Bucer, or Peter Martyr, or Hooker, or Beveridge, or all these together. *Cranmer* the *Archbishop*, and *Primate* in his day, of all England, speaks thus:—" In baptism are our sins taken away, and we from sins purged and cleansed, and regenerated in a new man to live a holy life, according to the spirit and will of God." " They [the Anabaptists] say that those that should be christened, must *first believe*, and *then* be christened. Children, they say, *cannot believe*, for faith is gotten by hearing, and hearing by the word of God. So *children cannot have faith*, say the Anabaptists. Wherefore they say that infants should *not be christened*.‡ To this reason I answer and say that *children may have faith*, although they have it not by hearing, yet *they have faith by the infusion of the Holy Ghost*, as the holy prophets had, and many holy men in the old law had. Also faith is the *gift* of God and the work of the Holy Ghost. Who should let [hinder] God to give his gifts *where he will*, seeing faith is the

---

\* Hooker's Works, vol. i., pp. 633–637.
† Church Catechism Explained, pp. 128, 129.
‡ And they say truly, and reason conclusively.

gift of God? He may give faith as well to *children* as to old men. Faith also is the *work* of God, and not of man, of man's will or reason. Who will let God to work *where* he lists? Therefore *it is not* impossible for children to have faith, as these Anabaptists falsely suppose." "God regardeth no persons, but giveth his gifts without all regard of persons. A *child*, or an *old man*, he counteth as *a person* in scripture. Wherefore it followeth plainly that he giveth not faith to an old man, or denieth faith to a child, because he is a child, for then God should regard persons, which he doth not." "And when they [the Anabaptists] say they must express faith before they be christened, what will they do with deaf and dumb men, that get not faith by hearing, nor express their faith by words? Will they exclude them from baptism, and condemn them to hell-pit?"* "Christ took little children in his arms and blessed them, and said, 'Of such is the kingdom of heaven.' Here are tokens that God loved these children, that they pleased him, and *that they had faith*, for without faith no man can please God."†

With all these testimonies before you, and the number might be increased indefinitely, can you doubt the teachings of the Episcopal church, in itself, and in all its sects? They hold with Lutherans, and Calvinists, that infants who receive the ordinance, are divinely en-

---

\* It is not at all surprising that this argument had no influence upon the hated Anabaptists. They would have been in a pitiable condition if they had had no more common sense on this subject than was shown by the Archbishop.

† Richmond's Fathers of the English Church, vol. ii., et seq.

dowed with repentance of sin, and faith in our Lord Jesus Christ; upon the reputed profession of which they are baptized!

The fact is now incontrovertibly established that *the practice of infant baptism perpetuates the superstitions by which it was originally produced.* Protestant pedobaptists, on all hands, still adhere to the old popish dogmas that baptism contains some mysterious divine efficacy, and that through it the spiritual state of infants is materially affected, both as regards their union with Christ in this world, and their salvation in the world to come.

The evil thus brought upon all the interests of truth and salvation is incalculable. Religion itself is degraded and caricatured. The minds of its votaries are besotted with miserable logomachy, such as that we have just examined. Fanaticism and bigotry reign triumphantly. Who that has not resigned his reason, can believe that the baptism of an infant conveys to its soul the quickening grace of God? Or that it is possible for an infant, at the age at which they are usually baptized, to exercise repentance, and faith in the Redeemer? All this is taught in the Papal church, and in the Protestant church, by the Catholic fathers, and by all the great Reformers. They were on many subjects wise and learned. On this subject they were neither. Do not, I pray you, oblige me to credit absurdities of any kind, and especially in religion. Not more insane than this is priestly pardon, the invocation of saints, transubstantiation, or purgatory. Infant baptism must, and does still look for support to the superstitions by which it was originally produced. Whoever submits to such superstitions in one department of religion, will soon be ready to give up his judgment, and common sense, in all the others. Thus a downward progress is commenced which cannot be arrested short of the dark caverns of popery.

# CHAPTER IX

INFANT BAPTISM IS AN EVIL BECAUSE IT SUBVERTS THE TRUE DOCTRINE OF INFANT SALVATION.

Doctrine stated; arguments in proof; manner in which subverted by infant baptism; authorities; conclusions.

DEATH is a relentless destroyer. He assails, without distinction, all classes and conditions of men. The young and the old alike fall beneath his power. Upon infancy, however, his shafts descend most frequently, and with a deadlier aim. How large the proportion of mankind who are hurried into eternity during the first years of their being! Where is the family that has not mourned infants loved, and lost? Bleeding hearts, and flowing tears, in all lands, tell of sorrows which no words can ever adequately express! Millions of infant spirits have gone into the unseen world. Each is an immortal intelligence. In that world they all possess the sensibilities common to humanity. With these facts before us, one question of surpassing interest, presses itself upon us all. *Of departed infants what is the eternal destiny? Are they happy, or miserable?* Parental affection *implores*, christian sympathy earnestly *solicits*, and ministerial faithfulness *demands*, that these inquiries receive a prompt, intelligible, and scriptural answer. *We believe that all infants are saved unconditionally, through the application to them, by the Holy Ghost, of the redemption of our Lord Jesus Christ.* No matter whether they are in the church or out of the church, whether they are baptized or unbaptized, whether they are the children of believers or unbelievers, of heathens, mohammedans, or christians, their everlasting blessedness is equally, and in all cases, secure. These, and all other such like circumstances, are irrelevant, and never can affect *their* relations with Christ. Consequently they can have no bearing upon their future destiny. *Every child dying in infancy is saved.* This is the doctrine of the Baptist denomination. Not of a *few only*, nor of our churches, and people, of the *present day* alone. It is the doctrine which has been invariably held by us in all countries, and in every age. It is the doctrine taught by the word of God. Having thus stated our position, I proceed at once, to the proofs of its truth.

*Infant salvation is guarantied, in the first place, by the nature of the divine government.*

God is infinitely good. His *benevolence* forbids the infliction of unnecessary suffering upon any of his creatures. Misery is never permitted, but when demanded by *justice*, as either the consequence, or the penalty of sin. The *government* of God is designed, not only to benefit his creatures, but also to manifest his glory. Through this medium, as well as through his works, and his word, he reveals his true character to all intelligent beings. Infants have no personal, or individual accountability. For the condemnation of the deliberate and impenitent rejecter of the gospel, and also of the wicked despisers of God, who violate the laws of nature, and of their own conscience, I can perceive ample reasons. In such a case I can readily comprehend how God, as the governor of the universe, will glorify his infinite *righteousness*. But I cannot see how this could occur in the case of infants. It is infinitely more in accordance with all our conceptions of God, to conclude that in them he will evince his special beneficence. It is, in truth, abhorrent to every feeling of kindness and love, to suppose that he will cast them off, or that he will not receive, and save them. There is no want of fulness in the redemption of Christ. The power of the Holy Spirit is not limited. God is infinitely gracious. What then is to hinder their salvation? Rather, does not every consideration connected with him, with his government, and his glory, seem imperatively to demand the salvation of infants?

*But infants are, I remark secondly, redeemed by our Lord Jesus Christ, and must therefore be saved.*

Their redemption is thus taught by an apostle:— "Death" [natural death] "reigned from Adam to Moses, even over them that had not sinned after the similitude of Adam's transgression." In other words, *infants*, who have not committed actual offences, as Adam did, have nevertheless all inherited his depravity, and are, therefore, subject to physical suffering and death. "As," however, "by the offence of one [Adam] judgment [sentence] came upon all men to condemnation, even so by the righteousness of one [Jesus Christ] the free gift [the offer of deliverance from condemnation under a better covenant] came upon all men, [upon as many as were involved in the consequences of

Adam's sin] unto justification of life."* Christ Jesus suspended the execution of the sentence of death under which men had fallen, and introduced another covenant in the place of the first, and so changed the relations of things that to man, though a sinner, destruction is not inevitable. The remedy is found in the satisfaction made to divine justice by Messiah, the promised "seed of the woman." In consideration of his atonement the ground of condemnation is changed. His interposition has placed the whole subject in an entirely new aspect. Previously, if I may so speak, all men were condemned. Their relation to Adam had involved them all in the curse. Subsequently the case was different. "This is [now] the condemnation, that light has come into the world, and men loved darkness rather than light, because their deeds were evil."† " *Ye* are condemned," "*because* ye have not *believed* on the name of the only begotten Son of God."‡ Not *now* it is not so much because of your relation to Adam, disastrous as that relation may be, as because you do not embrace Christ by faith. Hence all the counsels, the warnings, the commands, the invitations, the promises of divine revelation, are addressed to those who are capable of exercising intelligence. And its denunciations are hurled only against wilful rebellion, impenitency, and unbelief. What are we here taught concerning infants? They have not the capacity to know any thing of the gospel. They are not impenitent, or rebellious. They have not rejected Christ. They are clearly included in his mediation, since " by his righteousness the free gift came upon all men to justification

* Rom. v., 12-19.   † John iii., 19.   ‡ John iii., 18.

## THE DOCTRINE OF INFANT SALVATION. 179

of life." That free gift must of course have come upon them. They are redeemed by Christ. And again. The relation to us of our Lord Jesus Christ *in the work of redemption*, is clearly, *to man as man*. Adam and Christ, are alike, *heads of the race.* "The first man Adam was made a living soul; the last Adam [Christ] was made a quickening spirit. Howbeit that is not first which was spiritual, but that which is natural, and afterwards that which was spiritual. The first man is of the earth, earthy; the second man is the Lord from heaven. As is the earthy, such are they also that are earthy; and as is the heavenly, such are they also that are heavenly. And as we have borne the image of the earthy, we shall also bear the image of the heavenly."* Both, therefore, according to this apostolic exposition, are heads of mankind *as man.* The first Adam was the author of sin; the second Adam was the author of deliverance from sin. The same terms are employed to designate those who are involved in ruin by the former, and those to whom deliverance is offered by the mediation of the latter. Both events concern the whole race, of whom some reach maturity of life, embrace Christ by faith, and are saved; others reach maturity, do not receive Christ, and are lost; but great multitudes die in infancy, and do neither good nor evil. These last stand, according to Paul, in as strict a relation to Christ, as they do to Adam, with this difference, that "Where sin abounded, grace does much more abound." In bringing *them* into this world, divine *sovereignty* has justly, and without any act of theirs, entailed on them *the depravity*

\* 1 Cor. xv., 45–49.

*and corruption* of the first Adam. In taking them away from the world, the same divine sovereignty has *graciously*, and without any act of theirs, conferred on them *the salvation* of the second Adam. Thus it is that, redeemed by the blood of Christ, they are saved by the infinite grace of God.

But all infants are depraved and sinful. How then *can they be saved?* To prepare them for happiness, *it is evident that the redemption of Christ must be applied by the Holy Spirit, to their purification from sin. Otherwise they would be incapable of eternal life.*

Every one is obliged to exclaim with David, "Behold, I was shapen in iniquity, and in sin did my mother conceive me."* Truly may it be said, "The wicked are estranged from the womb. They go astray as soon as they are born."† All are depraved, and depravity necessarily incapacitates those who are under its influence for the enjoyment of happiness. From infants it must therefore, to secure their salvation, be removed, and their nature must be cleansed, and purified. This great work can be done only by the Holy Ghost. The work of *God the Spirit* is therefore, equally as necessary to their salvation, and ours, as the work of *God the Son*. None are saved by the abstract redemption of the Son, irrespective of the personal application of that redemption by the Spirit. Since, however, Christ died for all, and consequently for infants; and since the work of the Spirit is necessary to complete the designs of grace thus commenced; his sanctification is given in full measure, to every departing child. In all such instances, his merits and

* Psa. li., 5.   † Psa. lviii., 8.

righteousness are thus applied *personally*, to fit them for the change. *The scriptures nowhere teach that this is done through baptism*, nor any other ordinance ; *nor that it is withheld* for the want of it. Will not the Holy Ghost "quicken even your mortal *body*"* sleeping in the grave, to prepare you for the resurrection of the last day? "Why then should it be thought a thing incredible," and especially since they are redeemed by Messiah, that he should sanctify the spirits of departing children, and thus "make them meet to be partakers of the inheritance of the saints in light?"

*There are, I observe in the third place, instances of infant salvation on record in the word of God.*

Disease had laid his withering hand upon the infant child of David. He fasted, and wept, and prayed for the life of his beloved boy. All was in vain. It pleased the Lord to order otherwise than as he desired. The child died. Now his servants were alarmed on account of their master. They were afraid to communicate to him the melancholy intelligence : "For they said, Behold, while the child was yet alive, we spake unto him, and he would not hearken unto our voice. How will he then vex himself if we tell him that the child is dead! But when David saw that his servants whispered, he perceived that the child was dead. Therefore he said unto his servants, Is the child dead? And they said, He is dead. Then David arose from the earth, and washed and anointed himself, and changed his apparel, and came into the house of the Lord, and worshipped. Then he came to his own

* Rom. viii., 11.

house, and when he required they set bread before him, and he did eat! Then said his servants unto him, What thing is this that thou hast done? Thou didst fast and weep for the child while it was yet alive; but when the child was dead, thou didst arise and eat bread! And he said, While the child was yet alive I fasted and wept; for I said, Who can tell whether God will be gracious unto me, that the child may live? Can I bring him back again? I shall go to him; but he will not return to me."* What is the lesson taught us by this touching incident? David did not certainly console himself with the thought that he, too, should go to *the grave* whither his child had gone. This consideration could surely, have afforded him no special pleasure. The grave is cold, and silent, and dismal. Nor could it have been a grateful reflection that since God had taken him away, he must submit to the necessity. If these, or any similar feelings governed him, why were they not equally influential, since they were all fully as applicable, in the case of another son, slain in battle? When tidings of that unhappy event reached David, how then did he deport himself? Did he with calm and resigned acquiescence, say to those about him, Wherefore should I lament *him?* "Can I bring him back again? I shall go to him; but he will not return to me?" On the contrary, he was wholly inconsolable. Overwhelmed by the blow, he turned away from his friends, and trembling with agony, he "Went up to the chamber over the gate of the city. And as he went, thus he said: O my son Absalom, my son, my son Absalom!

* 2 Sam. xii., 15-23.

Would God I had died for thee, O Absalom, my son, my son!"* Why now this insupportable grief? The reason is obvious. Absalom was of mature age. He was a sinner against God. Besides, therefore, his affliction as a father on account of his death, he could entertain no hope for *him* in another life. Regarding his *infant child* the case was different. He had full confidence that he would, when the scenes of this world were over, "*go to him*" in the paradise above, where they would be associated in eternal glory. Therefore said he, in other words, He is happy now. He is in heaven. I will not grieve on his account. I also shall go ere long. Then I shall join him on high. This hope is most consolatory. It "is stronger than the grave." It is all radiant with joy and brightness. David undoubtingly believed that his child was saved.

Another instance, equally instructive, occurred in the family of Jeroboam. He, too, was a king of Israel, but a vile apostate, and wicked idolater. *His* child, also, was stricken with a deadly malady. He was greatly beloved, and his distressed father sought earnestly, but in vain, to save his life. The little sufferer sunk into the grave! In the midst of the tumult of sorrow produced by this event, the prophet Abijah, sent of God for the purpose, disclosed to the weeping mother, the designs of God in his removal at a period so early. "All Israel," said Jehovah, "shall mourn for *him*, and *bury* him. *He* only of Jeroboam shall come to the grave. In him there is found some good thing."† This child, therefore, was removed, when so

* 2 Sam. xviii., 33. † Kings xiv., et seq.

young that nothing of his personal history is recorded, as an act to him, of love, and blessing. But how could this be? Had he lived he would probably have been a king. If children—those of wicked parents, and of idolaters, as well as others—are not saved, he was lost. It is surely no blessing to a child, to take him away from the prospects of a kingly throne, and send him to destruction! It is implied in scripture that it *was* an act of kindness to this child to remove him from all these prospects. Therefore God received him to himself in heaven. And if he was saved, then the children who die in infancy, of other wicked men and idolaters, are also saved.

One other instance on record, of infant salvation, is worthy of our attention. The murder of all the children of Bethlehem and its vicinity, by the jealous Herod, perpetrated in the hope that thereby he might succeed in destroying Messiah, was a horrible tragedy. It was foreseen, and predicted by an ancient prophet, in language full of mingled pathos and encouragement: —"A voice was heard in Ramah, lamentation, and bitter weeping. Rachel weeping for her children, refused to be comforted, because they were not. Thus saith the Lord: Refrain thy voice from weeping, and thine eyes from tears." "They shall come again from the land of the enemy. And there is hope in thine end, saith the Lord, that thy children shall come again to their own border."* Is the design of this passage difficult to perceive? Does it refer merely to the captivity in Babylon, under which the Hebrews were then suffering? Is the Mother of Israel represented as

* Jere. xxxi., 15–17.

weeping in her tenderness, only over the woes of her children in a distant land, writhing under the oppressions of their masters? Does God comfort her merely with the assurance that they shall yet return from their bondage, and inhabit, in peace and prosperity, the fields and the cities of Judea? Whatever may have been the *primary* sense of the prophecy, inspiration itself has given it a still higher, and more exalted meaning. The evangelist Matthew furnishes the interpretation. He says:—" Herod, when he saw that he was mocked by the wise men, was exceeding wroth, and sent forth and *slew all the children* that were in Bethlehem, and in all the coasts thereof, from two years old and under." "*Then was fulfilled* that which was spoken by Jeremy the prophet, saying, In Ramah was there a voice heard, lamentation, and weeping, and great mourning. Rachel weeping for her children, and would not be comforted, because they are not."\* *This* cruel act of Herod, therefore, was in the mind of the prophet. Of the children slain by him, consequently, it was more especially said, *They* shall escape from the enemy; there is *hope* for them; *they* shall possess their land! For these reasons their bereaved parents were exhorted to " refrain their voice from weeping, and their eyes from tears." But how was it possible to fulfil such promises? These children were all dead! They remained in their graves. *Literally*, these promises could never be fulfilled. The prophecy must therefore necessarily refer to *another* life. It evidently teaches the *three* following facts:— First, that all these slain children should be delivered

\* Matt. ii., 16-18.

from the great *enemy, eternal death;* secondly, that there was *hope for them,* since they were all redeemed by Christ, that they should *enjoy eternal life;* and thirdly, that they should *possess the heavenly land,* of which the earthly Canaan was a type. *These are the grounds* upon which our Heavenly Father offers comfort to their parents, and exhorts them to subdue their sorrows. Their children had been foully murdered. The jealousy of the king had, with bloody and relentless violence, torn them from their bosoms. By this means, however, they had gone *speedily,* and *safely,* to eternal life. I have selected and laid before you these instances of infant salvation recorded in the word of God, and have drawn them from the children of the good and the pious, such as David; from the children of the idolatrous and wicked, such as Jeroboam; and from the children of all classes, such as were the bereaved parents " in Bethlehem, and all the coasts thereof," in order to prove to you that *all infants are saved,* without any regard to the *character of their parents,* or the *circumstances* under which they were removed from the present life.

We have now seen that all children who die in infancy, are saved by the grace of God; that they are saved through the redemption of Jesus Christ; that this redemption is applied to them personally, and directly, by the Holy Ghost; and that we have many instances of their salvation recorded in God's word; it remains only to be proved that *their salvation is unconditional.*

They are involved, it is true, on account of their connection with Adam, in the consequences of his fall.

## THE DOCTRINE OF INFANT SALVATION. 187

But provision has been made for their *unconditional* deliverance, in the satisfaction of the second Adam. One among the clearest demonstrations of this truth is presented to us in connection with the doctrine of *their resurrection* in the last day. "Since by man came death," says Paul, "by man came also the resurrection of the dead. For as in Adam *all* die; even so in Christ, shall *all* be made alive"* — *raised from the dead.*† It is true, then, that in the resurrection of the body, *all* will be raised. The righteous and the wicked, the christian and the idolater, the adult and the infant, will alike participate in that glorious event. Here there is no condition but that of humanity. Those who live to the age of personal responsibility, are saved only upon the conditions of *repentance*, and *faith*. The wisdom of this provision no one can fail to perceive. They have a conscious being, a personal accountability. Yet it is not *for* their repentance, and faith; nor *by* their repentance, and faith, as a *procuring* cause, that even they are saved. They, too, obtain salvation by the grace of God in Jesus Christ: "For by grace are ye saved, through faith, and that not of yourselves, it is the gift of God. Not of works, lest any man should boast."‡ But repentance and faith are acts of a mind enlightened, and comparatively mature. They are not demanded of infants. *Infants are saved unconditionally.*

Thus is the salvation of infants fully, and satisfactorily established. Wherever in the wide world, and whenever, any child dies in infancy, it enters immedi-

---

* 1 Cor. xv. 21, 22.     † πάντες ζωοποιηθήσονται.
‡ Eph. ii., 8, 9.

ately into the joys of eternal life in heaven. It thenceforth dwells forever with the Redeemer. How full of the richest consolation is this glorious truth! In no form more delightful, has Jehovah manifested to us his abundant mercy, and grace. "Thanks be to God for his unspeakable gift."

*With all these facts before us, we turn to hear the expositions on the subject of our Pedobaptist brethren.* We are immeasurably pained to find them in utter confusion! Their best conceptions of this subject are entirely inadequate, and unworthy. *All their teachings tend evidently to subvert the true scripture doctrine of infant salvation.* Most of them claim that *infants must be brought into the church,* since out of it there is no deliverance; and all of them insist that the merits of Christ's atonement and the sanctification of the Holy Spirit, without which no one can be saved, are *communicated to them through baptism.* Thus they make the salvation of infants dependent upon *conditions,* and *such* conditions as no child can control, but must be performed by parents, friends, and ministers! Infant baptism and infant salvation are, therefore, always found more or less intimately associated in the minds of all classes of pedobaptists. These, I know, are grave charges, but the testimony is at hand by which they are amply sustained.

Before I offer this testimony, however, I will refer to a singular imputation against Baptists, and properly account for its existence. You have many a time, doubtless, heard the declaration that "*Baptists believe in the damnation of infants!*" Some persons with whom you have met, have perhaps told you to your

face that they have themselves *heard* Baptist *people*, and Baptist *ministers*, avow the sentiment. Pedobaptists of all classes, repeat everywhere the charge, and declare with indignant eloquence, that "*Baptists* hold the damnation of infants!" If, as I have professed to do in this chapter, I have properly represented Baptist sentiment on the subject, how could such an accusation against us ever have originated? And when produced and put into circulation, how could it have been kept up for so many ages? The answers are easy. *Pedobaptists* believe that the baptism of infants is necessary to their salvation. According to *their* doctrines, therefore, if they are *not* baptized they must be *damned*. *Baptists* refuse to baptize infants. *Pedobaptists* instantly proclaim, as a consequence of *their own principles*, without waiting to hear *our* opinions on the question of their salvation, that therefore " Baptists hold the damnation of infants!" Nor will they give it up. To this day they insist that it must be so. Since we do not *baptize* infants, we surely believe that if they die in infancy they are damned! One example will probably be sufficient to establish and illustrate the correctness of this account of the origin of the charge. *Archbishop Cranmer*, in one of his discourses, speaks of the Baptists in the following language :—
" Children, of necessity, must be christened, or else they cannot be purged of their sins, nor yet saved by Christ, and come to life everlasting. Wherefore the Anabaptists that would not have children to be christened, they show themselves that they would not have children to be purged from their sins, and be saved. If they would have children saved, they would not

deny them the means whereby Christ purgeth his church from sins, and saveth it, which is baptism."* Thus the slander arose, and was continued. The authority for it was derived from Lords *Archbishops,* "Bishops, and other clergy." It is not, therefore, surprising that it was taken up by the multitude, and repeated without end. The whole Pedobaptist English mind thus became imbued with the odium, throughout Europe and America, and it remains with them to the present hour. If we needed a defence against these allegations, it might be drawn from *another class of our opponents,* the Lutherans of all the German states. By them we are, and ever have been, vilified and reproached for holding that "*Infants are saved without baptism.*" The Augsburg Confession of Faith contains the following passage :—"*They condemn the Anabaptists,* who disallow the baptism of infants, and *affirm that they may be saved without it.*"† The German charge against us is true. We do believe that infants are saved without baptism. But the English charge is false, and they might, if they would, know it to be so. But in respect to us they do not wish to know the truth. It is the object of both parties, not to do us justice, but, if possible, to cover us with reproach, and thus, if they may, retard the progress of our principles. But our principles are those of the gospel. They cannot be always, successfully resisted. They will ultimately find their way to the hearts of men. They must, in the end, gloriously prevail. Persecuted we may be, and perpetually denounced; still we are really, the

---

\* Richmond's English Fathers, vol. ii., &c.
† Augsburg Confession, Art. ix.

only christians whose doctrines on infant salvation are rational, scriptural, or true. We return to the argument.

Roman Catholics, as is well known, universally hold and teach that no child can be saved unless it is baptized, and within "the pale of the church." The Fathers and Standards, of the Lutheran church, and the Episcopal church, all maintain the same doctrine. They insist that "baptism contains the grace which it represents," and by its intrinsic efficacy conveys to the child that grace "ex opere operato." Of these facts the amplest testimony has been given in the preceding chapters. The authorities there adduced need not be repeated. Their truth will, by all intelligent men, be readily admitted. In this country, however, some Lutherans, and Episcopalians, are evangelical. *They* surely do not receive the absurdities believed by their Fathers! *Ask them*, if you please. Will they answer you at all? If they do, will it not be in evasive terms? Some of them will perhaps be indignant, and tell you infants may be saved without baptism. Press them for an answer as to the grounds of their salvation. They will respond thus:—*If*, in such a case, infants are saved, it is "*by the uncovenanted mercies of God.*" Ah, "The *uncovenanted* mercies!" It may be so; and it may not! The matter is in their minds, at best, very doubtful! But Methodists, Presbyterians, and others of those classes, surely *know better*. *They* believe that all infants are saved, baptized, or not baptized. You can readily *try* their faith upon that question. One form of the experiment may be seen at almost any time. They scarcely know themselves what they believe on the subject. They will certainly resent the suspicion that they suppose infants may, under any circumstances, be lost. But let an *unbaptized* child of any of them, be sick, and in danger of death. The utmost trepidation arises. Appalling fears of some disastrous consequences fill the bosoms of parents, and friends. Alarm reigns. The little sufferer must not continue an hour "*unsealed*," "*uninitiated*." The minister is sent for, and the child is baptized at midnight! The baptism quiets every foreboding, and is followed immediately by calmness, and resignation! Why all this apprehension, and haste? What if it *should die*—if die it must—*without baptism?* Can it suffer possible harm on that account? Ah! disguise it as you may, the old superstition is still in their hearts. They believe—and they thus evince the fact—that there is in baptism, some sort of a mysterious sacramental efficacy, that affects for good, the destiny of the child in another world!

But we will try their opinions by a surer and more tangible standard. *What do our Methodist brethren teach on the subject?*

The answer is found in the "*Doctrinal Tracts*," written by Mr. Wesley himself, and published by order of the "*General Conference*," as an authoritative exposition of Methodism. I invite you to examine the following passages:—"What are the benefits," says Mr. Wesley, "we receive *by baptism*, is the next point to be considered. And the *first* of these is *the washing away of original sin, by the application of Christ's death.* That we are all born under the guilt of Adam's sin, and that all sin deserves eternal misery, was the unanimous sense of the ancient church, and is expressed in the ninth article of our own. And the scripture asserts that we were shapen in iniquity, and in sin did our mothers conceive us; that we were all by nature the children of wrath, and dead in trespasses and sins; that in Adam all die; that by one man's disobedience all were made sinners; that by one man sin entered into the world, and death by sin, which came upon all men, because all had sinned. This plainly includes infants, for they too die; therefore they have sinned; but not by actual sin, therefore by original sin, else what need have they of the death of Christ? Yea, death reigned from Adam to Moses, even over those who had not sinned actually, according to the similitude of Adam's transgression. This, which can relate to infants only, is a clear proof that the whole race of mankind are obnoxious both to the guilt and punishment of Adam's transgression. But as by the offence of one, judgment came upon all men to condemnation, so by the righteousness of one, the free gift came upon all men unto justification of life." *"And the virtue of that free gift, the merits of Christ's life and death, are applied to us in baptism."* Here you have a plain statement. Mr. Wesley proves very clearly, that all infants inherit sin from Adam, and are redeemed by our Lord Jesus Christ. But where is the proof that "the merits of his life and death are applied to them in baptism?" None is produced. The *scriptures* contain none. But still proof is offered, satisfactory to Mr. Wesley. Hear him. "The *church* declares in the *rubric,*" that "it is *certain,* by God's word, that children *who are baptized,* dying before they commit actual sin, are *saved*. Here," he adds, " it is plainly *taught* that infants" " can be saved only by *the merit of Christ's death*, and that *this merit* is to be *applied in baptism*."\* The proof, then, is in the *rubric!* It is not in the Bible. *Christ's merits* can only be applied to infants *by baptism!* Is not the conclusion strangely absurd that, after having redeemed *all* children who die in infancy by his blood, Messiah should still be dependent *for the application of his merits to them, and without which they cannot be saved, upon the contingency of their baptism!* If not baptized, they remain corrupt and sinful, because his merits and righteousness can in no other way be applied to them. Corrupt and sinful beings must be lost. Unbaptized children die corrupt and sinful beings. Therefore, according to Mr. Wesley, unbaptized children must be lost. In another place the Father of Methodism gives us the following argument :—" If infants are guilty of original sin, then they are proper subjects of baptism, seeing, in the ordinary way, *they cannot be saved* unless this be washed away *in baptism*. Infants need to be washed from original sin. Therefore they are proper subjects for baptism."† And this is the *authorized* and established doctrine of the whole Methodist church, English and American, on the subject of infant salvation! It is approved by the people, and published for their instruction and guidance by the General Conference! Our Methodist brethren, therefore, believe that "The virtues of Christ's free gift—the merits of his life and death—are applied to infants in *baptism ;*" that " Infants can be saved only by the merit of Christ's

---

\* Doctrinal Tracts, p. 246. † Ib., p. 251.

death, and this merit is to be *applied* in baptism;" that "They cannot, in the ordinary way, be saved unless their *original sin be washed away in baptism.*" And what is this but the same old dogma, in substance, held by the Papists, the Lutherans, and the Episcopalians? They all teach that "Baptism *represents* pardon, sanctification, and salvation, through Jesus Christ; and that it *always conveys the grace* which it represents." What a revolting subversion we here have of the scripture doctrine of infant salvation!

We will now pay our respects to *the doctrines on the subject, of Presbyterians, and other Calvinists.*

These doctrines are set forth in the Westminster Confession of Faith, and Catechisms. We notice the following passages:—"The visible church" "consists of all those throughout the world, that profess the true religion, together with *their children,*" "and is the kingdom of our Lord Jesus Christ, the house and family of God, *out of which there is no ordinary possibility of salvation.*"* It follows, of course, necessarily, that the children of those who *do not* "profess the true religion"—and such, in their estimation, are the children of ninety-nine hundredths of the whole human race; are not of "the house and family of God;" are not *in* the church; are not to be baptized, and *for them* "there is no ordinary *possibility* of salvation!" But Calvinists also tell us that they confer "*benefits*" upon the children they baptize. What are these benefits? The Confession answers:—"Although it be a great sin to contemn, or neglect this ordinance, yet

* Westminster Confession, ch. 25, sec. 2.

grace, and salvation, are not so *inseparably* annexed unto it, as that *no person* can be regenerated or saved without it, [since there may be some unknown *extraordinary* possibility of salvation] or that all that are baptized are undoubtedly regenerated," [since some of the infants thus "*sealed*," may turn out to be of the "*non-elect*."] "The efficacy of baptism is not tied to that moment of time wherein it is administered; [all its sanctifying effects may not instantly be imparted] yet notwithstanding, by the right use of this ordinance, *the grace promised* is not only offered, but really *exhibited*, [conveyed] and *conferred* by the Holy Ghost, to such (whether of age or *infants*) as that grace belongeth unto [if they be *elect*] according to the counsel of God's own will, in his own appointed time."\* *The grace promised, is conferred upon the infant by the Holy Ghost, in its baptism!* What is the grace promised? We have the answer in the Catechism. It is "The engrafting into" Christ; "the remission of sins by his blood, and regeneration by his Spirit;" "adoption, and resurrection unto eternal life."† These constitute "the grace promised," and they are all, according to Presbyterians, and their kindred sects, *given to infants in their baptism!* Such infants, and only such, are *in* the church; and *out of* the church, "there is no ordinary possibility of salvation." Thus we have an exposition of Calvinistic doctrines on the subject. They hold baptism to be the medium through which, to the infant who receives it, are conveyed "the merits of Christ's death;" the blessings of grace and salva-

---

\* West. Conf., ch. 28, sects. 5, 6.
† Larger Cat., Quest. 165.

tion! Again we have precisely the same old Popish teachings maintained by all the other sects of Pedobaptists. We have also, a like falsification of the true scripture doctrine of infant salvation.

Those who study the several Pedobaptist Standards, and other authorities on this subject, must be struck with the fact that they frequently speak of "*the ordinary way*" of salvation, and of the "*ordinary possibility of salvation!*" What do they mean by such language? Do they intend to teach their people that there may be some other way of salvation than that which God has revealed in his word? Has not Jehovah himself told them that, apart from Christ Jesus, "there is *none* other name given under heaven among men, whereby we must be saved?"* There is but *one* way of salvation. Infants are saved in the same way that all others of the redeemed are saved, by the grace of God in Jesus Christ our Lord.

Am I told that the statements presented from the books may be true as to them, but after all, do not correctly represent the actual faith of the several communities involved? Is it affirmed that they do not, especially among us, credit this doctrine of baptismal efficacy, nor believe that baptism is necessary to the salvation of infants? If not, they do not believe their *books!* Why, then, do they continue to print and circulate these books, and to declare that they *do* believe them, heartily? If not, they do not believe their *teachers!* Why do they still hear, and sustain, and obey them? Say you they do not believe their own avowed baptismal doctrines? Why,

* Acts iv., 12.

then, do they still baptize their children? Why are they so alarmed when their children are in danger of dying without baptism? Why are they so impatient of any argument against infant baptism? Why this ceaseless effort to keep up infant baptism? Why all this, and much more, if they do not believe that their baptism has some sort of connection with the salvation of infants? Individuals among them are doubtless exceptions, but the masses still hold infant baptism as a condition of infant salvation. Their Standards teach it; their fathers believed it; they themselves cherish the same faith, more or less explicitly.

We have now seen that the whole Pedobaptist world make the salvation of infants *conditional*, and consign to destruction all those in whom these conditions are not fulfilled.

One of these conditions is, as we have seen, that they be within "the pale of the church." But where, in the word of God, can the authority be found to sustain this necessity for their church membership? None whatever exists. It is, besides, unreasonable in itself. The church was organized for special purposes, connected with the preservation of the christian character, the conversion of sinners, and the extension of the gospel among men. Only those, therefore, may enter it who are qualified to enjoy its blessings, and to perform the duties involved. You might as well tell me that it is necessary or beneficial to enlist infants to fight in our armies, as that it is advantageous to baptize them into our churches. Because the church sustains the character indicated, it is invariably required for admission that men give evidence of repentance for sin, faith in

## THE DOCTRINE OF INFANT SALVATION. 199

Christ, and a voluntary and cheerful obedience to all the demands of the gospel. No other class of persons can either receive good, or do good, in the visible church. The membership of infants can therefore neither benefit them, nor the church. And what advantage can they derive from the ordinances? They were instituted to designate believers, and to strengthen and confirm their faith. They never were enjoined upon infants. They are no more obligatory upon them than are repentance and faith. On such as possess no *ability*, rests no *responsibility*. God imposes no duty upon those to whom he has given no capacity to perform it. The church was not designed for infants. It is no place for infants. Their non-performance of obligations resting only upon adults, can never interpose a barrier in the way of their acceptance with God. The supposition that the church membership of infants is a condition of their salvation, is unscriptural, unreasonable, absurd, and not to be credited.

Another condition of the salvation of infants proclaimed by all pedobaptists, is, as we have seen, *their baptism*.

This, I remark, is fully as unscriptural, unreasonable, and absurd, as the other. What peculiar power is there in baptism, that with it they will be saved, and without it they will be lost? Is it the medium through which are conveyed to the child "the merits of the life and death of Christ?" Is the cleansing efficacy of the Holy Spirit given in baptism? Impossible! These blessings are never in any case, so conveyed, either to an infant, or to a believer. Grace and salvation are confined to and conferred by no ordinances whatever.

They are always given to dying infants, and to believing adults, by the direct action of God the Holy Ghost. The salvation of infants is in no way dependent on their baptism.

But further. The supposition that their salvation is dependent on any such conditions is *an impeachment of the righteous justice of God*. It is predicated on the supposition that he holds the dying child responsible for proceedings of which it can have no knowledge, and over which it can exercise no possible control. Whether it is baptized or not, depends entirely upon its parents, friends, and ministers. Even if it were obligatory, it would be *their* duty, not the child's. But it is the *child* that is to be saved, or lost. Shall the child be lost, because its parents were unfaithful, or unbelieving, or because the minister did not, or could not do his duty? The conclusion is nothing less than to charge God in the face of heaven, with cruelty, and injustice.

And lastly, the opinion that infant salvation is based on any of the conditions prescribed, and advocated, by pedobaptists, is horrible, on another account. It supposes that only those who are baptized, and in the church, are saved! What becomes of all the unbaptized who die in infancy? They of course must be consigned to eternal death! How countless the multitudes of children who go into the eternal world unbaptized! This is true of many, very many, in christian lands; and in Pagan, and Mohammedan countries, it is true of all. If Pedobaptist doctrines on this subject be true, untold millions of infants are damned! They could not be saved without "the merits of Christ's life and death." These are communicated to them only through baptism. They never were baptized. They are lost! But *their* doctrines are not true. They are, in themselves and in their results, wholly baseless. They are repugnant to every benevolent feeling of the soul. Never did the human mind conceive of sentiments more absurd and revolting.

Infant baptism, as these facts and considerations amply evince, subverts, and falsifies the true scripture doctrine of infant salvation, and thus proves itself *an appalling evil*, by denying the teachings of the word of God on that subject, and placing it upon fictitious grounds; by requiring that infants shall be in the church in order to be saved; by making baptism the means of removing original sin, and the medium of conveying to them "the merits of Christ's life and death;" by proclaiming that the purification of the Holy Spirit is obtained for them only through this ordinance; and by keeping out of sight the great truth that all infants are saved unconditionally, by the grace of God in Jesus Christ. For all this evil inflicted upon the *truth*, and for the boundless distress and anguish created by the *falsehood*, Pedobaptists of all denominations are responsible to God, and to men. Infant baptism has produced it all. They—not the Baptists—are the men really, who "*hold the damnation of infants!*" We would, if we could, heal the festering wound they have inflicted. We repudiate the doctrine of infant baptism, and of infant damnation. We denounce all their accompaniments, and consequences. If God is just and good, if reason deserves respect, if the gospel is true, if the merits of Christ are efficacious, if the Holy Spirit is not bound by the control of men, and tied down to forms and ordinances, then all children dying in infancy, irrespective of any relation with the church, and without regard to baptism, or any other ordinance, are saved with an everlasting salvation, by the grace of God in Jesus Christ our Lord, whose merits and righteousness, to fit them for the glorious change, are personally and effectually applied by the Holy Ghost.

## CHAPTER X.

INFANT BAPTISM IS AN EVIL BECAUSE IT LEADS ITS ADVOCATES INTO REBELLION AGAINST THE AUTHORITY OF CHRIST.

*Christ's authority paramount; infant baptism contemns it, in regard to the persons to be baptized, the required profession of faith, and the form of baptism; it prevents the obedience of believers.*

The authority of Jesus Christ is everywhere absolute. In his church he is the sole lawgiver, and ruler. His known will is, in all cases, decisive of your duty. His right to govern is unquestionable. He is your Creator and Redeemer, infinitely wise, good, and merciful. You are his people, ignorant, imperfect, and dependent. To enlighten and guide you he has given his most holy word, in which you have instructions on all subjects, and to the utmost extent. This perfect revelation you are obliged to receive as it is, and be governed by it in your heart, and your life. To attempt evasions in any respect; to practise as his what he has not commanded; or to substitute in place of his institutions any of your own; is to come directly into collision with his authority. Infant baptism offends in all these respects. It leads to the violation of divine commandments regarding the persons to be baptized, the preliminary profession of faith, the form of the ordinance, and the obligations to christian obedience.

1. Infant baptism leads its advocates into rebellion

against the authority of Christ in regard to the persons to be baptized.

These are described definitely, in the apostolic commission. When last the voice of Messiah was heard upon earth, it was in the utterance of the command, Go, and make disciples, not among the Jews only, but among all nations. Teach them the gospel, and those who believe it baptize in the name of the Father, and of the Son, and of the Holy Ghost. This duty imposed upon *them* is obligatory upon all their successors in the ministry " unto the end of the world." But infant baptism has introduced a condition of things that renders rebellion inevitable. In pedobaptist countries, such as Italy and Spain, an instance of compliance with the command of Christ has not occurred in a thousand years. In those lands, or among pedobaptists anywhere, who can " make disciples, and baptize them ?" All the people *have been baptized* in their infancy. There are, it is true, among them many *unbelievers ;* multitudes who are still " in the gall of bitterness, and in the bonds of iniquity ;" they ought to hear and believe the gospel ; but *they have all been baptized !* They are all *in the church !* Shall we exhort them as Peter, in his day, did those of the same character, " Repent, and be baptized, every one of you ?" This would be inappropriate. They have " every one" of them *been* baptized *without repentance !* Have any of them — a rare event — been instructed, and obtained faith ? May we then say to them, as Philip did to an interesting convert, " If thou believest with all thy heart thou mayest be baptized ?" No ; they have all *been* baptized *without faith !* And if any zealous preacher of righteousness should undertake to baptize one of these baptized infidels, after his conversion, he would subject himself to the disgrace and *the civil penalties* of being an Anabaptist. The Saviour requires that men shall first believe, and then be baptized. But the order *he* established is now *reversed*. The impenitent and unbelieving, as well as the holy and faithful, all have long ago *been baptized*. Thus infant baptism subverts the authority of Christ. *It baptizes exclusively* UNBELIEVERS, AND BELIEVERS NEVER! In proportion as it prevails the apostolic commission is contemned and violated. This remark may be illustrated by referring to a fact in the history of our fathers. In England, until after the restoration of the Stuarts, there was not in the established church, even a liturgy for the baptism of adult persons. During the Commonwealth, the citizens had enjoyed under Cromwell, a liberty of conscience before wholly unknown. With the Bible in their hands, great numbers of the people became Baptists. Their children were of course not baptized. After the return of the monarchy, these were compelled to submit to the ordinance, and for this purpose the liturgy was remodelled, and an "office" inserted, then for the first time, for *adults*. Dr. Wall narrates these events thus:—" It was by reason of this [the prevalence of the Baptist] opinion in those times, that the Convocation that set presently after the restoration of Charles II., when they made a new book of Common Prayer, found it necessary to add to it an office for the baptism of those who, having been born in those times, had not yet been baptized, whereof there were many that were now grown too old to be baptized as infants, and ought to make profession of their own faith. They gave in the preface to the said book an account of the occasion which made this necessary then, though not formerly, in these words, 'Together with an office for the baptism of such as are of riper years.' Which, although not so necessary when the former book was compiled, yet by the growth of Anabaptism, through the licentiousness [freedom of conscience] of the times, is now become necessary."\* From the period, therefore, that popery took possession of Britain in the seventh century, up to the reign of the second Charles, no believers, unless in secret, were ever baptized in all that realm! Thus completely and effectually, as to the persons appointed to receive this ordinance, does infant baptism lead to rebellion against the divine law, and subvert the authority of our Lord Jesus Christ!

2. Infant baptism offers an indignity to the authority of Christ by dispensing with the appointed profession of faith as a condition of baptism.

The previous profession of faith in Christ is made by the gospel itself, an indispensable condition of baptism. It can never be disregarded without a violation of the commandment of God. The apostles, and primitive christians, never departed from this principle in a single instance. So plainly is this fact set forth in the sacred word, and so firmly has it ever been fixed in the public mind, that, as we saw in a previous chapter, it has always been demanded even of infants! Papists, Lutherans, Episcopalians, and others, to this day, farcically pretend that little children do believe; and, since they

\* Hist. Inf. Bap., vol. ii., pp. 321, 322.

cannot themselves make their own profession of faith, sponsors are appointed to make it for them! But who that thinks at all, does not know that this is all a miserable fiction? It is absurd. It is ridiculous. Infants have no repentance, no faith, no religion. They are baptized without any profession of their own whatever. The law demands of all who are baptized a previous profession of faith. Infants make no such profession. Therefore infant baptism is rebellion against the law, and an indignity to the authority of Jesus Christ.

3. It also perpetuates the change of form, and thus wholly abolishes baptism itself.

As we have but " one Lord," and " one faith," so we have but " one baptism." There is no other. That "*one baptism*" is the burial in water, and raising again, by a true minister of the gospel, of a believer in our Lord Jesus Christ, upon a profession of his faith, in the name of the Father, and of the Son, and of the Holy Ghost. So ably and conclusively, by numerous writers, is this proposition established, that I deem it unnecessary here to enter into the argument. This is the form of christian baptism. It is its invariable form. Baptism itself is but a *form*. The form is the thing. Take away the form, and nothing is left. Destroy the form, and you destroy baptism. He who in baptism is not immersed, is really not baptized. The change of its form is the abrogation of baptism. But, except in the Greek church, infants are never immersed. They have water sprinkled, or poured upon them. The form is changed. No one, I presume, imagines that this desecration would ever have become general, had it not been to accommodate infants. "*Men and women"* who read, and believe the scriptures, who are governed by them, and act for themselves, would never think of submitting to any other than the scripture form. But to immerse infants would be, to say the least, very inconvenient, and not always perhaps entirely safe. Infant baptism has, therefore, perpetuated the change of form, and thus wholly abrogated baptism itself. Infant baptism is thus also in conflict with the authority of Jesus Christ.

4. Infant baptism prevents the obedience to Christ of believers.

He commands all believers, as believers, and when they become believers, to be baptized; but many who have been sprinkled in infancy, refuse to obey him; and they refuse upon the ground expressly that they *have been* sprinkled in infancy. Now infant sprinkling is certainly not baptism. And it prevents true baptism in a variety of ways.

Multitudes among sprinkled christians will not think, or converse on the subject. They are offended if it is even mentioned in their presence. A sermon they will not hear; a book they will not touch, unless it is designed to confirm them in their errors. If any one venture to present to them the truth, and admonish them to obedience, they will be at no pains to conceal their displeasure, and will probably never forgive him! They live and die unbaptized.

But there are many, very many who read the scriptures for themselves, and who cease to entertain pedobaptist sentiments. *They would*, if they might, most gladly be baptized. Will their own chosen and loved pastors baptize them? Never! Often have they been besought to do so, but they will not. They are immovable. What! refuse to administer the laws of Christ? How *dare* they refuse? His *commands* are upon them. "Teach," says the Redeemer, "and baptize those who believe." But no; they have sprinkled them in their infancy; therefore when they believe they will not baptize them! Infant baptism thus turns the professed *ministers* of Christ into rebels against him, and brings *them*, too, into collision with his authority!

In our country, however, there are large numbers who become enlightened, and consequently unhappy on this subject. They feel as if they must obey Christ, but how can they? In Europe, such an act was, for many a century, and in most transatlantic countries is now, a serious offence against the laws of the land. Both administrator and subject would this day, be persecuted, imprisoned, and, if they could not escape, be hurried by suffering possibly to an untimely grave. But in our own free land there are no such restraints. May not every one here do what he shall think to be his duty? Yes, it is his unquestioned right. But after all, is the exercise of that right practicable? Few who have no experience in the premises, or whose attention has not been especially called to the subject, can imagine how almost insurmountable are the difficulties such an one finds in his way. He cannot be baptized, as we have seen, in his own church. But he is at liberty to leave that, and join the Baptist church. Dare he venture such an act? Few, unless favored by peculiar circumstances, find themselves possessed of the requisite courage. *He* reject infant baptism! If he dare essay so bold an act, he is taunted and ridiculed as presuming to be wiser than the thousands of the great and the good who have gone before him. Reproached! Insulted! Scoffed! He shrinks appalled. *He* dare reject infant baptism! He is upbraided with a want of *respect for his parents* and friends, who believed in it, and who had him baptized in his infancy. Will he shame and scandalize those who of all others are dearest to his heart? *He* reject infant baptism! In this act he will renounce his family, and relatives, who will pursue him ever after with scorn and contempt, as unworthy and degraded. *He* leave his *own* church! He loves his church devotedly, and cannot abandon it. *He* think of forsaking his own, and uniting with *another* church! If he dare he will be at once denounced as weak-minded, vacillating, and unstable. It will be rung in his ears that not *much* confidence is to be placed in the religion or intelligence of those "renegades," who are going from one church to another. He join the *Baptist* church! For *that* church, above all others, he has been taught to cherish *disrespect!* He believes its members to be mostly ignorant fanatics, with whom intercourse must always be painful. All this, and only to be baptized! Had he not better give it up at once? These are some of the barriers that infant baptism throws in the way of obedience. They show that what our Lord Jesus Christ said on a memorable occasion, to the multitudes who surrounded him, is still true of all classes:—" If any man come to me, and hate not [love less than me] his father and mother, and wife and children, and brethren and sisters, yea, and his own life also, he cannot be my disciple. And whosoever doth not bear his cross, and come after me, cannot be my disciple."* I have known many, and from my heart have pitied them, who lamented in secret the obstacles in their way. They were always unhappy. Their consciences were perpetually upbraiding them. But they remained in disobedience!

There are persons, however, and I thank God that their numbers are rapidly multiplying, who rise superior to every restraint, and obey our Lord Jesus Christ at whatever hazard. They *know*, and *dare do* their duty. To them nothing is so precious as a consciousness that they please God. They are characterized by strong and independent minds, firmness of purpose, deep piety, and a readiness to sacrifice all for Christ. They count not their lives dear to themselves in comparison with the approbation of their adorable Redeemer. These can, and do, burst the bonds of infant baptism. But the thousands remain through life in slavery! They cannot move.

These are some of the forms in which infant baptism develops the evil inherent in its character; it leads directly to rebellion against the authority of Christ in regard to the persons to be baptized, receiving those he has prohibited, and rejecting those he has received; it dispenses with the profession of faith as a condition of baptism, which he has in all cases imperatively demanded; it has perpetuated the change of form in baptism, a form divinely instituted and commanded, and thus abolished baptism altogether; and it prevents those who have been sprinkled in infancy

* Luke xiv., 26, 27.

from obeying Christ when they become believers. It is now seen to be most true, that infant baptism is an evil because it brings its advocates into direct rebellion against the authority of our adorable Lord and Saviour Jesus Christ.

## CHAPTER XI.

INFANT BAPTISM IS AN EVIL BECAUSE OF THE CONNECTION IT ASSUMES WITH THE MORAL AND RELIGIOUS TRAINING OF CHILDREN.

*Importance of correct training for children; how infant baptism connects itself with it; the injuries thus inflicted.*

THE correct moral and religious training of children, is immeasurably important. No subject is more worthy of our careful attention. We are all, and especially those of us to whose charge these little ones have been providentially committed, called upon to study it with prayerful assiduity. The great business of parental life is the proper training of the next generation. Material errors here, must always result more or less disastrously, while true principles, prosecuted with fidelity, invariably secure the richest blessings. This most interesting and responsible work, however, is not permitted to proceed unembarrassed. With it infant baptism boldly connects itself, and confidently claims to be necessary to its faithful and successful prosecution. This connection, and the evil it inflicts, it is my purpose in the present chapter, briefly to consider.

On the general subject of the moral and religious training of the young, Paul thus exhorts:—" Ye fathers, provoke not your children to wrath, but bring them up in the nurture and admonition of the Lord."* Regarding the benefits to be expected from compliance with this injunction the wisest of men instructs us thus:—" Train up a child in the way he should go, and when he is old he will not depart from it."† In approval of the domestic fidelity of Abraham Jehovah said:—" I know him that he will command his children, and his household after him, and they shall keep the way of the Lord."‡ All those upon whom our heavenly Father has devolved this great duty, are held accountable to him, and to society, for its true and faithful performance. How strong, too, are the other motives which impel them! Who can look upon the children around him, and especially upon his own offspring, without feeling in his heart a firm purpose, for their sake, to discharge the obligation to the utmost extent? These infant minds are so many blank sheets upon which you may write almost whatever you please. Ere, however, the work is commenced, let the startling fact be duly weighed that impressions, when once given, can never be entirely effaced. They are to a greater or less extent indelible. If evil, or adverse to purity, and truth, an injury, probably an irreparable injury, is done to the children themselves, to all the social interests with which they may afterwards be connected, and to whatever pertains to human happiness in this world, and in the world to come.

The *principles* to be instilled are all contained in the " sacred oracles." They ought to be preserved as far as possible from all evil influences, to have constantly before them a pure and holy example, and every oppor-

* Eph. vi., 1–4.    † Prov. xxii., 6.    ‡ Gen. xviii., 19.

tunity should be improved to fix in their hearts the lessons of heavenly wisdom. The great object must be—since piety includes morality, and fits them both for the duties of this life, and the glory of the life to come—to lead them to Christ, and to seek for them pure vital religion. Until this end is gained, very little comparatively, has been accomplished. The *manner* in which the proposed end is to be sought, is perspicuously stated by God himself:—" These words which I command thee this day, shall be in *thy* heart, and thou shalt *teach* them *diligently* unto thy *children;* and thou shalt talk of them when thou sittest in thy house, and when thou walkest by the way, and when thou liest down, and when thou risest up."\*

On this *general* subject there is, as far as known to me, among christians of all classes, no difference in sentiment. The moment, however, we descend to *particulars,* we are the poles asunder. Baptists insist that the successful moral and religious training of children can only be fully attained by adhering strictly to the teachings of divine inspiration. And since their baptism and reception into the church in infancy, are measures not authorized in the gospel, nor consonant with reason, they must be productive not of good, but of evil. Pedobaptists, on the contrary, earnestly insist that it *is essential* to a happy result in the premises that all infants be baptized, received into the church, and be there brought up with the people of God. Here we join issue, and shall proceed to examine the merits of the controversy. I consider myself the more imperatively called upon to do this, because Baptists have

\* Deut. vi., 6, 7.

heretofore thought it scarcely worth their while on this topic, to defend their opinions, or practice, with any special carefulness. We *have been*, and *are*, fiercely attacked, and violently denounced, in sermons, books, tracts, newspapers, everywhere, as wanting in affectionate attentions to our children, and paying little or no regard to their moral and religious training! This odious charge is rung perpetually in the public ear, and it is thought to be sufficiently proved by the fact that we refuse to baptize, and receive them into our churches. The clamor has been kept up from age to age, and with so much zeal and pertinacity, that out of our own circles the calumny is almost universally believed! Justice and truth demand of us a temperate but firm defence.

Baptists wanting in affectionate attentions to their children! Pay very little regard to their moral and religious training! Let *facts* speak. Do the children of Baptists in their general conduct, evince less moral propriety than others? Are they, when of the same social grade, less polished in their manners, less intelligent as men, or less patriotic as citizens? Are a smaller number of them in proportion, found to be truly religious, and active, and useful as followers of Christ? Who dare affirm any of these things? No man certainly, who has any respect for his own character, or veracity. By reliable statistics, collected at different times, and in several cities of our Union, it has repeatedly been proved, that a much *larger* proportion of the children of Baptists become religious than of the children of Pedobaptists. During the early part of last year, a report was made, after accurate examination, by the Baltimore Sabbath-school Superintendents' and Teachers' Association, with the following results:—In the Protestant Episcopal Church Sabbath-schools of that city, among all the pupils, about *one* in every *forty-one* had professed religion; in the Sabbath-schools of the Presbyterian church, Old School, about one in *ninety,* and New School, about one in *fifty;* in those of the Lutheran churches one in *fifteen;* in those of the Methodist Episcopal churches, one in *twenty;* in those of the *Baptist* churches, ONE IN FIVE.* A sim-

* True Union, June 12th, 1851. A correspondent writes as follows:—

"A few months ago you published the statistics of the Baltimore S. S. Superintendents' and Teachers' Association, to disprove the oft-repeated fallacy that Baptists are cruel to leave their children without 'the seal of the covenant,' and thus exposed more than those who have enjoyed that 'privilege' to live and die without Christ. We then showed that in the Sabbath-schools of this city, the proportion of converts was more than twice as large among the Baptists as in any other school, and more than ten times as great as in some of them. The report for the present year is still more conclusive, and I humbly trust it will tend to dissipate the fears and silence the complaints of those who say our children are left 'to the uncovenanted mercies of God.' Would that all the children were taught as ours are, that they are 'by nature children of wrath,' needing the work of the Spirit and the application of the blood of Jesus to their hearts, before they are fit for a place in his holy church. Then we might see more than we do converted in their early days, and consecrating the bloom of their youth to God. To teach an unconverted person (man or child) that he is a member of the church, and embraced within the covenant, simply because a rite with which he had nothing to do, was performed upon him, can have no other effect than to lull his conscience to sleep, and to make him comparatively contented with his favorable position. God grant that the day may soon come when such dangerous and unscriptural teaching shall cease, and when the church shall be as she is described by inspiration, 'a cho-

ilar investigation has been made in Cincinnati, with like results. In New York some years since, a scrutiny was instituted in a large number of families of all the prevailing denominations, and it was found that very many more of the Baptist than of any others, had been brought savingly to Christ. These are facts. What do they prove? Not that the baptized children around us have an advantage over ours, but the contrary. Every theory must be judged by its results, and both the reasons and the facts in this case, prove that of infant baptism is worse than *useless*. The public mind is beginning to be enlightened on this subject, and will not much longer bear with patience, the reproaches, and defamations with which we are so untiringly pursued.

What moral and religious advantages are, in the training of children, *claimed* as arising from their baptism, and admission as members into the church?

sen generation, a royal priesthood, a holy nation,' 'a *peculiar people.*'

" But to the Report :—

| School. | No. attending. | Prof. of rel'gn. | Proportion. |
|---|---|---|---|
| Protestant Episcopal | 1161 | 28 | 1 in $41\frac{1}{2}$ |
| Presbyterian, Old School | 726 | 8 | 1 in $90\frac{3}{4}$ |
| Do. New School | 300 | 6 | 1 in 50 |
| English Lutheran | 553 | 37 | 1 in 15 |
| Methodist Episcopal | 4556 | 220 | 1 in $20\frac{3}{4}$ |
| Baptist | 761 | 143 | 1 in $5\frac{1}{3}$ |

" It will be seen by this table that the Baptists have nearly *three times* as many professors of religion in their schools as any other denomination, and about *seventeen* times as many as are in the Old School Presbyterian church, one of the strongest advocates of infant baptism. These are eloquent facts, and we trust that their language may not be forgotten."

Are we told that when the children are baptized, sponsors, or parents, or both, come before the church, and there in the presence of God and men, enter into the most solemn vows that they will " bring them up in the knowledge and admonition of the Lord ?" All this we know. And we know more than this. *Sponsors*, it is plain, must be conscious when they assume these vows, that they cannot redeem them. It is notorious that not one in fifty ever even attempt it. The whole paraphernalia of *sponsorship* is in fact, a mere matter of form and show, without authority, and without benefit. But what of the vows of *parents?* Are they not substantial, and valuable ? Upon *them* surely, every reliance may be placed. And *what* do *they* vow ? Why, that they really *will do* what God Almighty has commanded them to do ; in other words, that they will discharge an obligation which no *vows* of any kind can either absolve, or render more binding ! Who has required this at their hands ? To me it is most evident that if without these vows they will not obey the divine injunction, they will not obey it at all. If the authority of the Most High is not sufficient of itself, vows and pledges will add nothing to its force. But even if the vows in question were effective and desirable, why connect them with baptism ? For this relation I can perceive no especial reason. No benefits, therefore, on this ground are, or can be, secured to the children.

These baptized children, however, are members, we are told, of the church. They have, in consequence, thrown around them a strong moral influence, which without this relation, they could not enjoy. This is looked upon as giving them superior advantages. But are they, after all, any more intimately associated with the people of God, or under the influence of the church, than they would have been had no such proceedings ever have transpired? Certainly they are not. In either case they are under precisely the same control and direction. The children of Baptists are surrounded by all the moral influences and christian associations, that are enjoyed by those of pedobaptists, and their salutary results are felt to fully as great an extent. We have therefore all the benefits which have been supposed to attach to infant baptism, without incurring any of its evils.

It is most evident that no good arises from the engagements of sponsors, from the promises of parents, from associations with the people of God, from the moral influence of the church, from any circumstances or sources whatever, connected with their baptism, which they would not have enjoyed, and which our children do not enjoy without it. On the contrary, they incur the most serious and dangerous evil, in *two* respects: they are deceived on vital tenets relating to salvation, and they are thereby placed in circumstances extremely unfavorable to the reception of gospel truths.

Infant baptism leads, in moral and religious training, directly into deceptions regarding the way of salvation.

These baptized children will, as soon as they are capable of thought, inquire, if they care to think at all on the subject, what relation this ordinance has given them to Christ and salvation. They can find in the Book of God no answer. The Bible is silent. To what quarter, then, must they look for information?

To their catechisms, of course. And what do these same catechisms teach them? If they are *Calvinists*, they teach them that they were born in the covenant of grace, and members of the church of Christ, and that in their baptism they had, sealed and made over to them, "all the benefits of the death of Christ!" If they are Methodists, their catechisms teach them that their baptism cleansed them from the defilements of original sin, united them with the church, and enrolled them among the faithful people of God! If they are Episcopalians, (and so in substance of Catholics, Lutherans, and others,) that by "their baptism they were made members of Christ, the heirs of God, and inheritors of the kingdom of heaven." A great portion of their moral and religious training consists in teaching them these very catechisms, together with their creeds, confessions, and other standards. If they believe them, they are unquestionably deceived as to the great principles of true religion. They must conclude that they are safe. What more is necessary? If now they live moral and correct lives, they cannot fail of heaven! And is this true? No. It is wholly false. Their minds are miserably perverted! They have mistaken the very nature of vital christianity. If they would look into the Bible, they would find its teachings on this subject the opposite of those contained in their catechisms. And would they examine their own hearts and lives, they would find them, in the light of the holy word, not pure, not sanctified, but still depraved, sinful, criminal. *Their* moral and religious training has *betrayed* them! It *may* lead them to ruin.

These deceptions imposed upon the infant mind, are

fostered in riper years, and strengthened, and deepened, and fixed, by the press, and the pulpit of all classes! "Baptized young people" are addressed by their pastors, not as sinners, but as "children of the covenant." They are "peculiarly favored." Dr. Miller, for example, observes:—"The only question they [baptized young people] can ask themselves is not, Shall we enter the church, and be connected with Christ's family? But shall we continue in it, or act the part of ungrateful deserters?" He maintains that:—"Such children are to be registered as members; as such they are to be specially taught; their own relation to the church tenderly pressed. There are to be meetings exclusively for their parents, and for them as members with their parents, and in those meetings they are to see their schoolfellows admitted into full communion." Thus "they will be brought to recognize their own membership."* Alluding to these views of the venerable Princeton professor, Dr. Campbell of England, in a recent work, remarks:—"Under such a system it is hardly extravagant, with Richard Baxter, and Dr. Miller, to believe that in nineteen cases out of twenty, our children would grow up dutiful, sober, orderly, serious, and before they reached mature age, recognize their membership in a personal act, with sincerity and edification."† This is the moral and religious training prompted by infant baptism, and taught in the books. Not the *conversion* of these children is sought, but "the unfolding of the elements of the holy heart with which they were born," or which was imparted in baptism! Other sinners may require to be "born again," but these have been "pu-

* Stovel's Hereditary Claims, p. 24.     † Jethro, p. 219.

rified by baptism." It remains only that they "recognize their membership" in the church, and they are in "full communion." They are not exhorted to "personal religion," but warned against "personal apostasy," "the part of ungrateful deserters!" It is a calamitous mistake to connect infant baptism with the moral and religious training of children. Its doctrines deceive millions. It creates false hopes. It leads them to conceive themselves favorites of heaven, when in truth they are "in the gall of bitterness, and in the bonds of iniquity."

The children of Baptists are led into no such deceptions, but are carefully guarded against them. No mists are thrown around them which prevent them from understanding the gospel of Christ. They are not obliged to perform the double labor of "unlearning what they have learned amiss," and then learning the truth. They set out in the right direction, and industriously pursue it. They learn that all, whether baptized or unbaptized, are by nature, depraved and sinful, and that in order to be saved they must repent, and believe in our Lord Jesus Christ; that all true religion is personal; that every man must account individually to God; and that each must for himself think, decide, and obey our Lord Jesus Christ. Their minds are not preoccupied by error, but open to receive the truth without prejudice, and to practise it without hindrance. These advantages are priceless. They are of unspeakable magnitude and importance! Of them all, however, our brethren of the several denominations around us are unhappily deprived. The hearts of their children have been withdrawn from the truth, and "turned unto fables." Infant baptism, therefore, unfits parents, and others, for the successful moral and religious training of children, and it disqualifies the children under their charge from embracing the truth, by previously imbuing their minds with error, and implanting prejudices against the simple gospel of the Son of God.

We have now submitted for your consideration the importance of the moral and religious training of children as enjoined in the word of inspiration; the obligations it imposes upon parents, and others; and the claims to fidelity preferred by the interests of society, and urged by the spiritual and eternal destiny of the children themselves. We have seen that from their baptism, and church relationship, no good is secured of any kind, but on the contrary, that they are seriously and permanently injured. We have ascertained that the evil inflicted consists, in part at least, in the false impressions made upon their minds in regard to the teachings of the gospel, in regard to their own character as sinners, in regard to the way of salvation, and in regard to the true nature of the religion of Christ. And we have also shown that parents thus place both themselves and their children in a position in which they lose all the advantages of being guided by the divine word, of receiving originally just conceptions of themselves, and of preserving the mind free from prejudices of all kinds in relation to both truth and duty. Most fearful, therefore, and often we apprehend fatal, is the evil of infant baptism, evinced in the connection which it arrogates with the moral and religious training of children.

# CHAPTER XII.

INFANT BAPTISM IS AN EVIL BECAUSE IT IS THE GRAND FOUNDATION UPON WHICH RESTS THE UNION OF CHURCH AND STATE.

Testimony in proof; origin and nature of the union; destructive of true religion.

INFANT baptism is inseparable from the union of church and state. They are essential to each other. This fact will, I presume, be admitted by all. In a late learned work, Dr. Williams, (of England,) remarks:—
"Without it [infant baptism] those prophecies can never be fulfilled that predict the conversion of nations to God. National conversions must be pedobaptistical conversions, because there must be children included in these nations. A national church must therefore be a pedobaptist church. Indeed, those who aim at a national church must have some principle upon which the whole of its inhabitants may be compressed within its pale. This infant baptism alone renders possible."\*
"Dr. Wall justly asserts that all national churches have practised infant baptism. Nothing is plainer than that where national churches are maintained, infant baptism must be practised, because the nation is brought into the church in its infancy."† In Europe, this is in

---

\* In Stovel's Chr'n Discip.
† Hinton's Hist. of Bapt., p. 368.

fact, one of the principal arguments in support of infant baptism, that it is the grand foundation upon which rests the union of church and state, and that without it such union cannot be maintained. The following canon law of England is prompted by a conviction of the truth now stated:—" No minister shall refuse or delay to christen any child, that is brought to him upon Sundays, or holy-days, to be christened;" " and if he shall refuse to christen, he shall be suspended by the Bishop of his diocese from his ministry by the space of three months."* All who belong to the nation must belong to the church. To be in the church, all must be baptized. And to baptize all, they must receive the ordinance in their infancy. Were only those who repent, believe in Christ, and live holy lives, admitted into the church, then indeed would it be as Christ designed, pure, elevated, sanctified, but it never could be national, and particularly would it very seldom contain the kings, and princes, and great men of the earth. These can find their way into the church by no other medium than infant baptism. But they must be in the church in order to make it a national church. Infant baptism is essential to the union of church and state.

Upon what arguments do the friends of a state church rely to prove its lawfulness? The very same by which they defend infant baptism. To this fact I briefly alluded in a former chapter. Judaism in both cases, furnishes the required testimony. The Jewish society before Christ, and the christian society after Christ, are one and the same church under different

* Ch. Can., 68.

## FOUNDATION OF ALL STATE RELIGIONS. 227

dispensations. The Jewish church was national. The christian church must also be national. Every Hebrew was born in the Jewish church, and to confirm him in his rights and immunities, he was circumcised. In like manner every christian child is born in the church, and receives baptism. "If infant baptism is legitimate, a national church, and priesthood, necessarily follow."* Infant baptism, therefore, as is maintained, both by its friends, and its enemies, is the grand foundation upon which rests the union of church and state. This fact having now been fully determined, we proceed to consider the origin and nature of the union in question.

Our Lord Jesus Christ foresaw that his holy religion would meet, in all lands, the condemnation of men in power, and that in its progress it would agitate society to its very foundations. He therefore said to his disciples:—"Think not that I am come to send peace on the earth. I am not come to send peace, but a sword. For I am come to set a man at variance against his father, and the daughter against her mother, and the daughter-in law against her mother-in-law. And a man's foes shall be they of his own household."† "And ye shall be hated of all nations for my name's sake."‡ Accordingly, the religion of Christ no sooner began to be preached than it had arrayed against it all the princes, priests, and officials of every government upon earth. Its advocates were pursued, hunted down, persecuted, and destroyed everywhere. Resistance, however, but added to its strength. God was in his truth. His purposes no earthly power can successfully frustrate. The people heard, and believed. Disciples mul-

* Henry Denne.   † Matt. x., 34–36.   ‡ Matt. xxiv., 9.

tiplied. Heathenism waned. True religion spread itself into all the ramifications of society, in all places and countries. At this moment peculiar events were transpiring in the Roman empire. Lucinius and Constantine were in conflict for the imperial crown. Politicians are ever sagacious to perceive, and avail themselves, of any element in society which may bear them on triumphantly to their desired end. Lucinius identified himself with the pagans, and rallied to his support all classes who composed the opposition to the religion of Christ. Constantine linked his fortunes with the christians. Battles were fought. Constantine was victorious. He ascended the throne of the Cæsars. Numerous reasons show that of doctrinal religion this emperor knew very little, and of experimental religion nothing. His connection with christianity originated in a far-seeing policy, and afterwards continued from similar considerations. The result was the adoption of the christian religion, and its establishment in the place of paganism, which had gone down with Lucinius, as the religion of the empire.

The model upon which the union of church and state now brought into being was framed, was strictly pagan. The union itself was subsequently advocated by the priests as scriptural, upon the ground that Judaism was a national religion, and established by law. This consideration, however, did not at first, if it ever did afterwards, weigh in the mind of the emperor. He very well knew that in every nation, of whatever grade, before that period, and it is still true of them all, the prevailing superstitions were, and are, established by law, as the religion of the state. "Despotic rulers,"

## FOUNDATION OF ALL STATE RELIGIONS. 229

says Noel, "have ever sought to extort from their subjects all possible advantages for themselves, and to this end to retain them in the most complete servitude. They have chiefly depended on their armies. But the fears and the hopes of superstition, have been too obvious a support not to be largely employed. Well-paid soldiers have been their first instruments of power. Their second has been a well-paid priesthood. Priests have lent to despots in aid of their selfish designs, the portents, and the predictions of superstition. Despots have in return, invested the superstition with splendor, and punished non-conformity with death." "By the aid of the superstition the despot fortified his tyranny; and by the aid of the despotism the priest gave currency to his falsehoods." "Neither party was strong enough to rule alone. But when the priest preached for the despot, and the despot governed for the priest, both the more easily kept their feet upon the necks of the people, and made the universal degradation subservient to their greatness."* This was the policy established in Egypt, and Babylon, and Persia, and Greece, and Rome, and all other countries. All this was well understood by Constantine. He therefore combined in himself, and in his successors, as had been the practice, the highest ecclesiastical with the highest civil power. He governed not only the state, but also the church. He regulated its discipline, assumed to decide all controversies, by judges of his own appointment, and, except those called by himself, interdicted the assembling of any council whatever. Thus the whole form and character given to his church by Jesus Christ

* Union of Church and State, pp. 35, 36.

were destroyed and lost. It was erected into a great hierarchy. Messiah was dethroned. It was no longer the church of Christ. Such was the union of the church with the state, when that alliance was first brought into being. It was fashioned upon the principles of paganism, and advocated upon those of Judaism. And upon this substantially, has been since modelled the union of church and state in every other country!

The results of this union now demand our calm attention.

Those which *immediately* arose were most disastrous. Wealth and honors poured into the church; and with them came impiety, spiritual ignorance, ceremonies and superstitions of all kinds. Frequent pilgrimages, for example, were undertaken to Palestine, and to the tombs of the martyrs. Absurd doctrines and idle ceremonies daily multiplied. Dust and earth, brought from Judea, were sold and bought at high prices, as the most powerful remedy against the violence of wicked spirits. The old heathen habiliments, and processions, were brought into christian worship. And the virtues which had formerly among pagans been ascribed to their temples, their lustrations, and the statues of their gods, were by the baptized now attributed to their churches, their holy water, and the images of their saints.* To this deplorable condition was the cause of Christ at once reduced by the calamitous union of the church with the state.

Another result was to give increased prevalence to infant baptism, as a practice required by this new relation.

* Noel, Union of Church and State, pp. 87–89.

The introduction of infants, though in primitive times unknown in the christian church, was not a new policy in bodies ecclesiastic. The children of the ancient pagans had been ever, by appropriate forms, soon after their birth, solemnly presented to the gods. Infant dedication was therefore continued, and its form of course was now baptism. Policy demanded that christianity should be as much as possible, and particularly in its ceremonials, conformed to paganism, in order that the masses might be the more readily transferred from one religion to the other. On this subject Mr. Hinton remarks:—"We find it indelibly recorded on the pages of history, that the practice of baptizing infants did not spread extensively till after christianity became the state religion of the Roman empire."*

The last result I shall mention is, that any established religion ceases instantly to be the true religion.

Christianity, as revealed by Messiah, necessarily involves individual inquiry, belief, and profession. An established religion is exactly the opposite, since it demands unexamining conformity. The gospel defers every thing to the conscience:—"Let every one be fully persuaded in his own mind," and "whatsoever is not of faith is sin." A state religion disregards the conscience altogether. The gospel requires men to reject every false religion. A state system compels men to embrace, right or wrong, the religion of their country. The gospel invites men to form a voluntary society upon conviction as men. An established religion herds them together by law, as animals, within the inclosure of a national ritual. The gospel binds every man to search

* Hist. of Bapt., p. 368.

after truth, to receive it, to maintain it, and to promulgate it, in opposition to error, however venerable and popular. All this is by every state religion denounced and prohibited. The union of church and state is therefore, in all cases, inevitably, and necessarily, iniquitous in itself, and full of evil in all its bearings, and relations, social, political, and religious. It is unscriptural, it binds the consciences of men, it suppresses inquiry, it subjects the wise and good to be governed by the ignorant and vicious, it is a horrible engine of persecution, it is an injury to the state as well as to the church, and impedes and prevents the extension of the gospel, and the conversion of the nations. "I am thoroughly convinced that this *unchristian* connection between the church and the state [which has ever prevailed in Europe] has done more mischief to the gospel than all the ravings of infidelity since the crucifixion. It converts good christians into bad statesmen, and political knaves into pretended christians. It is at best, but a foul and adulterous connection, polluting the purity of heaven with the abominations of earth, and hanging the tatters of a political piety upon the cross of an insulted Saviour."*

Such is the union of church and state, in its origin, character, and results. Ours is the first christian country, and the only one, since the reign of Constantine, in the government of which this union has been repudiated and denounced as a monstrous evil. In the sentiments, therefore, which I have here expressed, I expect to have the concurrence of every true-hearted American christian. But the union of church and state rests for its foundation upon infant baptism, without which it cannot

* Dr. Philip.

exist. Destroy infant baptism, and you destroy the union of church and state. That unhallowed relation is no longer possible. Is it consistent to repudiate and condemn the connection, and at the same time uphold the platform that supports and perpetuates it? Can you deprecate the result while you continue to defend the cause? He who defends infant baptism defends the union of church and state. For the enormities of every state religion, Catholic and Protestant, infant baptism is, as we have fully shown, justly chargeable. Therefore infant baptism is an enormous evil.

# CHAPTER XIII

INFANT BAPTISM IS AN EVIL BECAUSE IT LEADS TO RELIGIOUS PERSECUTIONS.

Testimony from the nature of pedobaptism; from its political associations; from the sources upon which it relies for support; from facts.

Infant baptism leads to religious persecutions. Of this fact I shall proceed at once to submit the amplest testimony.

The first argument to which I call your attention in proof of the proposition before us, is found in the nature of pedobaptism itself. It brings into the church the whole population of the country where it prevails. All are baptized, and admitted to membership. Every class and condition are necessarily included. Such a church must inevitably, and to a great extent, be ignorant of spiritual things, and essentially irreligious. The great mass, we all know, of every community, grow up without religion; and although, according to Pedobaptism, in the church, and entitled to all its privileges, are full of sensuality and worldliness. The majority of members, therefore, especially in countries where infant baptism is fully carried out, know nothing of the renewing grace of God, and are governed in their feelings and pursuits by considerations entirely of earth. It cannot be expected, therefore, to feel much interest in holy things, or to exercise that love and forbearance towards others inculcated in the word of God, and especially if they appear to them to manifest disrespect or stubbornness. The persons who compose its several departments have their ambition to consult, their hatred to gratify, their superiors to please, and their schemes of personal aggrandizement to accomplish. This is the character and spirit with which infant baptism must in the nature of things imbue the church. Woe to him, therefore, who shall be found in the way of any of its purposes or designs. He must, he will be crushed. Such a church infant baptism makes. It will inevitably be a persecuting church. This conclusion is confirmed by the history of all ages. Previous to the reign of Constantine, no such thing existed as the persecution of christians by each other. They were all full of affection, forbearance, and kindness. Whatever might be the errors of their brethren, the thought did not occur to them that they might do more than express their disapproval, and formally withdraw from them. Immediately after that period infant baptism became general, and persecutions commenced. The scenes of cruelty and blood which have since been enacted, fill all who contemplate them with the deepest horror! It is unquestionably true, therefore, that infant baptism leads to religious persecutions.

A second proof is found in the political connection which, when practicable, infant baptism always assumes. We have just seen in the last chapter, that it is the grand foundation upon which rests the union of church and state. Without infant baptism, no such union is possible. And the fact is well known that *every state church* in all ages, and in all countries, has been a persecuting church. This is true even of heathenism, as well as of christianity. Nebuchadnezzar compelled his subjects, of whatever creed, upon pain of death, to bow down to his golden idol. Darius thought it excellent policy to establish a royal decree that no prayer should be offered to any god but himself for thirty days. The Greek legislators forbade the exercise of any but the national religion. Draco punished departures from the established faith with death. Plato thought that every such act should be denounced to the magistrate as a crime. Aristotle allowed but one national form of religion. Socrates was sentenced to drink the hemlock, and died for the crime of heresy. Established religions in christendom have been conducted on the same principles, and have been equally as exclusive, as intolerant, and as bloody as paganism. Heathens, in common with Jews, persecuted the followers of Christ, as long as they had any ability. Infant baptism was introduced, the church was united with the state, and Christianity immediately began to walk in the footsteps of Heathenism and Judaism. From that to the present day, the history of every *state church*, popish and protestant, has been the same. But no state church could ever have existed without infant baptism. Infant baptism, therefore, is justly chargeable with all their persecutions.

A third proof is derived from the source of the main argument upon which infant baptism relies for support. The appeal of its friends is now, and has been for many ages, to Judaism. In Judaism they find their "*scripture* testimony," for the union of church and state. In Judaism also they obtain ample authority for all their persecutions. Judaism is now the grand platform upon which all these principles stand. There all of them are alike sustained. If infant baptism is right, a state religion is right, and persecution is right. Look into pedobaptist standards, popish and protestant, and you will find that they maintain their doctrines, and defend their proceedings, by appeals to the laws of the Hebrews. Does any man dare to differ from the established religion? Each priest is another Samuel, and armed with the same powers. He therefore hews the presumptuous Agags to pieces before the Lord. In the same scriptures that support their forms of ecclesiastical organizations, they find commands to punish those who depart from the doctrines, or violate the precepts of their religion. Can we be surprised, then, that such a church should practise persecution? It would be wonderful if it did not.

In proof that infant baptism leads to religious persecutions, I, in the last place, appeal to facts.

Popery before the Reformation, poured out upon our *Baptist Fathers* all the fury of its malignant heart. Nor could any thing better have been expected, since the oath taken by her Bishops at their consecration, and similar ones are made by every inferior priest, is as follows:—" I will persecute and oppose all heretics, and schismatics, to the utmost of my power."* And most fully do they perform their vows. I will not, however, here recount the horrid details of her cruelties, practised in every disgusting and execrable form. They may be read in the Histories of the Church by Ivimy, Jones, Benedict, and others. From the third to

* Hereticos et schismaticos pro posse persequar et impugnabo.

the fifteenth century they were hunted down and destroyed like wild beasts. They "had trials of cruel mockings and scourgings, yea, moreover, of bonds and imprisonment. They were stoned, they were sawn asunder, were tempted, were slain with the sword. They wandered about in sheepskins, and goatskins, being destitute, afflicted, tormented, (of whom the world was not worthy.) They wandered in deserts, and in mountains, and in dens, and caves of the earth."* This was the measure meted *to us* by popery. And *after* the Reformation, did our Baptist Fathers receive kinder treatment from *protestants?* No; in no respect whatever. They were still pursued with the same relentlessness. The papists and the protestants *destroyed each other*, in every possible manner. Never were enemies more bitter, or uncompromising. In but *one thing* upon earth was it possible for them to agree, and that was in *persecuting the Baptists*. This was carried so far that in several of their treaties, both in Germany and Switzerland, as D'Aubigné confesses in his History of the Reformation, a special article was inserted binding both parties to use every possible effort to destroy all the Baptists in Europe. Let us briefly enter into this history, and see how far the protestants fulfilled their part of the obligation they assumed. Thus we shall have laid open before us more fully the persecutions into which infant baptism hurries its friends.

"Luther, on his return from Wittenberg," says D'Aubigné, "*extinguished* in Germany the fanaticism of the Anabaptists."† How he did this is, for his own fame, but too well remembered by every reader of history.

---
\* Heb. xi., 36–38.   † Hist. Ref., vol. iii., p. 305.

## LEADS TO RELIGIOUS PERSECUTIONS. 239

Nor were he, and his friends, content to destroy them in their own land. They followed them with cruel hatred even into other countries. For example, Dr. Cox says:—"The princes of Germany, having discovered by means of *intercepted letters*, a secret correspondence between the German and English Anabaptists, wrote an epistle to Henry VIII., containing a statement of their pernicious doctrines, and warning him of danger likely to result from their fanatical proceedings, unless prevented by a bold and timely interference."* This "epistle" of "the princes of Germany," we are specially informed, was advised by Luther, and written by Melancthon. It was their work. How attentive Henry, and his successors, were to the advice it contained, the prisons of the "United Kingdom," and especially the fires of Smithfield, bear ample testimony.

In Switzerland our brethren met the same fate as in other countries. "This fanaticism," says the pedobaptist chronicler of the Reformation, "*reappeared* in Switzerland, where it threatened the edifice which Zuingle, Haller, and Œcolampadius had erected on the word of God." "Grebel [a Baptist minister] *endeavored* to gain over *Zuingle*. It was in vain that the latter had gone further than Luther. 'Let us,' says Grebel, 'form a community of true believers, for it is to them alone that the promise belongs; and let us establish a church that shall be without sin.' But Zuingle would neither hear Grebel himself, nor permit him to speak to the people." He then turned in another direction. Roubli, an aged minister of Basle, Brodtlein, minister of Zollikon, and Lewis Herzer, welcomed his advances. They resolved

* Life of Melancthon, p. 218.

on forming an independent body in the centre of the general community, or church within the church. A new baptism\* was to be their instrument for gathering their congregations, which were to consist exclusively of true believers. "The baptism of infants," said they, "is a horrible abomination,† a flagrant impiety, invented by the evil spirit and by Pope Nicholas II. The Council of Zurich, in some alarm, directed that a public discussion should be held, and as the Anabaptists still refused to relinquish their errors, some of them who were natives of Zurich were imprisoned, and others who were foreigners were banished. But persecution only inflamed their zeal." "Fourteen *men*," he remarks, "and seven *women* were arrested," "and imprisoned on an allowance of bread and water, in the heretic's tower. After a fortnight's confinement, they managed, by removing some planks in the floor, to effect their escape during the night." "They were joined by George Jacob Coira, surnamed *Blourock*, a man of distinguished powers, and many others. While Zuingle was attempting to stem the torrent of Anabaptism at Zurich, it quickly inundated St. Gall. Grebel arrived there, and was received by the brethren with acclamations; and on Palm Sunday he proceeded to the banks of the Lithe, attended by a great number of his adherents, whom he there baptized." "Zuingle wrote a tract on baptism, which the Council of St. Gall ordered to be read in the churches." To this the only answer of these Baptists was, "Give us the word of

---

\* He means that nothing but the immersion of believers upon a profession of their faith was by them allowed to be baptism.

† Most true.

God, and not the words of Zuingle." "Do you keep the doctrines of Zuingle; as for us, we will keep the word of God." The Council, overcome in argument, and put to shame by the truth, now resorted to other measures. They condemned Mentz to be *drowned*, and the sentence was immediately executed. Blourock was *scourged with rods*, and *banished* by these pious *protestants*. Soon afterwards, falling into the hands of the *papists*, he was *burned at the stake*. Multitudes of others also suffered in various ways little less severely than did Mentz and Blourock. But do Lutherans and Zuinglians now justify such conduct? D'Aubigné, the writer I have recited, and who is of our own day, apologizes for it thus:—"Undoubtedly the *spirit of rebellion* existed among these Anabaptists; undoubtedly the *ancient ecclesiastical law* which condemned heretics to capital punishment was still in force, and the Reformation could not in the space of one or two years *reform every thing;* nor can we doubt that *the catholic states* would have accused their protestant neighbors of encouraging insubjection, if the latter had not resorted to severe measures against these enthusiasts."\* "Rebellion!" What rebellion? The refusal to submit their consciences to the magistrate? Of this the Baptists were guilty. It was rebellion! Then there was an "*old ecclesiastical law*," forsooth! But *this* was a *popish law*, and it condemned *Zuingle* as clearly as it did Mantz or Blourock. They were just now especially desirous not to scandalize their *catholic* neighbors! They *must* therefore imprison, banish, drown, and burn these Baptists! And I regret to say that

\* D'Aubigné's Hist. Refor., vol. iii., pp. 306-319.

similar persecutions are thus carried on until *the present hour*. In which of the prisons on continental Europe, where Baptists are found, have not our ministers, and our people, within the last five years, been incarcerated? But tell me, what impulse moved, and still moves them to all this? Was it not infant baptism? Their denial of infant baptism was expressly assigned as the main cause! Infant baptism undoubtedly, therefore, leads to religious persecutions. It undoubtedly produced all these evils.

Let us turn for a moment to England. There, from the day of the burning of Sawtre and Brute,* almost to our times, persecutions against Baptists, have raged with the utmost violence. Protestants in our fatherland, could bear almost any thing else with more patience than opposition to infant baptism. Our sympathies have been moved a thousand times in our childhood, and we have wept over Cranmer, Ridley, Rogers, and others, who fell martyrs under the hands of the papists. By pictures, easy lessons, and essays, in primers and Sabbath-school books, in our infancy and by declamations in riper years, our sorrows have been called forth for their sufferings. I refer to this fact not to condemn it. These great men were cruelly butchered. But I am obliged to say that our feelings have been abused in this matter. Where are our sympathies, and our tears, for our own brethren whom these very men murdered in cold blood as really as David did Uriah? Ah, of this no primers, or other schoolbooks, have told us! And yet these men had before dealt to many a Baptist, the cup that they were at last

* A. D. 1400.

obliged themselves to drink from the hands of the Roman Catholics. Take, if you please, an example or two in illustration. Laws were passed in England to search after Baptists, and to bring them to punishment. "The bishops named in the commission" for the performance of this work, "were *Cranmer*, *Ridley*, Goodrich, Heath, Scorey, and Holbrach," who executed their bloody office with singular ferocity.* Joan of Kent, a distinguished *lady*, and a Baptist, was among the first apprehended. She was unceremoniously condemned to be burned alive at the stake. The death-warrant was laid before the young King Edward. He refused to sign it. *Cranmer* was deputed to persuade him to do so. How did the archbishop discharge his office? He "argued," says the annalist, "from the law of Moses, according to which blasphemers were to be stoned." He said "that there were impieties against God which a prince, being his deputy, ought to punish just as the king's deputies were obliged to punish offences against the king's person." "Plied with such arguments," Burnet says,† "the young king was rather silenced than convinced." "He set his hand to the warrant with tears in his eyes, telling Cranmer that if he did wrong, as it was done in submission to his authority, he [the archbishop] should answer for it to God." And most sternly, and soon, did he answer for it. Again: In whose mind is not the picture of *John Rogers* at the stake, with his wife and children around him, indelibly imprinted? A distinguished gentleman,

---

\* See this whole matter in Neal's Hist. Puritans, N. Y. ed., vol. ii., pp. 353–380.

† Hist. Ref., vol. ii., p. 110.

when the lady spoken of, who is called by the historian "an illustrious female," was condemned, *went to Rogers,* and besought him to exert his influence to *save* her, or at least to procure her a *less dreadful death.* Rogers manifested much indifference, said "*she ought* to be put to death," and jestingly observed, "Burning alive is not a cruel death, but easy enough!" On hearing these words, which expressed so little regard for the poor woman's sufferings, his friend replied with great vehemence, at the same time striking Rogers' hand, which before he had held fast, "Well, perhaps it may so happen that you yourselves will one day have your hands full of this mild burning." And so indeed, in the providence of God, it did happen. And yet more. In a sermon before Edward VI., Bishop *Latimer* speaks of the fearless intrepidity with which went to the stake "the Anabaptists that were [then] lately burned in divers towns in England." These were the men, Cranmer, and Ridley, and Latimer, and Rogers, who burned Baptists by scores, and who were afterwards themselves burned by the papists. *They* were *no better*, and died no more *unjustly*, or *cruelly*, than their Baptist victims. "What measure ye mete it shall be measured to you again." *Our* sympathies should be at least as warm for our *own* brethren and sisters, as for the titled dignitaries by whom *they* were so cruelly destroyed.

Of the horrible details of persecutions practised in after years, in England, in which thousands fell who were among the best and holiest men the world ever saw, I will not speak. I add only, that their principal crime was the denial of infant baptism. This was an offence so enormous that they could not be forgiven.

If favors were extended to other criminals, Baptists were always excepted from their provisions. Whoever else escaped, they were sure to suffer. "The [solemn league and covenant] Confession of Faith" of "the Church of Scotland"—Presbyterian—contains the following passages, which were subscribed, and sworn to by every minister who entered their pulpits :—" The defence of Christ's church appertaineth to the christian *magistrate*, against all idolaters and heretics, as papists, and Anabaptists, &c., to root out all doctrines of devils and men, &c."\* "The examples of scripture do plainly declare that the abusers of the *sacraments*, and contemners of the word, are worthy of *death*."† We "ordain the spreaders, or makers of books, or libels, or letters"—"repugnant to any of the articles of the true religion publicly preached, and by law established"— "to be punished. All *magistrates, sheriffs*, &c., are ordained to *search for, apprehend*, and *punish*, all contraveners."‡ We "give our public testimony against the dangerous tenets of *independency*, and what is falsely called *liberty of conscience*."§ Such were our persecutions before the Reformation, and have been since that event among protestants in Germany, Switzerland, England, and Scotland. Nor were they confined to the other side of the Atlantic. They came with our ancestors to America, and prevailed alike among the puritans of New England, and the cavaliers of Virginia. Happily, our glorious Revolution put them down, and gave freedom of worship and of conscience to our beloved land. Need I here recite the laws, and describe

\* Sect. 1. † Sect. 3.
‡ Sect. 6, act 2, part 1. § Sect. 17.

the cruelties practised upon us, by the Episcopalians of the South, and the Congregationalists of the North? I need not, since they cannot but be to all most familiar. Our fathers have been denounced by every religious faction, condemned in all the Confessions of Faith, led everywhere to prison and to death, and covered with opprobrium in all nations. *Politicians* as well as religionists have believed that in putting them to death they did God service.

Thus we have shown incontrovertibly that infant baptism leads to religious persecutions. It necessarily makes an ignorant and worldly church, which if it has the power will persecute; it unites the church with the state, and every such church has been and is guilty of religious persecutions; the source from which infant baptism mainly draws the arguments for its support leads the church to acts of persecution; and history shows that all pedobaptist churches having the power have engaged in persecution, and that their persecutions have been always most violent and bitter against Baptists, principally because we deny, and refuse to practise, infant baptism. The world has never been visited by a more dreadful evil than religious persecutions. No man can read the details of their enormities without shuddering. All feel the deepest disgust. I shall attempt here no description of them. But let it be remembered that persecution is one of the results of infant baptism.

The converse of this proposition is also true. *Baptist principles are inimical to persecution.* They, in their very nature, repel it in all its hateful forms. And when these principles shall spread themselves over the earth—and they ever have advanced, and ever will advance *pari passu* with political freedom—religious persecution shall be known no more among men.

It is not a little remarkable that historians, and others, have attributed the first true conceptions of *religious liberty* to Roger Williams, the Governor of Rhode Island. In this they all evince their total ignorance of Baptist history. Of Williams Bancroft says:—" He was the first in modern christendom, to assert in its plenitude, the doctrine of the liberty of conscience, the equality of opinions before the law, and in its defence he was the harbinger of Milton, and the precursor, and the superior of Jeremy Taylor."* I honor Roger Williams for his enlightened conceptions, and his bold action regarding religious liberty. But he was only the representative of all the Baptists who had gone before him, many of whom had written as wisely, as learnedly, and as conclusively as he. When, for example, Calvin had succeeded in bringing Servetus to the stake—one of the most horrid *blasphemies* alleged against whom, by the way, was his *denial of infant baptism*—a protest against the proceeding was published by a learned and pious Baptist minister, Mr. David Joris. "It is," said Joris, "an incredible blindness that the servants of Christ, who are sent to give life to the dead through the knowledge of the truth, should condemn the erring to death, and through temporal death expose their souls to eternal ruin. The right to pass such a sentence belongs to Him alone who gave life, and suffered death for our redemption. Were it lawful to put heretics to death, there would be a *general* slaughter, since all re-

* History, &c., vol. i., p. 375.

ligious parties regard their opponents as guilty of heresy."* In Calvin and Joris, you see Presbyterian and Baptist principles regarding religious liberty, in full contrast, long before the days of Roger Williams. Thomas Helwys was another example equally as striking as the Governor of Rhode Island. If the latter stated and defended in the new world, the doctrine of *"soul liberty,"* with great skill and force in his writings, and honorably illustrated it in the planting of a civil state where consciences, however diverse or eccentric, were never oppressed, the former gave in his publications, in the old world, full form and expression to the same sentiments, and maintained them with singular personal boldness, and magnanimity. Helwys was spurned from society, and driven into obscurity. Williams was more fortunate. The small territory that he planted, scarcely noticeable upon the map of the great confederacy of states of which it now forms a part, furnished the example of religious freedom which that confederacy has copied, and which across this wide continent, the millions of our people now account "their highest honor." This was, however, only the embodiment of the great Baptist principle which, from the apostles' times, our churches have all maintained, and defended.

In a Baptist Confession of Faith published in 1611, may be seen the following passage:—" The Magistrate is not to meddle with religion, because Christ is the King, and Lawgiver of the church."† Let also a few sentences from the distinguished confessor already

---

\* Henry's Life and Times of Calvin.

† Struggles and Triumphs of Religious Freedom, pp. 6, 7.

mentioned, be here pondered. "The power and authority of the king"—he wrote in England—"is earthly, and God hath commanded us to submit to all ordinances of man. Therefore I have faith to submit to what ordinances of man soever the king commands, if it be not against the manifest word of God. Let him require what he will, I must of conscience obey him with my body, goods, and all that I have. But my *soul*, wherewith I am to worship God, *that* belongeth to *another King*, whose kingdom is not of this world, whose people must come willingly, whose weapons are not carnal, but spiritual." Again, says Helwys:—"I acknowledge unfeignedly, that God hath given to magistrates a sword to cut off wicked men, and to reward the well-doers. But this ministry is a worldly ministry; their sword is a worldly sword; their punishments can extend no further than the outward man; they can but kill the body." "Their ministry is appointed only to punish the breach of outward ordinances, which is all that God hath given to mortal man to punish. The king may make laws for the safety and good of his person, state, and subjects, against which whoever is disloyal, or disobedient, he may dispose of at pleasure. The Lord hath given him the sword of authority, foreseeing in his eternal wisdom, that but for this his ordinance of magistracy, there would be no living for men in the world, and especially for the godly. Therefore the godly have particular cause to glorify God for this his blessed ordinance of magistracy, and to regard it with all reverence." And again:—"The breach of Christ's laws of the which we all this while speak, which is the only thing I stand upon," how is it to be punished? "His kingdom is spiritual; his laws are spiritual; the transgression is spiritual; the punishment also is spiritual—everlasting death." "No carnal or worldly weapon is given for the support of his kingdom."\*

These are Baptist sentiments, and they consequently have never, in any country, been engaged in the nefarious work of persecution. To this fact it has, however, sometimes been objected, that their circumstances have always been such that they never possessed the power to persecute. Have we not reason to be surprised at a statement like this? Had Roger Williams and his associates, no such power? Could they not have persecuted the puritans as safely, and as successfully, as the puritans persecuted them? Is it responded that they did not do so because they were just out of the fires of persecution themselves? But were not the puritans also just out of the fires of persecution? They persecuted the Baptists. The Baptists never persecuted them, but received them into their territory, and though differing with them in opinion, gave them the same religious liberty which they themselves enjoyed. That the Baptist never *can* become a persecuting church is guaranteed by the very nature of its organization. It is composed of none but those who give satisfactory evidence of a change of heart by the Holy Spirit, and voluntarily seek admission to its membership. None others can be received. "A church without a Bishop" to concentrate its designs; steadfastly adhering to the full independence of each particular separate organization; offering to ambitious men

\* Struggles and Triumphs, &c., pp. 11, 12.

no distinctions, and to its members, of whatever grade, no secular advantages; how can she ever engage in the business of persecution? She persecute? *Who* would she persecute? Not her own communicants, since to them she is bound by the strongest ties of affection, and can, besides, do nothing without their consent. Not those who are out of the church, since over them she has no control. *Why* would she persecute? To bring men into her communion? She would not *have* them, until convinced that they were truly converted, nor then, unless it was their unbiased pleasure to come, professing that they did so from a desire to obey our Lord Jesus Christ. She can never be a persecuting church. To become such she must cease to be Baptist.

These are, and ever have been, Baptist principles. They are the principles taught by Christ and his apostles. They demand the freedom of the conscience. They have long been overborne, and trodden under foot; but they are not destined to die. "God is in his truth." It must at length triumph. Our people are rapidly filling the world. They carry with them the Bible. They study it for themselves. They form their own opinions. They submit their consciences to no man. They oppress the conscience of no man. They act upon their convictions of duty. This mental independence, commenced in childhood, soon becomes a habit, and is inevitably extended into every department of life. The character of the people is thus elevated, their powers of thought invigorated, their conceptions purified, and they become truly formidable to tyranny in the state as well as in the church. By such they must always expect to be denounced. But they never can be enslaved. Their principles have ever rendered them obnoxious to despots, and in every absolute government they have been put to death, as the enemies of magistrates and rulers. Light is now, thank God, breaking in upon the world. Truth, political and religious, is gaining ground. The nations must ultimately sever the yoke of their oppressors. And as national liberty extends itself, Baptist principles, and Baptist people, will cover the whole earth.

## CHAPTER XIV.

INFANT BAPTISM IS AN EVIL BECAUSE IT IS CONTRARY TO THE PRINCIPLES OF CIVIL AND RELIGIOUS FREEDOM.

Nature of freedom; infant baptism destroys civil freedom; it destroys religious freedom; it enslaves the mind in all respects.

FREEDOM is a state of exemption from illegal control. We enjoy *civil freedom* under a government in which our persons, our property, and all our rights, are secured, and protected, by just and equitable laws, promptly administered, and duly obeyed. *Religious freedom* is immunity from the dominion of men over our faith. He is free who worships and serves God without molestation, according to his own convictions of duty. Freedom has no affinity with lawless license. It cannot, on the contrary, be possessed without submission to the law. Government is essential to the condition of man. God has therefore instituted government, both civil and religious. Between these departments there is no conflict. They never contravene each other. As citizens of a common country, and moral and accountable beings, we are subject to both divine and human laws. Ours are the blessings of both. In the obedience rendered we are admonished by Messiah himself, to "give unto Cæsar the things that are Cæsar's, and unto God the things that are God's."

Civil government is of divine appointment. "The powers that be are ordained of God." As members of the body politic, every man is obliged scrupulously to conform to its legal requirements, in all cases in which they do not come into collision with his obligations to God. His duty to the Most High is more exalted and imperative than any other. Jehovah has not delegated *his* authority to earthly rulers of any class, whether they be officers of state, or ministers of religion. In faith and worship every man, as long as he infringes the rights of no other man, is accountable to God only. The disciples were forbidden to call any man on earth master. Messiah is himself sole Lord. Nor are they permitted illegally to rule each other. Even the apostles of Christ disavowed any authority in this respect. "Not," said they to their brethren, "that *we* have dominion over your faith, but are helpers of your joy;"* and "Who art thou that judgest another man's servant? To his own master he standeth or falleth."† Freedom, political and religious, thus defined and understood, is, as we now see, not only the *just* right of every man, but, I will add, it is his *inalienable* right. He is not permitted to resign it even if he were so disposed; nor can he, by any power, be deprived of it without the grossest violence, and wrong. "Religious freedom is *inalienable*," says the distinguished and lamented Dr. Robert B. Semple, "because the opinions of men depending only on the evidence contemplated by their own minds, cannot follow

* 2 Cor. i., 24. † Rom. xiv., 4; James iv., 12.

the dictates of other men. It is inalienable, also, because what is here a right towards man, is a duty towards the Creator. It is the duty of every man to render the Creator such homage, and such only, as he believes to be acceptable to him. This duty is precedent both in order of time, and degree of obligation, to the claims of civil society. Before any man can be considered as a member of civil society, he must be considered as a subject of the Governor of the universe. And if a member of civil society who enters into any subordinate association, must always do it with a reservation of his duty to the general authority, much more must every man who becomes a member of any particular civil society, do it with a saving of his allegiance to the universal Sovereign. We maintain, therefore, that in matters of religion, no man's right is abridged by the institution of civil society, and that religion is wholly exempt from its cognizance."* These great facts and principles will be readily conceded by all enlightened *American* christians, of every denomination. The time is past when, in this country at least, they will be called in question. Yet with them all infant baptism, as I shall now demonstrate, is wholly incompatible.

It is contrary to the principles of *civil freedom*.

It is the first step in a process which soon enslaves the mind, and throughout after life, leads captive all its powers. The child, without its own knowledge or consent, has been subjected to the ordinance in which he makes a profession of religion. As soon as his reason begins to dawn, he is, in popish countries and commu-

\* Semple's Hist. of Virginia Baptists, p. 436.

nities, obliged at regular intervals, to *confess* to his priest, all the actions of his life, and thoughts of his heart. He dare not entertain any opinion, which his confessor condemns. To him he must submit in all things. Thus a feeling of dependence and subjection is created in his earliest years, which is fostered in all subsequent life. He must receive upon *authority*, as *true*, propositions which to his own judgment and reason, if he may venture to exercise them, are absurd; and he must hold as *false* those which appear to *him* incontestably *true*. He must adopt no sentiment but by permission of his spiritual guide. Habits of self-distrust, and submission to superiors, thus formed, are soon indelibly *fixed in the soul*. They can never be eradicated. In Catholic countries, and communities, children are thus reared. As a natural consequence, they are *mentally*, through life, inevitably, and irrecoverably *slaves*. His habits are characteristic of the man, and are, as a matter of course, carried into all the relations of life, *civil* as well as *religious*. Every citizen is sedulously trained to refuse the formation of any judgment of his own, or if he chance to do so, to *distrust*, and *renounce* it, the moment it is contradicted by those to whom he is accustomed to defer. Can such a man be free? He is necessarily, *politically*, a slave. His soul is bound in such fetters that he can no more recover from them than he can change his nature. Infant baptism places men in this condition. Therefore infant baptism is contrary to the principles of civil freedom. Occasionally, I grant, as an exception to a general rule, a man may be found who is capable of breaking these chains, and rising above the evils of his condition. But he is almost alone. The great mass are content to remain in their bondage. *No popish nation, therefore, ever has been, or ever can be, free.* The people are so trained that they must have masters. They demand to be ruled. How dare they form an independent opinion upon politics, or any other subject? They never did such a thing. The act is above their reach. They shrink from it with alarm. If, as lately in France, they arise, and achieve their liberty, it is done in tumult, and they remain in tumult, until, as that nation did once before, and so will again, we fear,* they sink back into despotism. The states of South America are called republics, but they are not free. They never can be, under existing circumstances, because all these destructive influences are embodied in their organic laws. Infant baptism is at the foundation of the slavery of the nations.

Infant baptism is contrary to the principles of *religious freedom.*

The deteriorating causes just noticed are also influential here. A people incapable of civil, must also be incapable of religious liberty. But there are here additional reasons. The very first act in religion is a gross violation of the great principle of freedom. No choice is left to the child. He is baptized, and placed in the church, as soon as he is born. His faith, his religion, his relation to God, is not a subject upon which he is ever to exercise his own powers of reason or judgment. His church is selected for him, and he is committed to the principles of that church, no matter what they may

---

* This prediction, hazarded in the first edition, recent events have given us no ground to retract.

be, in its polity, in its doctrines, or in its forms. To question the truth of any thing he is taught, is presumptuous and criminal. He is not to doubt whether his church may in some things be wrong. He may prove her right if he can, but not wrong. In most countries it is at the risk of his reputation, his fortune, and his life, that he adopts any opinions, or practices, not sanctioned by authority. Talk to such a man about studying the scriptures to learn the true faith, and to gain correct knowledge of his duty! His faith and duty are prescribed. He dare not dissent. Why should he study the scriptures? He is prohibited from giving them any other than the authorized interpretation. He is obliged to believe what the church believes, and to do what he is commanded by her priests. Religious liberty is to him, utterly impossible. He is bound hand and foot, in hopeless slavery. And what is true of one man is true of a whole community, or of an entire nation, since it is composed of men all of whom are of the same character. Such a nation never can possess, they never can even understand religious freedom. Into this condition of things they are thrown by infant baptism. Therefore infant baptism is contrary to *religious* no less than to political freedom.

Am I told that the evil we are now considering might exist without infant baptism? If it might, then infant baptism cannot be justly regarded as its legitimate cause. But no, it could not exist, and would not, without it. To this cause it is truly and necessarily traceable. Without infant baptism there could have been no overshadowing and oppressive hierarchies; without it there could have been no degenerate nominal christianity; without it there could have been no union of church and state; there could have been no lording it over the consciences of the people of God by men in power; there could have been no destruction of religious freedom. Let infant baptism be at once blotted out, and all of every successive generation of children taught the true principles of religion as set forth in the word of God; put the Bible into their hands, and teach them that in their faith and practice they must exercise their own judgment; that they cannot be members of the church unless they have repentance of sin, and a living faith in the Redeemer; and that no obedience can be acceptable to God which is not rendered from love to our Lord Jesus Christ, voluntarily, and intelligently; let all this be instilled into their minds, and religious freedom will instantly spring up, and spread itself over the face of the earth. Infant baptism is the true origin of the evil, and it must be banished from the world before the nations can be emancipated.

But these facts and arguments, I am reminded, are predicated of infant baptism as it exists in connection with popery, and that it does not necessarily follow that they are true of it when practised in connection with protestantism. Infant baptism, I answer, made popery, and it will carry protestantism back to the same point. Out of Great Britain, what is protestantism at this hour in Europe? So far as *religious freedom* is concerned, it differs almost nothing from popery. Our facts and arguments are therefore true and applicable also to protestantism.

In England, however, and in our own country, do not men think and act freely in religion? How, then, can it be said infant baptism fetters their freedom either in politics or religion? In England, I answer, infant baptism is very extensively renounced, and a corresponding liberty prevails. But does England enjoy full religious freedom? That she does no one will for a moment pretend. Public sentiment is brought to bear on the subject by means of the establishment, and the influence of fashion, wealth, and aristocracy. An enslaving power is thus exerted which few have the moral courage to encounter, and which all must confess is contrary to the principles of religious freedom.

In America, the very atmosphere we breathe is essentially anti-pedobaptistic. Here infant baptism is comparatively a dwarfish and inefficient thing. A distinguished minister of that class—Rev. Dr. Bacon of New Haven—in a recent official paper, thus speaks of the decay of the practice:—"A wide neglect of infant baptism prevails" in the Congregational and Presbyterian churches. "How does this happen? We commend the inquiry to the earnest attention of all whom it concerns, and especially of pastors, and the teachers in the theological seminaries." "Is it true that the views on the subject which have been gaining authority in our churches for more than a century, are essentially anti-pedobaptistic in their tendency, and that this tendency is revealing itself in a growing disuse of infant baptism? The question of the fact, and the question how to explain the fact, ought to be fairly and frankly considered. Our Baptist brethren on the one hand, and the believers in baptismal regeneration on the other, are constantly telling us that the baptism of an unconscious infant is incongruous with our theory of religion." This witness is true. There is among all classes in our country "a wide neglect of infant baptism!" It can never flourish here. It is out of its element, and does not produce its mature fruits. It is in the old world that its results are felt in all their power. But is it not in the nature of the same cause to produce the same effects? These effects may be so modified by other influences, as to be less painfully felt, but as far as they go they are precisely the same. It is in the nature of infant baptism here as elsewhere, to destroy civil and religious freedom, and that it has not its full effect among us is attributable mainly, if not wholly, to the Baptist element which everywhere so strongly pervades the public mind, and even enters the Pedobaptist churches themselves.

Thus have we seen the nature of freedom, political and religious; that it is the inalienable right of all men; and how it is destroyed by infant baptism in the state, and in the church. It is true, therefore, beyond question, that infant baptism is contrary to the principles of civil and religious freedom. It follows that by how much civil and religious freedom is an unspeakable blessing, by so much is infant baptism, which destroys it, an evil, and a curse.

## CHAPTER XV.

INFANT BAPTISM IS AN EVIL BECAUSE IT ENFEEBLES THE POWER OF THE CHURCH TO COMBAT ERROR.

Design of the church; to accomplish it, it must be pure; weakening effect of infant baptism; illustrated by its influence on the Reformation; by daily occurrences.

Jesus Christ designs to destroy sin among men. His church is mainly, the instrumentality by which this great work is to be achieved. By the gospel, she is to enlighten the world, to instruct the nations, to subdue the hearts of all men to the truth, and to bring them under the glorious dominion of Messiah. This is a fundamental feature in the faith of all christians. Its correctness no one doubts.

Contemplate the extent, and the nature of the work proposed. To accomplish it, must not the church herself be clothed with all her strength? Her power is in her conformity in all things, to the laws of Christ. He has therefore sanctified his church, "that he might present it to himself a glorious church, not having spot, or wrinkle, or any such thing, but that it should be holy, and without blemish."* Is it possible for a Pedobaptist church to maintain this character? We have already amply seen that it is wholly impracticable, since infant baptism necessarily robs it of its purity,

* Eph. v., 27.

and spirituality, and consequently of its ability to fulfil the purposes of its organization. A corrupt church may become great, and learned, and powerful. It may rule over the world. The papacy has done all this. But to *rule* the nations is one thing, and to *convert* the nations to Christ is another thing. This last she cannot do, because she is not herself converted. To accomplish the work assigned her, is to her impossible. Infant baptism, whenever operating without restraint, inevitably corrupts the communities that practise it. It fills the church with the worldly and unregenerate, and thus gives her either a dead and soulless faith, as in Spain, or a living and active infidelity, as in Germany. It is manifest that such a church has no longer any power successfully to combat error in herself, in her sister denominations, or in the world around her.

Of this important truth we have no more striking exemplification than that which is presented in the history, and results, of the Lutheran reformation. This great moral revolution was characterized by many defects. Painfully was it mingled with the passions, and prejudices, and fanaticism of men. It fell far short of restoring religion to its original Bible standard. Yet it was productive, during a long period, of many great and most happy consequences. "*Indulgences*," as they are familiarly called, first attracted the attention of the reformers. By *indulgences* is meant to be described a peculiar appendage to the popish "sacrament of penance." They had regard to the pardon of the sins of the baptized. The baptized were conscious that they committed daily sins, from the guilt of which it was necessary they should be absolved. In this way only could that favor be dispensed, and for such pardon the frivolous, the gay, and the criminal, were disposed to pay liberally. But they would pay much more liberally, when their pardon included, as it frequently did, permission for subsequent crimes which they desired, and intended to perpetrate. Priests only could administer sacraments; consequently priests only, could grant indulgences. Lucrative indeed, did they find the monopoly. These indulgences, with some others of the outworks of popery, were vigorously attacked. Not long, however, did the conflict rage before nearly every department was involved. The citadel itself of popery— the power of sacraments to convey the grace of God, and their consequent necessity to the salvation of all, whether adults, or infants—they soon gallantly assailed. With the Bible in their hands, which they professed to regard as the standard of truth, and duty, Luther and his coadjutors exploded, and overwhelmed with obloquy, the whole fabric of superstitions which had been imposed upon the world as the religion of Christ. Terrible indeed, for a season, was the battle. Upon which standard victory would ultimately perch seemed doubtful. It was soon perceived that the conquest could not be gained unless the word of God, in their vernacular, was put into the hands of the people, and disseminated throughout the whole land. This was done. The spell by which men had been bound, was broken. The papacy writhed like an expiring monster. Its power was overcome. The great doctrines of salvation by grace, not through *ordinances*, but through *faith*, were again proclaimed to the world.

This was the first period of the Reformation. During

its continuance the simple force of truth was the sole reliance of its friends. No exterior aid was invoked. The gospel, unencumbered by any of the traditions, or commandments of men, was everywhere in the ascendant. No power could resist its progress. Religion was no longer a dead formality for the masses, but a spiritual energy pertaining to *each individual* personally. It concerned his own heart, and life. Thus the hopes of men were removed from the old popish theory of *grace expected* through *sacraments*, to the gospel scheme of *grace received* through *faith* in our Lord Jesus Christ. This was then the character of protestantism. It was the character of the religion of the apostles. Errors of all kinds, fled before it. It rapidly spread into all the nations of Europe. England, and France, and even Spain, as well as the German nations, felt its power. They were all agitated as by the throes of an earthquake. Never was there a movement so popular. Not the *people* alone, but the *princes* also embraced the gospel. O, if the *gospel had continued to guide them*, what might not have been the result! But here a *second era* in the Reformation commences. A national establishment of religion was unhappily, considered by them all, as a matter of course. Popery was abolished. Protestantism must be adopted, and furnished with the sceptre of worldly dominion, which had just been snatched from Popery's bloody hand. It was done. Here was the *first false step*. "A vital question," says Stovel, " at once arose to be considered. It was how the uninformed and unconverted masses of the people, might be most peacefully transferred from a papal to a protestant government, and most effectually united under its rule. In determining this question, to every worldly politician it would appear, that the less change they introduced in the external ceremonies, and popular rites of religion, the more their difficulties would diminish, since the change would thus become less obvious to the people." They supposed themselves, therefore, obliged "to *retain infant baptism*, always pleasing to the masses, and *as much* of the other papal ceremonies, and sacramental doctrines, as they could *possibly tolerate.*"\* Here was *the next false step.* How lamentably had they *now, already* receded from their original ground! To render their religion *national*, they had given up the essentials of its purity, and to fix it in the affections of the people, they had embodied in it the elements of its destruction. Thus they placed themselves voluntarily, in a position in which it was impossible long to retain their character, as the representatives of Christ upon earth! How could the reformers consent to *such* desecrations? How could Luther, and Melancthon, and Zuingle, and their associates, fail to see that the *union of church and state*, and *infant baptism*, a necessary concomitant of that union, must, sooner or later, be ruinous to all true religion? Did they not anticipate that these influences, if permitted to operate, would ultimately destroy all the advantages to gain which they had labored and suffered so nobly? No. They *all* concurred with *the princes*. Protestantism was established by law. Infant baptism was fixed upon the church! The power of the church vanished. It had no more ability successfully to combat error.

\* Christian Disciple, pp. 17-20.

Another fact here claims our attention. The Baptists saw the approach of the Reformation with unmingled joy. During its first period they warmly sympathized with the movement, and heartily co-operated with its friends. They were found in every place, gallantly battling in the cause. When, however, to settle protestantism as the religion of the state, infant baptism was confirmed and established, they stood appalled. They paused. They protested. They said to their brethren, "Christianity is not a mere expansion of Judaism. Its great end is not again to envelop man, as the papacy seeks to do, in the swaddling-bands of outward ordinances, and man's teaching. Christianity is a new creation. It takes possession of the inward man, and transforms him in the innermost principles of his nature, so that he needeth not human teaching, but by God's help he is able of himself, and by himself, to discern that which is true, and to do that which is right." Balthazar Hubmeyer, for example—one of the noble army, whose souls ascended to heaven from amidst the martyr-fires of Vienna—was a pious, learned, and eloquent Baptist. Before the dawn of the Reformation he had sought to revive the spirit of religion in the Catholic church, of which he was then a priest, and multitudes had flocked to his preaching, and had been moved by his appeals. When Luther and Zuingle lifted their voice for reform, an animated echo was instantly heard from Hubmeyer. He had already translated portions of the scriptures into the language of the people, and was by the side of the foremost in the battle. When the leaders halted, considered, hesitated, and acquiesced in *infant baptism*, and the *union of church and state,* he dissented, and planted himself upon the eternal principles of the word of God. He knew that nothing was gained until the church was restored to its primitive form, as set forth in the gospel. " Write to me again," said he to Zuingle, his early friend, but afterwards his bitter foe, " Write to me again, for God's sake, on baptism." " I believe and know, that christendom shall not receive its rising aright, unless baptism, and the Lord's supper, are brought to their original purity." Zuingle had once doubted himself, as had Melancthon, and Carlstadt, and most of the others, about infant baptism; but they were now committed. The fatal step was taken. But he could not pause, until he saw the church composed, as Jesus Christ commanded, of believers only, and a pure, and spiritual body. Blourock, and Grebel, and Mantz, and Hubmeyer, and the others, reminded the reformers of their own previous doctrines. What response did they receive? Zuingle pettishly answered:—" It is impossible to make a heaven upon earth. Christ has taught us to let the tares grow among the wheat!"* Our brethren, determined that no effort should be wanting on their part, still pressed the subject. They were answered only by imprisonments, persecutions, and the stake! For the great Swiss leader, however, D'Aubigné ventures this apology:—" He designed a complete religious reformation, but he was resolved not to allow the least invasion of *public order* or *political institutions.* This was the limit at which he discovered written by the hand of God, that word from heaven, ' Thus far shalt thou go,

* D'Aubigné, Hist. Ref., vol. iii., p. 806.

## THE POWER OF THE CHURCH. 269

and no further.' Somewhere it was necessary to make a stand, and it was at this point Zuingle, and the reformers, took their stand, in spite of the efforts made by rash and impetuous men [the Baptists] to hurry them beyond it."\* In other words, infant baptism was necessary to a state religion, and as such had entered into the *"public order, and political institutions."* It was the law of the land. Our brethren, therefore, who refused to conform to it, were denounced as *rebels;* they were covered with reproach as violators of the law; they were, by princes and magistrates, imprisoned, scourged, banished, put to death! And for their persecution christian men still rise up as apologists!

The *progress* of the Reformation *ceased.* It was stationary for a season. The current then turned back, and flowed towards the corruptions from which it set out. In France, England, and other countries, it followed in the same direction, and reached the same results. Infant baptism has now had time to work its legitimate effects, and they have been full of calamity. It is actually *announced* from some quarters, and by *Protestants* themselves, that "The Reformation has proved itself a failure." And so believing, what measures are being adopted by *these same Protestants?* Do they compare the principles of the Reformation with the Bible, ascertain in what they are deficient, correct their errors, and thus go forward into the light of truth? Far from it. They give up even what had been gained, and take up their march back again into popery! How large a portion of the Episcopal church, especially in England, has already returned to the embraces

\* D'Aubigné's Hist. Ref., vol. iii., p. 311.

of "the Man of Sin!" Infant baptism made popery what it is, and infant baptism will carry protestantism again into popery.

What power has *popery*, what power has *protestantism now*, either permanently to reform itself, to extirpate error from other christian communities, or to convert the nations to Christ? They cannot make others purer than themselves. Were all men of their principles, they would not therefore be the humble, converted followers of Christ. They would not be christians in the true gospel sense. What can the English church do at present, in the combat with error? She is enfeebled to a hopeless degree. What can Lutheranism do, in any of the numerous governments where it prevails? She is powerless. And Calvinism? Ah, what is to be hoped from the Arianism of Geneva, or the Unitarianism, and Universalism of New England? Scattered among all these classes are to be found many individuals who really love our Lord Jesus Christ, and serve him with a sincere heart. Their piety I respect and honor. I speak here not of these few, but of the great mass of the popish, and the protestant world. In them all infant baptism has evinced the essential evil of its character, by either wholly destroying their ability, or greatly enfeebling their power to combat error. "Will it be said that, in the present depraved state of humanity, communities might easily be pervaded by an irreligious and infidel spirit, even if infant baptism had never existed? We grant it. But then the destructive element would have been out of the church. Now it is within the church. However high the tide of ungodliness may rise, all is safe while the church preserves the model ordained by its divine founder. Planted on the rock against which the gates of hell shall not prevail, it presents an embankment to the swelling waves, which breaks their force, and turns them harmless back. In a pure church there dwells a recuperative power that can renovate the most degenerate lands. Living and spiritual; in the world, yet distinct from the world; such a church acts as a correcting and restoring agent, reproving iniquity, confounding unbelief, and holding forth the word of life to a reckless and profligate generation. But if its own light becomes darkness, how great is that darkness! When the church itself engenders the disease; when its own bosom is the fountain that sends out the contagion; then the last hope disappears. It must be taken down, and give place to one built on a scriptural foundation. Otherwise the land which its presence blights, must sink beyond recovery, into the gulf of corruption."* It can never reform itself; it can never reform others; it will retard and obstruct the conversion of men.

It may be objected, however, that these facts and considerations are too sweeping, and are not applicable to the *evangelical* pedobaptist denominations among us. Let us, then, descend to more of particularity, and trace in the *minutiæ* of society, and among the best classes, the influence of infant baptism in destroying the power of the church successfully to combat error.

Indulgences, auricular confessions, priestly celibacy, purgatory, and similar doctrines and practices of the *papacy*, are revolting abuses. They are theological monstros-

* Ide, in Gill's Part and Pillar, &c., pp. 79, 80.

ities which ought to be banished from the world. But what *protestant* pedobaptist has power to reach them? He may show them to be destitute of any countenance from the word of God. His arguments may be logical, and conclusive. But what has he accomplished? His popish brother effectually puts down all his essays by a single question :—Where do *you* get your infant baptism? He tells him in the face of the sun, and he tells him truly, that the Bible gives just as much support to the papal rites which he condemns, as it does to the protestant rite which he approves and practises. They all rest upon the same ground, and must stand or fall together. No man can consistently receive one, and reject the others. They must, for the same reasons, be all received, or all rejected. This appeal to his own principles comes with resistless power. He is *silenced*, and silenced *forever*. Infant baptism has wholly incapacitated *him* successfully to combat the *errors of popery*.

Among Episcopalians, *confirmation*, and *orders*, are among the most striking abuses. Our Presbyterian and Methodist brethren declaim against them eloquently. They pronounce them unauthorized in the Bible, and injurious to religion. Their verdict is true. But while they learnedly discuss, and clearly prove these propositions, their Episcopal brother hears them unperturbed. He knows that he is armed with a weapon they cannot resist; it is the *argumentum ad hominem.* Our authority, he calmly responds, for confirmation and orders, is the same with yours for infant baptism! Are these corruptions, and injurious to religion, because they have no direct scripture warrant? Then so is infant baptism a corruption and injurious to religion, for the same reason. With what consistency can you practise one, and condemn the others? They dare not contradict him. They are necessarily silent.

Among Methodists, a very painful corruption is the baptism of "*seekers*," and their reception to their communion. And who are these "*seekers?*" They are persons who desire to be saved, and manifest feeling on the subject of religion, but who professedly, have not a living faith in Christ, nor any well-grounded hope of eternal life. Against this practice Presbyterians of all classes protest. They pronounce it a gross error, palpably unscriptural, and not to be countenanced! Their Methodist brother is not at all disconcerted. He tells them plainly, and tells them truly, that, The baptism of *seekers* is, to say the least, as lawful as the baptism of *infants*. It is, in truth, attended with prospects even more encouraging, since these seekers may soon be rejoicing in hope, but of infants no such expectation is reasonable. The scriptures favor one as much as they do the other. His assailants cannot answer him. They are silent. He is thenceforth uninterrupted.

The doctrine of "hereditary claims to the covenant of grace," is an appalling abuse among Presbyterians, and Calvinists generally. Other pedobaptists pronounce it an absurdity, and wholly incredible. Dare they openly assail it? If they do, they are quietly reminded that their theory of infant baptism is as scriptural as any other. Thus they are all put to flight each by the other. Every denomination is so enfeebled that it cannot combat error in any other. The invariable and effectual answer to every argument is, "Physician, heal thyself."

Let no one consider these views of the subject as of small importance. The method of argument here sketched has ever been, and is now, a favorite resort of both papists and protestants. It was employed by Cardinal Du Perron in his reply to the first King James; by John Ainsworth against Henry Ainsworth; by Fisher the Jesuit against Archbishop Laud; and by Bossuet, Bishop of Meaux, against De La Roque of Rouen. Bossuet's object was to defend the withholding of the cup from the laity in the Lord's supper, upon the authority of the church, and he urged that *infant baptism*, both as to subjects and mode, was maintained not by scripture, but by church authority only, with which, nevertheless, the reformed complied. Why, then, he asked, should they refuse compliance in the other case?"* De La Roque was dumb. Dr. Whitby employs this argument with special force against the English pedobaptist dissenters. When, after pleading for some condescensions in their behalf, he says:— "And on the other hand, if, notwithstanding the evidences produced that baptism by immersion is suitable to the institution both of our Lord and of his apostles, and was by them ordained to represent our burial with Christ, and so our dying unto sin, and our conformity to his resurrection by newness of life, as the apostle clearly maintains is the meaning of that rite;† if, I say, notwithstanding this, all our dissenters do agree to sprinkle the baptized infant; why may they not submit

---

\* Stennet's Answer to Russen, p. 173, et sequitar.
† Rom. vi., 3–6.

to the significant ceremonies imposed by our church? For since it is as lawful to add to Christ's institutions a significant ceremony which he or his apostles instituted, as to use another in its stead which they never did institute, what reason can they have to do the latter, and refuse submission to the former? And why should not the peace, and union of the church, be as prevailing with them to perform the one, as is their mercy to the infant's body to neglect the other?"* Thus infant baptism is used as the grand plea for compliance with the ceremonies both of the church of Rome, and of the church of England. It is their chief prop to support these hierarchies, the appeal to which they resort for countenance. And so triumphant is this appeal, that no pedobaptist ever has been able to stand before it.† They *must* all either *submit*, be *silent*, or *renounce* infant baptism. While they retain this unauthorized rite, they have no power to resist error on the part of others.

Nor are they untrammelled even in their efforts *to bring the unconverted to Christ*. Infant baptism tends to close the hearts of sinners, and does close the hearts of thousands, against those great doctrines of the gospel, the reception and belief of which, are essential to their salvation.

Is it asked—How does infant baptism prevent men from embracing the fundamental doctrines of the gospel? Preach as they are revealed in the word of God, the doctrines of universal and total depravity, the work of the Holy Spirit in regeneration, justification by faith,

---

\* Protestant Reconciler, p. 289.
† Gill's Part and Pillar, &c., ch. 2.

and other doctrines of this class, and press them upon those who have been taught to believe the baptismal doctrines of the Standards. They will gaze in your face with a look of self-confident incredulity. If they answer you at all, it will be in language like this:— "We believe that children are born in the church, and covenant of grace, or that their original sin was washed away in baptism. In either case, they are consequently holy. We are all, therefore, originally pure. No one can be holy and depraved at the same time. Those, at least, who are baptized in childhood are not depraved. We were baptized in childhood. Your doctrine of depravity we do not believe!" But the work of the Holy Spirit in regeneration, they *surely* will not deny! You see before you a company of men "without God, and without hope in the world." You affectionately warn them that, if they would be saved, they "must be born again"—"born of the Holy Ghost." Do they believe your message? They have studied their catechisms too well. We, they answer, were *baptized* in our infancy, and in that ordinance we were *then*, and *there*, "*born again* of *water*, and of *the Holy Ghost*." Why do you tell *us*, who have been long ago "*born again* of the *Holy Ghost*," that we must *yet* be born again of the Holy Ghost? Are people *twice born again?* They pronounce your teaching nonsense! They profess that they believe in the regenerating efficacy of the Holy Spirit, but they confine it to the medium of baptism! They *adhere to the catechisms*. In the form in which the doctrine is revealed *in the Bible*, they do not believe it. And regarding *justification by faith*, what are their impressions? They are confident that in their baptism, in infancy, they "were cleansed from the defilements of original sin," and had "*conferred* upon them *all the benefits* of the death of Christ." They must *then*, have been accepted of God, and of course, *justified!* Men are justified *but once.* They have no idea that they are *again* to be justified. Infant baptism has encased them all in a covering of steel. You cannot approach them. They are impervious to truth! Why, say they to their pedobaptist teachers, what do you mean? We were brought up in the church. We have never forfeited our birthright. "We are not sinners of the gentiles." "We are Abraham's seed," "the children of the covenant." They are confirmed in sin and deception! Infant baptism has been their ruin. These, alas! are no fancy pictures. They are realities which are daily occurring all around us. These deceived men boldly tell you that if you taught them the truth concerning baptism, you now teach them *falsely;* and if you now teach them the truth, you *then* taught them *falsely!* What can you answer them? Their declaration is true. You have betrayed them! You cannot justify yourself. Infant baptism has closed their hearts against the gospel.

Thus does infant baptism destroy the power of the church to combat error, and prove itself a most lamentable evil. By adopting it she takes away her own purity, and places herself in a position in which she can do nothing effectually, either to reform herself, or to remove the errors of her sister churches. This is shown conclusively, by the history and results of the Reformation; by the present attitude of Lutheranism,

Episcopacy, and Calvinism; by the inconsistencies of even evangelical Episcopalians, Methodists, and Presbyterians; and by the influence of the rite upon the minds of unrenewed men. Such a church ceases necessarily, to be an effective instrumentality for the destruction of sin among men. She cannot teach the nations the gospel. She cannot enlighten the world. She cannot subdue the hearts of men to the reign of truth. She can never bring a rebellious universe under the dominion of Messiah. She has lost forever, the locks of her strength.

## CHAPTER XVI.

INFANT BAPTISM IS AN EVIL BECAUSE IT INJURES THE CREDIT OF RELIGION WITH REFLECTING MEN OF THE WORLD.

*It is irrational; it is without authority; it throws suspicion upon all religion; its purposes are sectarian.*

THE honor of religion is dear to every true christian. To cherish and to love it, is both his duty, and his interest. He can never see it tarnished, but with deep pain. The gospel is consistent both with itself, and with reason. It is to be proposed to men of the world. Their salvation depends upon their believing, embracing, and obeying it. They are not always ignorant of its truths. The utmost care should be exercised that they be not repelled from its teachings. They are capable of reasoning on religious subjects. What you attempt to teach them must correspond with the divine word. Otherwise christianity will, in their minds, be discredited, and your approaches will be resisted. To honor the cause of Christ, therefore, and to gain men to truth and salvation, such must be your faith, and your practice, that none may be able to point to them, and say, this is irrational; this is without authority; this is suspicious in its character; this is a sectarian device. You must be above reproach. "Let your light so shine before men, that they may see your good works, and glorify your Father which is in heaven." But infant baptism does not *honor*, it inevitably *injures* the credit of religion, with intelligent reflecting men of the world.

It does so, in the first place, because it is really in itself *irrational*.

You bring forward a child to be sprinkled. An intelligent man will naturally inquire your reasons. He asks for the *rationale* of the practice. Do you tell him that thereby it is cleansed from original sin; or that it receives all the benefits of the death of Christ; or that it is regenerated, and fitted for heaven? He solicits your proofs. You can give him none that deserve the name. With his Bible in his hand, and his eyes open to behold the objects around him, does he believe your teaching? It is impossible. He does not. He cannot. He may not answer you. He may believe you honest, and sincere. But he does not assent. The baptism of a little infant! What sense or reason is there in it? He perceives none. There is none. It commemorates nothing. It signifies nothing. What good does it accomplish? None for the child; none for the parents; none for the church; none for religion; none for the world; none in any respect whatever. What reasonable man can believe that the child, or any other human being, is the better for it, either in this life, or in the next? It in reality confers no privileges, or advantages, temporal, or spiritual. It is, in truth, utterly irrational, and in the estimation of intelligent, thinking, unprejudiced worldly men, must detract painfully from the credit of religion.

Infant baptism, in the second place, injures the credit

## INFANT BAPTISM DISHONORS RELIGION. 281

of religion, because *it is practised without any authority whatever.*

The Bible contains not one passage in its support. This fact has been before sufficiently demonstrated. No man, however carefully he studies the sacred record, can find one there. And do you place at the very threshold of religion an irrational institution, unauthorized by God, and hurtful to men? And do you demand compliance with it as an essential part of the divine service? What must be the impression thus made upon intelligent men of the world? The credit of religion inevitably suffers.

Infant baptism, in the third place, injures the credit of religion by *casting suspicion upon the whole subject.*

Religion must be set forth and practised in a plain, candid, open, ingenuous, honest manner. If I find a man equivocating, and double dealing with me on one subject, I suspect he may on another; and if I detect him so acting in several instances, I withdraw my confidence from him entirely. So it is in religion. Men must not be trifled with, nor deceived by its professors, and teachers. But infant baptism is inconsistent both with scripture and reason. Yet, in this country, its advocates vehemently maintain that religion in *all* its parts, *is reasonable,* and that *they* are governed in their whole faith, and obedience, exclusively by *the word of God!* What must be the effect upon the mind of a discriminating hearer? Will he conclude that these pedobaptists are sincere, but ignorant? This may be true of many, but cannot be true of all. He will certainly reason in his own heart thus:—*This,* I know, *is irrational,* and *unauthorized.* I *know not* how many other *like things* christians may teach and practise. If one irrational and unauthorized principle be advocated, why not another? And if two, why not twenty? *Suspicion is awakened*, and men of the world are repelled by it from religion. Thus infant baptism casts suspicion upon the whole of the religion of Christ.

Finally, infant baptism, as practised among us, is a well-arranged sectarian device.

It appeals not to the judgment, but to the feelings; not to reason, but to prejudice in favor of an old and venerable custom. It wears very much the appearance of an essay to take undue advantage of all the parties concerned. You receive the *babes* into the church! You then have certainly such a hold upon the *parents* as commits *them* to that particular *denomination* of which their cherished loved ones are thus made members. If the children go, the parents will follow them. Thus both are secured. But how? Not by reason; not by the force of religion; but by a mere sectarian fiction! The whole proceeding *seems* to argue a consciousness that religion will not bear the test of examination! Otherwise why do they impose what implies a profession of it, upon these children, before they are capable of exercising their reason? Why not allow all parties an opportunity to study the Bible before their dogmas are forced upon their acceptance? Why hurry parents and children into the church in violent haste, as if they could not otherwise be saved? Can men of the world, can any class of men, believe that an intelligent, a holy, a reasonable religion, a religion that addresses the judgment and the heart, can be propagated, and honored, by means like these? They cannot. Infant baptism among us is a sectarian device, and as such unworthy of the religion of Christ.

From all these facts and considerations it is most evident that infant baptism injures the credit of religion with reflecting and unprejudiced men of the world, and is therefore a great evil. They must see that it is irrational in itself, that it is wholly without authority from the word of God; they must be led by it to suspect, in all its other departments, the integrity of religion; and they will thus be tempted to regard as compatible with its morals, and honor, any sectarian trap, or management which may swell the numbers of an ecclesiastical party. Need we be surprised, therefore, that among persons of this class, so strong a tendency to skepticism should prevail; that they should feel inclined to repel the gospel of Christ; and that they should so often want confidence in the ministers of religion? Infant baptism is inimical to the honor and prevalence of the gospel of Christ. With regard to it, therefore, we may with emphasis repeat the divine admonition:—"Cast ye up, cast ye up, prepare ye the way, *take up the stumbling-block out of the way of my people.*"

# CHAPTER XVII.

### INFANT BAPTISM IS AN EVIL BECAUSE IT IS THE GREAT BARRIER TO CHRISTIAN UNION.

*Nature of christian union; its importance; the principles upon which it is maintained; incompatible with infant baptism.*

CHRISTIAN union, and infant baptism, never can exist together. Between the millions of Baptists and pedobaptists this rite interposes a barrier which is, and must forever remain impassable. But christian union is imperative upon us all. Whatever prevents it is an evil. Infant baptism prevents it. Therefore infant baptism is an evil.

It is in the very nature of true religion to produce, and perpetuate christian union. God is one; his religion is one; and his people are one. All who love Christ are guided by the same gospel; are partakers of the same Spirit; have in view the same great ends; and are heirs of the same immortal inheritance. How can they be otherwise than united? In asserting these scriptural propositions, I am not unmindful of the fact that diversities of sentiment on nearly every subject, will exist. They arise inevitably, from the differences in natural capacity, in acquired knowledge, and the modes of thought, of different minds. These, however, will always refer to minor considerations, and therefore be unimportant in their nature, extent, and influence. They will be such as intelligent and holy men may indulge without offence, without alienation of affection, and without detriment to the most perfect christian union. Nor is the requisition met when all who compose one particular church, or denomination, are in harmony. Christian union embraces all christians throughout the whole universe. All who are one with Christ, and governed by his word, are inevitably one with each other. The law of gravitation in the natural world, does not more certainly attract to its centre the objects within its range, than does the religion of Christ bring into unity all those who are within the circle of its influence. It knows no names, or distinctions. It is complete. It is universal.

Christian union, I have said, is imperative upon us all. Our Saviour himself commands it, as an object to be sought, with unremitted earnestness. He deemed it also of such importance as to receive a place in that memorable last prayer offered by him in behalf of his ministers and people. "I pray," said he, "that *they all may be one;* as thou, Father, art in me, and I in thee, that they also may be *one in us;* that the world may believe that thou has sent me. And the *glory* which thou gavest me, *I have given them*, that they may be one; I in them, and thou in me, that they may be made perfect in one; and *that the world may know* that thou hast sent me."* Christian union among *all* the people of God is therefore essential to the glory of the Redeemer, to the honor of his truth, to the spread of the gospel among the nations, and to elicit and confirm the

* John, ch. xxvi.

faith of believers. Well then did an apostle thus admonish us:—" Now I beseech you, brethren, by the name of our Lord Jesus Christ, that ye all speak the same thing, and that there be no divisions among you, but that ye be perfectly joined together in the same mind, and in the same judgment."* How imperative! Dare any of us disregard this injunction?

But christian union is not to be governed by feeling merely, however ardent that feeling may be. Like every other duty, it must be guided by fixed principles. And what are these principles? It may be sufficient to say, without descending to particulars, that they are all plainly and fully laid down in the gospel. "The word of God, the whole word of God, and nothing but the word of God," is the grand "platform." There is no other. This must be embraced, believed, loved, practised, and all christians will as naturally flow together as the waters of the whole earth will find their way into the ocean. A union upon any other principles would not be christian union, but a conspiracy against true religion, offensive to God and injurious to his people.

Such is christian union, in its nature, its obligations, and its principles. It is implanted in the renewed heart by the Holy Spirit; it is demanded by the gospel for the honor of truth, and for the extension of the kingdom of Christ among men; and governed exclusively by his holy word, it is practicable, natural, and easy. But infant baptism interposes and destroys it wholly, indeed, renders it impossible. It destroys christian union by changing the laws of membership in his church, established by Christ; by receiving into that sacred body the un-

* 1 Cor. i., 10.

holy and profane; by admitting men without the ordinance ordained and enjoined as the initiatory rite; and by the corruptions which invariably attend the practice of infant baptism. Thus the lovers of Christ are thrown hopelessly asunder. While the barrier remains, the separation must continue.

Infant baptism is therefore an offence against Christ; an offence against the peace and harmony of his people; an offence against the souls of men. And who is responsible for this monstrous evil? Those, of course, who introduced it, and who still adhere to its practice. For all its calamities they must account to God, and to men. We solemnly declare ourselves innocent of its enormities. We never can approve it. We never can believe in the principles upon which it is maintained. Were we, therefore, to unite for the sake of union, or from any other motive, with pedobaptists, it would not be christian union. It would be a sin against God. It would be a combination against the truth and purity of religion. While infant baptism continues, christian union is utterly impracticable.

## CHAPTER XVIII.

INFANT BAPTISM IS AN EVIL BECAUSE IT PREVENTS THE SALUTARY IMPRESSION WHICH BAPTISM WAS DESIGNED TO MAKE UPON THE MINDS BOTH OF THOSE WHO RECEIVE IT AND THOSE WHO WITNESS ITS ADMINISTRATION.

*Impressions made by baptism; lessons it teaches; contrast; infant baptism turns them all aside.*

BAPTISM, like all the other ordinances of religion, was designed to make a deep and salutary impression upon the heart, both of those who receive it, and those who witness its administration. It teaches important lessons, and holds up perpetually before the mind the most glorious truths of the gospel. But the sprinkling of a babe turns them all aside, and destroys every salutary result.

Baptism is an ordinance of singular dignity, and impressiveness, especially when considered in its various bearings, and relations. Give it, if you please, a moment's thought. An intelligent and humble believer stands before you. He has been instructed in the gospel; he has embraced its truths; and deeply penitent under a sense of his guilt and condemnation, he has given himself to Christ, on whom by divine grace he has been enabled to rest his hopes, and confidence. He cherishes a holy assurance of pardon and acceptance.

"Justified by faith, he has peace with God through our Lord Jesus Christ." His soul exults with gratitude and joy. He is "a new creature." His will, his affections, his inclinations, his desires, his purposes, are all changed. He now presents himself, as is his privilege, and his duty, and in accordance with all his desires, that he may confess Christ before men, and be united with his people. With indescribable emotion he approaches the ordinance in which this confession is divinely appointed to be made. He is to be baptized but once in his life. He desires, therefore, to cherish in that hour especially, the spirit of ardent devotion, and full consecration, which so important a service demands. Christ died for his sins, was buried, and rose again for his justification. He is now dead to sin, and according to his commandment, is about to be buried with Christ by baptism into death, and like as Christ was raised up from the dead by the glory of the Father, even so he also, is to arise to walk in newness of life. How unspeakably solemn is that moment! With what fervor he renounces the world, the flesh, and the devil! How earnestly he scrutinizes his own heart, and reviews the reasons of the hope by which he is animated! How thrilling his vows to be the Lord's; to devote himself to the glory of him "who hath called him out of darkness into his marvellous light!" How fervent his prayers for the divine grace and blessing! The act is performed. He retires. The scenes of that hour are indelibly engraven upon his soul. They can never be erased. The salutary practical results are as lasting as his earthly existence.

With this scene compare that of the sprinkling of a child. The little innocent, unconscious of all that is passing, is brought forward, bedizened, possibly, with ribbons and lace. Some forms are recited. Questions and answers are read from books. The wet finger of the minister is laid upon the forehead of the child. Startled by the nervous shock, it perhaps shrieks convulsively, and is hurried away from the altar! The spectacle is over. What have you looked upon? A lamentable desecration of an ordinance of Jesus Christ! Who is benefited? Who is impressed? Who is taught? And this is called baptism!

The baptism instituted by Jesus Christ teaches us, I have said, important lessons. It holds up to our view incessantly, Jesus as our only Saviour; it instructs us that he gave his life for our life, and that the great acts by which we are redeemed, were his death, burial, and resurrection. This redemption is made ours personally, by the work of the Holy Spirit in regeneration. We are one with Christ by faith. For this reason in Christ's death for sin, we died; in his burial, we were buried; in his resurrection, we were raised up; and in his victory we are glorious conquerors. All this we are regarded by the Father as having done, not in ourselves, but in Christ, since what *he* as our *representative* did *for* us, is justly regarded as having been done *by* us. For Christ's sake, therefore, he pardons, sanctifies, adopts, and crowns us with eternal salvation. In this form occurred the acts of our redemption; this is the form of our spiritual change, a death to sin, a burial to the world, and a resurrection to a new life; and this, as the apostles repeatedly declare, is therefore the form of our baptism. "Buried with him in baptism, wherein also we are risen with him through the faith of the operation of God who hath raised him from the dead." In baptism, therefore, those great truths are ever before the mind that constitute the sum of the gospel. How, then, can a Baptist ever become a Unitarian, a Universalist, a legalist, or a cold formalist? As a Baptist he never can. Our very baptism teaches us salvation by grace, through faith in our Lord Jesus Christ. But what does *infant baptism teach?* Nothing, that is salutary. Absolutely nothing.

A believer makes in his baptism a solemn profession of his faith. He has avowed his belief in the doctrine of the Trinity, in whose name that ordinance was administered; in " the freeness of the Father's love, the all-sufficient atonement of the Son, and the regenerating and sanctifying influences of the Holy Spirit;" and he has recognized his obligations, in all things according to the divine word, to walk with the people of God, in newness of life. Nor can he ever renounce these tenets without at the same time, renouncing his baptism. His baptism also implants all the strongest motives to holy living, since it was his own voluntary act, in which he declared himself dead to sin, buried to the world, and alive to God in Jesus Christ our Lord. Such a separation was then pledged between him and sinful things, as is found between the dead and the living. Even the common desire to maintain consistency of character, bears in favor of the christian life, since he has been publicly and solemnly baptized. Such are his professions, and declarations, and their practical influence, the benefit of all which, in infant baptism is totally lost. The child professes nothing, promises nothing, feels nothing.

Such is baptism as to the impression it was designed to make upon those who receive it, in the case of a *be-*

*liever* contrasted with that of an *infant*. When you witness the baptism of a believer, in the form instituted by Jesus Christ, your heart is moved. There is an imposing solemnity in the whole scene. You cannot restrain your tears. Many a sinner has by this means been convicted of sin, and afterwards given himself to Christ. But who ever was convicted of sin, or led to Christ, by witnessing the sprinkling of an infant? Who ever, under such circumstances, felt the solemn grandeur of religion? Infant baptism prevents the salutary impression upon the minds of those who witness the ordinance, which was designed to be made by baptism.

But infant sprinkling seeks to supplant the baptism of believers altogether, and does so, as far as it prevails. Should it universally prevail, it would thus banish from the world some of the best influences connected with the religion of Christ. The salutary practical impression made by baptism upon the minds of both those who receive the ordinance, and those who witness its administration, is of the utmost importance. Infant baptism prevents this impression. Therefore infant baptism is a great evil.

## CHAPTER XIX.

INFANT BAPTISM IS AN EVIL BECAUSE IT RETARDS THE DESIGNS OF CHRIST IN THE CONVERSION OF THE WORLD.

Christ designs to convert the world; it is to be done by the gospel; the work hindered by the conflicts of christians; consequences; conclusion.

THIS whole world is to be converted to God. As yet most of the nations are in darkness, and the shadow of death. But they shall all ultimately be delivered from their thraldom. Joy, and peace, and salvation, shall at length, reign universally. God himself has taught us this glorious truth. Hear the language of his inspired prophets. "*All kings* shall fall down before him. *All nations* shall serve him."\* "And it shall come to pass in the last days, that the mountain of the Lord's house shall be established in the top of the mountains, and shall be exalted above the hills, and *all nations shall flow unto it.*"† "For *the earth shall be full of the knowledge of the Lord*, as the waters cover the sea."‡ "And the kingdom, and dominion, and the greatness of the kingdom under the whole heaven, shall be given to the people of the saints of the Most High, whose kingdom is an everlasting kingdom, and *all dominions shall serve and obey him.*"§

\* Psal. lxxii., 11.  † Isa. ii., 2.
‡ Isa. xi., 9.  § Dan. vii., 9.

These declarations cannot be readily mistaken. If all kings, and nations, shall acknowledge and worship the true God, and flow as a stream *unto* his house; if the earth shall be full of the knowledge of him, and if all dominions shall serve and obey him; and than this, no less is here assumed; then surely the entire universe will have been converted, and brought fully under the reign of our adorable Redeemer. These are the reasons of our confidence in this result. The Lord Most High has declared that it shall be so, and his infinite wisdom, and power, are pledged for its accomplishment. Heaven and earth shall pass away, but his word shall not pass away unfulfilled. They were "*voices in heaven*" which were heard by an apostle, saying, "The kingdoms of this world have become the kingdoms of our Lord, and of his Christ, and he shall reign forever and ever."[*] The round earth, "instead of being a theatre on which immortal beings are preparing by crime, for eternal condemnation, shall become a universal temple in which the children of men are learning the anthems of the blessed above."

But how is this amazing moral revolution to be achieved? How are the hearts of all men, now so corrupt, so obdurate, so fixed in sin, to be changed, and brought to love and worship the Saviour? There is but one power capable of producing this result. It is the simple unadulterated *gospel of Christ*. Reason cannot do it. Philosophy cannot do it. Civilization cannot do it. The forms and ceremonies of religion, apart from its vitality, cannot do it. Nothing can do it

---
[*] Rev. xi., 15.

but *the cross of Christ.* "This alone has power to bend the stubborn will to obedience, and melt the frozen heart to love." The lost children of men are to be taught that, "God so loved the world that he gave his only begotten Son, that whosoever believeth in him should not perish, but have everlasting life." They will receive the message. They will believe it. They will embrace the Redeemer, and live. Nor will they " henceforth live unto themselves, but unto him who died for them, and rose again." The remedy provided in the gospel is effectual. " It has been tried by the experience of eighteen hundred years, and has never failed in a single instance. Its efficacy has been proved by human beings of all ages," from the youthful penitent " to the sinner a hundred years old. All climates have witnessed its power. From the ice-bound cliffs of Greenland to the banks of the voluptuous Ganges, the simple story of Christ crucified has turned men from darkness to light, and from the power of Satan unto God. Its effect has been the same with men of the most dissimilar conditions." It has alike elevated and purified the degraded and abandoned, " and the dwellers in the palaces of kings. It has been equally sovereign amidst the scattered inhabitants of the forest, and the crowded population of the metropolis. Everywhere, and at all times, it has been, and still is, and ever must be, 'the power of God unto salvation to every one that believeth.' "\*

Such are the designs of our Lord Jesus Christ in the gospel, and such is the power by which they are to be

\* Wayland.

executed. The church, we have before seen, is the appointed instrumentality by which these purposes of grace are to be accomplished. Is she ready for her exalted mission? The nations are in her presence. They are covered with misery and death. In her hands is the power by which they are to be delivered and saved. The command from heaven is sounding in her ears, "Preach the gospel to every creature." Each day that obedience is delayed, hurries thousands down to irrecoverable destruction! What is she doing? Springing forward to the duty? Grappling with the powers of darkness? Hurling back the hosts of iniquity? Proclaiming Jesus Christ the deliverer? Alas, no! She has ingloriously turned away from her mission! She has indeed, herself become worldly, and corrupt. She is engaged almost solely, in theological conflicts with her fellow-disciples! She is quarrelling about fictions! She has abandoned the nations to perish in their sins! Infant baptism, like the touch of a torpedo, has benumbed all her powers. What to her are the designs of Christ in the conversion of the world? She is, for the present at least, incapable of their execution!

Infant baptism retards the designs of Christ in the conversion of the world, by placing Baptists and Pedobaptists in conflict with each other. Endless controversies occupy the time, and powers, of the very men who are under infinite obligations to be united in heart, and harmoniously to co-operate in this enterprise of love. Nor is the battle which has been proceeding during so many centuries, relaxing in any degree. It is becoming each day, more and more warm and vigorous. In what is it possible for the contending parties to harmonize? Alas! they cannot agree even upon such *a version of the Bible* into the languages of the people, as both parties are willing to place in their hands!* Not only is the living preacher detained from the nations, but the written word is withheld, and confessedly on account of this very question of baptism! The heathen must not, therefore, even have the Bible! Say you that the designs of Christ in the conversion of the world, are not thus retarded?

Infant baptism retards the designs of Christ in the conversion of the world, by diverting from the work the time, the talents, the learning, and the money of the church. These are, to a painful extent, occupied not in endeavoring to destroy sin; not in enlightening the nations by sending them the written and preached word; not in labors to save the souls of men; but in counteracting, and preventing the success of each other! How much larger the number of meeting-houses which must be built, and of pastors, and other ministers, who must be supported, than would otherwise be necessary! All these powers, and labors, and vast sums, might, but for this evil, be appropriated for the extension of the kingdom of Christ.

Infant baptism retards the designs of Christ in the conversion of the world, by detaining large numbers of ministers from the foreign field. Were Baptists and Pedobaptists united, as but for infant baptism, and its concomitants, they would be, a much

---

* See the conflicts between the American and American and Foreign Bible Societies.

smaller number would be sufficient for christendom, and the remainder might "go far hence to the gentiles." What an immense army of heralds of the cross, in such a case, might at once depart! And "the wilderness, and the solitary place, would be glad for them, and the desert would rejoice, and blossom as the rose."

Infant baptism retards the designs of Christ in the conversion of the world, by giving the name of christians to the abandoned and profligate merchants, and sailors, and soldiers, and others, in foreign lands. These men, wicked as they are, covered with every crime, *claim to be christians!* Heathens, and mohammedans, *recognize them* as christians, and as true representatives of the religion of Christ! They really are, for the most part, members of pedobaptist churches, into which they were received in infancy. In these distant and dark lands, a man seldom dwells who is really born again, and even when he does, the natives naturally confound him with the mass of foreigners. Forming their conceptions of christianity by the moral character of the men before them, nearly all of whom are swearers, drunkards, adulterers, gamblers, and abominably depraved, is it surprising that they look upon christianity with loathing, and reject it with disdain? How can true religion ever be impressed upon their hearts? A barrier all but impassable, is thus presented in the way of any successful effort abroad. A missionary finds his way among the people, but what can *he* do? He preaches to them "of righteousness, temperance, and a judgment to come." *They* point him to his *countrymen*, and ask, Have they not been *baptized?* Are not *they* christians? The man of God tells them of a Saviour who died for them, and of the Holy Spirit, by whom men are purified. They answer him by asking, Have not your *christian* countrymen, who cheat, defraud, and abuse us, been redeemed by Christ, and purified by the Holy Ghost? *They* have been baptized! *They are christians.* Does he attempt to explain the difference between nominal and real christians? They do not understand it. Their answer is, You are all alike. *We see* the practical influence of your religion. We do not want such a religion! They will hear no more. Their hearts are closed against the truth.

Infant baptism retards the designs of Christ in the conversion of the world, by creating everywhere, strifes, and sectarian prejudices. How effectually do these *embarrass* and *obscure* the conceptions of men of all classes! How can those who are under *their* influence, ever see the truth? They give constantly recurring occasions for reproach and alienation. They turn away the hearts of multitudes from Christ, from his religion, and from his people. In this way the moral force of all parties is greatly weakened, and the progress of the gospel proportionally retarded.

Thus it is seen how infant baptism retards the designs of Christ in the conversion of the world, by enfeebling, through her own errors and worldliness, the church herself; by placing Baptists and Pedobaptists in perpetual conflict with each other; by diverting from the work the time, the talents, the learning, and the money of the church; by detaining large numbers of ministers from the foreign field; by giving the name of christians to the abandoned and profligate in heathen lands; and by creating among men everywhere, perpetual strifes, and the bitterest sectarian prejudices. How lamentable the evil in this respect which infant baptism inflicts upon our world! What multitudes has it left uninstructed, to perish forever! With such an incubus hanging upon the church, diverting her energies, corrupting her principles, and destroying her life, how can the world ever be converted to God? But this impediment will be taken away, this baleful influence which has poisoned christianity, will be removed, and "the kingdoms of this world become the kingdoms of our Lord, and of his Christ."

It must now, I think, be evident that infant baptism is the most pernicious heresy that has ever found its way into the church of Christ. Are there still those who think it a small matter? Say you that it cannot be so very iniquitous? You are perhaps willing to admit that, "It does no good." Do you yet claim that it "does no harm?" You are, I trust, undeceived. You now see that it is really the source from which have sprung most of the corruptions that afflict the cause of Christ. "And it is the more dangerous from the slow, and insidious manner in which it accomplishes its results. It acts, I confess, silently. It covertly reaches its ends. Its steps are so circuitous, and its progress so imperceptible, that the consequences are not seen till the catastrophe comes. And even then, they are nearly always referred not to the primal cause, but to some one of the intermediate agencies which it has set in motion! Infant baptism has done more, directly and indirectly, than all other corruptions combined, to overthrow truth, to turn men away from vital religion, to pollute christianity, to enfeeble her power, and to keep back the hour of her final triumph."

# CHAPTER XX.

### RECAPITULATION, WITH CONCLUDING ADDRESSES.

*Recapitulation; addresses to Pedobaptists; to Baptists in Pedobaptist churches; to Baptists.*

THE evils of infant baptism have now, in most of their forms, passed successively in review. They have been considered calmly, dispassionately, but faithfully, and as demanded by the truth of our Lord Jesus Christ. If I have "nothing extenuated," neither have I "set down aught in malice." Let them be here briefly recapitulated.

Infant baptism is an evil, because its practice is unsupported by the word of God; because its defence leads to most injurious perversions of scripture; because it engrafts Judaism upon the gospel of Christ; because it falsifies the doctrine of universal depravity; because it contradicts the great fundamental principle of justification by faith; because it is in direct conflict with the doctrine of the work of the Holy Spirit in regeneration; because it despoils the church of those peculiar qualities which are essential to the church of Christ; because its practice perpetuates the superstitions that originally produced it; because it subverts the scripture doctrine of infant salvation; because it leads its advocates into rebellion against the authority

## RECAPITULATION, ETC.

of Christ; because of the connection it assumes with the moral and religious training of children; because it is the grand foundation upon which rests the union of church and state; because it leads to religious persecutions; because it is contrary to the principles of civil and religious freedom; because it enfeebles the power of the church to combat error; because it injures the credit of religion with reflecting men of the world; because it is the great barrier to christian union; because it prevents the salutary impression which baptism was designed to make upon the minds both of those who receive it, and of those who witness its administration; and because it retards the designs of Christ in the conversion of the world. These, mainly, are the charges I prefer against infant baptism, and I believe that I have proved each one of them conclusively. If so, it is a great and unmitigated evil. It not only does no good, but it does evil, immense evil, and only evil.

In closing this discussion, may I not, in the first place, address a few words to my *pedobaptist* brethren?

Will you not here pause, and with the Bible in your hand, prayerfully re-examine this whole subject? You have probably never, at any time, given it a careful investigation. You found it in your church, and feeling, very naturally, a prejudice in favor of whatever she approves, and observes, you received and adopted it. You have since practised the rite under a sort of indefinite impression that, although you do not yourself comprehend with any clearness how, yet it is defensible by the word of God. This, I know, is the position occupied by thousands. You do not design to depart from the gospel. Least of all do you imagine that in this matter you are committing an injury in any way. The enormous evil it brings upon *you*, upon *your children*, upon *the church*, and upon *the world*, is a great fact to which your attention has not hitherto been called. You have regarded it with favor because it is observed by your church; because great men practise, and defend it; because it is a time-honored institution which has come down to you through a period of fifteen centuries; and because you have thought that "If it does no good, it will do no harm!" But great men, and good men, as great, and as good, as any that have defended, and practised infant baptism, have also defended, and practised, all the corruptions of popery. If on this account you receive infant baptism, you are obliged, for the same reasons, to receive all the corruptions of popery. That, too, is a time-honored institution, clothed with the sanction of more than twelve centuries. High position; great learning; venerableness; never can give authority to any thing which is in itself false, and injurious. Ours is neither the age, nor the country, nor is religion the theme, in which such arguments can be respected. Because our fathers were governed by kings, and emperors, who, as they were taught by great, and good, men, "*ruled by divine right,*" shall we be *monarchists?* We choose in politics, to exercise our own judgment, and we reject as baseless, all these antiquated pretensions. Shall we be less wise in *religion?* Here, too, we will look not to men, but to God; not to antiquity, but to divine revelation. Our appeal is, " to the law, and to the testimony. If we speak not according to these, it is because there is no light in us."

Does infant baptism do no harm? I persuade myself that no one who reads these pages, will ever again urge that fallacious plea. Every departure from truth must be an evil, and this is one of the most melancholy of them all. Will you not, my brother, ascertain for yourself, its character, and renouncing it, return cheerfully to the word of God? It is "a perfect rule of faith and practice." If you, and all others, do so, no more will be heard of this injurious and deprecated custom. Even now, in our country at least, it is losing its hold. Among all evangelical christians it is rapidly waning. Multitudes of the best members in pedobaptist churches of all sects, utterly refuse to have their children baptized. Will not you also abandon it? In maintaining this, or any other error, *you cannot* possibly have any interest. Review prayerfully, and in the light of the divine word, your opinions, and practice in the premises. I am sure you must desire to know the truth, and to obey the truth. It may cost you some labor, and may perchance, demand sacrifices at your hands. But will you shrink from it on these accounts? Let the "love of Christ constrain you" in this work. And may God enlighten, and guide you into the knowledge of his will, and into an humble, holy, and ready obedience in all things.

May I, in the second place, appeal to persons who, although Baptists in principle, are yet members of Pedobaptist churches?

This class of persons is much more numerous than has generally been imagined. Many of them are not themselves fully aware that they approximate our principles. They have derived all their knowledge of them through Pedobaptist channels, and such have been the representations that they suppose us to be almost any thing else than what we really are. It has ever been our lot to be traduced, and exhibited in false lights. Even their ministers—this is the most charitable construction—are strangely ignorant of us. Not a few, however, know that they really do hold our opinions. By all those who occupy the contradictory position now indicated, I would gladly be heard. What apology do you offer for practising in your religion, one set of principles while you really believe another? Do you tell me that it is more convenient for you to be a member of a Pedobaptist church; or that your family are members of such a church, and it is not desirable that you should separate from them; or that there is no Baptist church near your residence; or that there are some things among Baptists that you do not like; or that its social relations are not congenial; or that you are not sectarian in your feelings, and wish to evince your liberality? One or another of these, or some like reason for the abandonment of your faith, is, alas, but too often heard! Are any such sufficient to reconcile you to a relation which must result in serious injury, since it violates your own principles, and aids in the perpetuation of the most disastrous of evils? Can you continue to believe one thing, and to profess, and practise another and opposite thing? Such inconsistency speaks little for your christian conscientiousness. You probably require baptism for yourself. You think every other believer, as a believer, ought to be baptized. But you at the same time, refuse your countenance to those whose opinions and practice agree with your own; and you uphold those who maintain the contrary! By your presence, your influence, and your money, you support what you do not believe, and are convinced Christ does not authorize; and by withdrawing them all, you oppose what you do believe, and are assured your Saviour has enjoined! You renounce infant baptism, and you at the same time vigorously uphold it! You believe it is wrong, and an abuse; and you meantime do all in your power to fasten the evil upon the church, and the world! When remonstrance is offered on the subject, you reply that it is not *convenient* for you to do otherwise; that you cannot separate from your family and friends; that you do not like the Baptists; that you are no sectarian; or that you professed religion among Pedobaptists, and cannot leave them! Can you suppose yourself thus justified in departing from what you believe the law of Christ?

I appeal to your judgment and your heart. I ask you affectionately, but candidly, whether you can reconcile it with your sense of duty, and consistency, longer to continue in your present contradictory position? How can you be happy, or useful, as a christian, thus daily sacrificing truth, and conscience, to mere worldly considerations? Do you ask what you must do? I answer, be true to Jesus Christ. Be honest with yourself, and with others. Will this require that you change your church relations? And what then? You may feel that it will be a painful sacrifice. It probably may be painful. It may be most difficult. Pride will oppose it. You will be appalled by the odium it will

will bring upon you. The love you bear to those with whom you are now associated, and who will frown upon you, will plead against it. How can you surmount such barriers? Nothing but the firmest purpose, sustained by the grace of God, can carry you forward. On the other hand, however, you have the most animating encouragements. Christ, who died to save you, demands your fidelity. Truth claims your love and obedience. The honor and advancement of religion, call upon you to act, and to act promptly, vigorously, and effectually. The cause of Christ protests against your present course, and claims your protection. These are sufficient. They will bear you on triumphantly. Do not, I entreat you, refuse to consider this subject. Dare to be consistent. Dare to honor, and to obey, as well as to love our Lord Jesus Christ.

And now, my beloved Baptist brethren, what, in conclusion, shall I say to you? During many a weary century has our venerated church struggled onward, against every opposition. She has been denounced and proscribed by every despotism, national and ecclesiastical, popish and protestant. All the powers of earth have been perpetually combined, and have exerted their utmost energies, for fifteen hundred years, to destroy her. She has lived on, "like a spark amid the raging billows of the ocean. God has supported her. God has been our refuge, and strength, a very present help in trouble." " From the time of the first departure from apostolic purity, even down through all the darkest eras of the subsequent apostasy, there has always been a succession of men who, abjuring all communion with Rome, have under different names, and in different countries, kept the word, and the testimony of Jesus."* Latterly that little band has become a great and mighty army. "The days of our mourning are ended." The time of triumph has come. Your advanced position, your disciplined array, your growing power and resources, furnish significant indications that God is about to introduce, through your instrumentality, that general return to primitive order, which is to herald the final conversion of all nations. This work is to be done, and it must be, for the most part, done by you, since it never can be accomplished by those who adhere to infant baptism. "How can they hope to demolish *popery*, while they strive to perpetuate in their own organizations the very key-stone of its strength?" Infant baptism was the chief instrument which "brought it into being, and if continued, will inevitably build it up again, the same in substance, if not in name. Who can reasonably look for ultimate triumph in a conflict with *infidelity*, by those who cherish among themselves, a traitor that, as fast as they can drive one army from the field, will bring a fresh one into it? This is but the labor of Sisyphus repeated. The stone of victory, rolled almost to the mountain-top, will rebound, and fall back into the abyss. Such efforts, to be successful, must begin at the foundation. The axe must be laid at the root. Infant baptism—that old Upas-tree, which, with its death-distilling branches, ungodly church-membership, state religions, popery, prelacy, and skepticism, has, for fourteen centuries, shaded and blasted the world—must come down, before the pure light of heaven, and the sweet breath of

* Gill's Part and Pillar, p. 109.

life, can circulate freely, over the expanse of darkened, and diseased humanity."\* You must not only enlighten and guide the heathen and mohammedan nations to Christ, but you must also purify christendom, papal and protestant, nor will you find the latter achievement less difficult than the former. How exalted is the mission assigned you from on high! How gloriously it is to affect the destinies of the world! Yours is a loftier aim than mere patriotism, and philanthropy. You seek the temporal good of nations, and of the whole race. But you stop not here. You labor for the eternal salvation of men. It is yours to convey the news of everlasting life to all the perishing; to furnish every family upon the face of the earth with the word of God in its own language; to send to every neighborhood a preacher of the cross, and to erect there, a temple in which the children of men shall learn the anthems of the blessed above, and become meet to join the General Assembly and Church of the First Born, whose names are written in heaven. Do you properly appreciate your obligations? Up, then, and to your high and holy calling. God himself is with you. He will be your strength. He will honor your "works of faith, and labors of love," with triumphant success.

\* Dr. Ide.

THE END.

# A Biographical Sketch of Robert Boyté Crawford Howell
## (1801-1868)

### By John Franklin Jones

# A Biographical Sketch of Robert Boyté Crawford Howell (1801-1868)

Robert Boyté Crawford Howell–missionary, pastor, writer, editor, historian, denominational leader, helped lay the foundations of the Southern Baptist Convention--was born in Wayne County, North Carolina, on March 10, 1801. Though his heritage was Episcopal, he united with a rural Baptist church fourteen miles from his home in 1821. He enrolled at Columbian College, Washington, D.C. but left after the 1825-26 session to become a lawyer. He was awarded an honorary D.D. by Georgetown College, Kentucky, ca. 1844 (*ESB*).

Howell committed himself to become a missionary at Portsmouth, Virginia, and was ordained in January 1827. He forthwith became pastor of Cumberland Street Baptist Church, Norfolk, Virginia (*ESB*) and labored there until 1834 (Cathcart).

He accepted an appointment from the American Baptist Home Mission Society as missionary to the West and became pastor of the Nashville church January 1, 1835. The church had lost its pastor, nearly all its members, and its building to Campbellism May 24, 1828 and had ceased to exist. The church reconstituted October 10, 1830 and erected a building dedicated late in 1837 or early 1838. Howell restored respect to the Baptist name. The church excluded about 100 antimissionary members June 18, 1838 (*ESB*).

## JOHN FRANKLIN JONES

Howell began *The Baptist*, a monthly paper, in January 1835. He edited the paper most of time prior to giving it to the Tennessee Baptists in June 1848. He revived Sunday School and organized societies for education/ministerial improvement, Bible distribution, publication, and colportage. He resuscitated a missionary society organized by Luther Rice in December 1816 in Tennessee (*ESB*).

He led in establishing Union University. He also led in organizing (May 1842) the Baptist General Association of Tennessee and North Alabama to replace a convention, organized in 1833 and destroyed by antimissionary Baptists (*ESB*).

Howell championed early efforts proposed by the Southern Baptist Convention in 1849 to organize a Baptist seminary. That seminary became Southern Baptist Theological Seminary at Greenville, South Carolina. Ten years later it moved to Louisville, Kentucky (*ESB*).

He became pastor at Second, Richmond, Virginia July 5, 1850. He returned to Nashville July 1857 to find the churches controverted by Landmarkism under the influence of J. R. Graves. Opposing Landmarkism, he worked actively to free the Bible Board, Nashville, from Landmark domination (*ESB*).

He opposed creating the Southern Baptist Sunday School Union at Nashville by Graves and his followers. Howell was loyal to the Southern Baptist Publication Society, Charleston, South Carolina. The Graves-Howell controversy threatened First Baptist Church, Nashville, the third time the church's existence had been threatened in its thirty-year history (*ESB*).

Shortly after the Union army captured Nashville in February 1862, Andrew Johnson, the Union military governor, possessed for the military the building of the First Baptist Church. Howell and three or four other ministers refused to take an oath of allegiance to the Federal government, and Johnson imprisoned the refusant ministers for two months. His health failingly affected by the imprisonment, Howell resigned in July 1867 and died some ten months later (*ESB*). He died on Sunday April 5, 1868 at Nashville, Tennessee following a week of speechlessness, but consciousness (Cathcart). He was buried at Mount Olivet Cemetery, Nashville (*ESB*).

He was the second man elected to be president of the Southern Baptist Convention, presided four years (1851, 1853, 1855, 1857) over that body, and was a vice-president at the time of his death. He was elected a fifth time as president in 1859 over the "prolonged and bitter opposition of Graves," but immediately resigned to prevent that controversy further intruding into the Convention (*ESB*). He served as vice-president of the American Baptist Historical Society, a member of the Historical Society of Tennessee, and president of the trustee board of the asylum for the blind in Tennessee. He was also frequently the moderator of the Concord Association and other deliberative bodies (Cathcart).

Howell married Mary Ann Toy, in April 1829. Of ten children born to that union, two died in infancy (*ESB*).

Howell authored *Terms of Sacramental Communion* (1841), in later editions, *Terms of Communion at the Lord's Table* (1846) (*ESB*). The Tennessee Baptist Convention requested the work be published, resulting in the 456-page *Terms of Christian Communion* (1854). The book was reprinted several times in the United States and in England (Cathcart).

His *The Deaconship* (1846) (*ESB*), issued by the American Baptist Publication Society, quickly transited six editions (Cathcart). Other works included *The Way of Salvation* (1849); *The Evils of Infant Baptism* (1851); and *The Cross* (1854). *The Covenants* (1856) was later revised in ms. as "The Christology of the Pentateuch" (*ESB*);

JOHN FRANKLIN JONES

*The Early Baptists of Virginia* began as an address at the 1856 American Baptist Historical Society, was published in a tract; enlarged to book form in 1856, enlarged again in 1864, and was published posthumously by the American Baptist Publication Society. *A Memorial of the First Baptist Church, Nashville, Tennessee from 1820-1863* is a two-volume mss. edition of the church's history. The author's sermons exist in thirty bound mss. volumes (*ESB*).

## BIBLIOGRAPHY

*2000 Annual of the Southern Baptist Convention.* Nashville, TN: Executive Committee, Southern Baptist Convention, 2000.

Cathcart, William, ed. *The Baptist Encyclopaedia: A Dictionary of the Doctrines, Ordinances, Usages, Confessions of Faith, Sufferings, Labors, and Successes, and of the General History of the Baptist Denomination in All Lands, with Numerous Biographical Sketches of Distinguished American and Foreign Baptist, and a Supplement.* Philadelphia, Louis H. Everts, 1881; reprint, Paris, AR: Baptist Standard Bearer, 1988.

*Encyclopedia of Southern Baptists.* S.v. "Howell, Robert Boyté Crawford," by Homer L. Grice.

BY JOHN FRANKLIN JONES
CORDOVA, TENNESSEE
JULY 2004

# THE BAPTIST STANDARD BEARER, INC.

a non-profit, tax-exempt corporation
committed to the Publication & Preservation
of the Baptist Heritage.

## CURRENT TITLES AVAILABLE IN
## THE BAPTIST *DISTINCTIVES* SERIES

**KIFFIN, WILLIAM**  A Sober Discourse of Right to Church-Communion. Wherein is proved by Scripture, the Example of the Primitive Times, and the Practice of All that have Professed the Christian Religion: That no Unbaptized person may be Regularly admitted to the Lord's Supper. (London: George Larkin, 1681).

**KINGHORN, JOSEPH**  Baptism, A Term of Communion. (Norwich: Bacon, Kinnebrook, and Co., 1816)

**KINGHORN, JOSEPH**  A Defense of "Baptism, A Term of Communion". In Answer To Robert Hall's Reply. (Norwich: Wilkin and Youngman, 1820).

**GILL, JOHN**  Gospel Baptism. A Collection of Sermons, Tracts, etc., on Scriptural Authority, the Nature of the New Testament Church and the Ordinance of Baptism by John Gill. (Paris, AR: The Baptist Standard Bearer, Inc., 2006).

| | |
|---|---|
| CARSON, ALEXANDER | Ecclesiastical Polity of the New Testament. (Dublin: William Carson, 1856). |
| BOOTH, ABRAHAM | A Defense of the Baptists. A Declaration and Vindication of Three Historically Distinctive Baptist Principles. Compiled and Set Forth in the Republication of Three Books. Revised edition. (Paris, AR: The Baptist Standard Bearer, Inc., 2006). |
| BOOTH, ABRAHAM | Paedobaptism Examined on the Principles, Concessions, and Reasonings of the Most Learned Paedobaptists. With Replies to the Arguments and Objections of Dr. Williams and Mr. Peter Edwards. 3 volumes. (London: Ebenezer Palmer, 1829). |
| CARROLL, B. H. | *Ecclesia* - The Church. With an Appendix. (Louisville: Baptist Book Concern, 1903). |
| CHRISTIAN, JOHN T. | Immersion, The Act of Christian Baptism. (Louisville: Baptist Book Concern, 1891). |
| FROST, J. M. | Pedobaptism: Is It From Heaven Or Of Men? (Philadelphia: American Baptist Publication Society, 1875). |
| FULLER, RICHARD | Baptism, and the Terms of Communion; An Argument. (Charleston, SC: Southern Baptist Publication Society, 1854). |
| GRAVES, J. R. | Tri-Lemma: or, Death By Three Horns. The Presbyterian General Assembly Not Able To Decide This Question: "Is Baptism In The Romish Church Valid?" 1st Edition. |

|               |                                                                                                                                                                 |
|---------------|-----------------------------------------------------------------------------------------------------------------------------------------------------------------|
|               | (Nashville: Southwestern Publishing House, 1861).                                                                                                               |
| MELL, P.H.    | Baptism In Its Mode and Subjects. (Charleston, SC: Southern Baptist Publications Society, 1853).                                                                |
| JETER, JEREMIAH B. | Baptist Principles Reset. Consisting of Articles on Distinctive Baptist Principles by Various Authors. With an Appendix. (Richmond: The Religious Herald Co., 1902). |
| PENDLETON, J.M. | Distinctive Principles of Baptists. (Philadelphia: American Baptist Publication Society, 1882).                                                               |
| THOMAS, JESSE B. | The Church and the Kingdom. A New Testament Study. (Louisville: Baptist Book Concern, 1914).                                                                 |
| WALLER, JOHN L. | Open Communion Shown to be Unscriptural & Deleterious. With an introductory essay by Dr. D. R. Campbell and an Appendix. (Louisville: Baptist Book Concern, 1859). |

For a complete list of current authors/titles, visit our internet site at:
www.standardbearer.org
or write us at:

## he Baptist Standard Bearer, Inc.

NUMBER ONE IRON OAKS DRIVE • PARIS, ARKANSAS 72855

TEL # 479-963-3831          FAX # 479-963-8083
EMAIL: Baptist@centurytel.net    http://www.standardbearer.org

*Thou hast given a standard to them that fear thee; that it may be displayed because of the truth. — Psalm 60:4*

www.ingramcontent.com/pod-product-compliance
Lightning Source LLC
Chambersburg PA
CBHW021802220426
43662CB00006B/161